MAHLER

Series edited by Stanley Sadie

The Master Musicians

Titles available in paperback

Berlioz *Hugh Macdonald*
Brahms *Malcolm MacDonald*
Britten *Michael Kennedy*
Bruckner *Derek Watson*
Chopin *Jim Samson*
Grieg *John Horton*
Handel *Donald Burrows*
Liszt *Derek Watson*
Mahler *Michael Kennedy*
Mendelssohn *Philip Radcliffe*
Monteverdi *Denis Arnold*
Purcell *J. A. Westrup*

Rachmaninoff *Geoffrey Norris*
Rossini *Richard Osborne*
Schoenberg *Malcolm MacDonald*
Schubert *John Reed*
Sibelius *Robert Layton*
Richard Strauss *Michael Kennedy*
Tchaikovsky *Edward Garden*
Vaughan Williams *James Day*
Verdi *Julian Budden*
Vivaldi *Michael Talbot*
Wagner *Barry Millington*

Titles available in hardback

Bach *Malcolm Boyd*
Beethoven *Barry Cooper*
Chopin *Jim Samson*
Elgar *Robert Anderson*
Handel *Donald Burrows*

Schubert *John Reed*
Schumann *Eric Frederick Jensen*
Schütz *Basil Smallman*
Richard Strauss *Michael Kennedy*
Stravinsky *Paul Griffiths*

In preparation

Bartók *Malcolm Gillies*
Dvořák *Jan Smaczny*

Musorgsky *David Brown*
Puccini *Julian Budden*

THE MASTER MUSICIANS

MAHLER

Michael Kennedy

OXFORD
UNIVERSITY PRESS

OXFORD
UNIVERSITY PRESS

Great Clarendon Street, Oxford OX2 6DP

Oxford University Press is a department of the University of Oxford.
It furthers the University's objective of excellence in research, scholarship,
and education by publishing worldwide in

Oxford New York

Athens Auckland Bangkok Bogotá Buenos Aires Calcutta
Cape Town Chennai Dar es Salaam Delhi Florence Hong Kong Istanbul
Karachi Kuala Lumpur Madrid Melbourne Mexico City Mumbai
Nairobi Paris São Paulo Shanghai Singapore Taipei Tokyo Toronto Warsaw

and associated companies in Berlin Ibadan

First published 1974 by J. M. Dent & Sons Ltd

Published in the United States
by Oxford University Press Inc., New York

First paperback edition 1977
Second edition 1990

First published in paperback by Oxford University Press 2000

British Library Cataloguing in Publication Data

Data available

Library of Congress Cataloging in Publication Data

Data available

ISBN 0–19–816480–7

1 3 5 7 9 10 8 6 4 2

Printed in Great Britain
on acid-free paper by
Butler & Tanner Ltd
Frome, Somerset

To Christopher Bishop

'Those who are born after such great spirits as Beethoven and Wagner, the epigones, have no easy task. For the harvest is already gathered in, and there remain only a few solitary ears of corn to glean.'

'In forty or fifty years, they will play my symphonies at orchestral concerts as they now play Beethoven's.'

GUSTAV MAHLER

Preface

'We cannot see how any of his music can long survive him,' a New York critic wrote in 1911, a few days after Mahler's death. This short-sighted Olympian pronouncement will raise nothing but a derisive laugh today, when his music is popular to a degree that no one could have foreseen in, say, the 1950s. But Mahlerians must not exaggerate the extent of his neglect in the years from 1911 to about 1960. A devoted group of conductors, several of whom had known Mahler – among them Klemperer, Mengelberg, Walter, Bodanzky and Fried – kept his name before the public. Research shows that there were more performances than is perhaps realized. These devotees kept the pot simmering, as it were, so that when the time came for the gas to be fully turned up, the contents came quickly to the boil. Less fortunate composers have had to start from stone-cold.

The critical rehabilitation of Mahler's reputation is a fascinating study. There have always been impassioned champions of his cause, but for nearly half a century they were a minority. The musical atmosphere in England during my adolescence was predominantly anti-Mahler. He was not to be taken seriously. Mr Donald Mitchell has written of how a leading critic of yesteryear said to him: 'We don't want Mahler here', and I could give a parallel example from my own experience. It is a warning to critics to temper their judgments with humility; no doubt many of those to whom Mahler is now an open book are guilty of misjudging some other composer as he was misjudged. What was particularly heinous in his case was that many adverse verdicts were recorded on the sparsest of acquaintance with the music. There was also an attitude among the arbiters of English taste which implied the most extraordinary choices: if you liked Stravinsky, you couldn't like Mahler; if you liked Mahler, you couldn't like Vaughan Williams; even, if you liked Vaughan Williams, you couldn't like Elgar. Ludicrous, but true. Thank heavens that has gone today.

Symptomatic of the former English attitude to Mahler was the decision that his inclusion in the 'Master Musicians' series should be on a sharing basis – with Bruckner, of course! Each of these great figures now receives a volume to himself, but it would be remiss of me not to pay a tribute to my old friend Hans Redlich's book, which has made such a valuable contribution to a fuller understanding of both composers. He would surely have been delighted that J. M. Dent have now freed them from double harness.

Mahler is not entirely free of misunderstanding, though, even now. I believe that there is a tendency towards too strong an emphasis on supposed defects in his personality arising largely from inaccuracies and distortion in Alma Mahler's book and partly from amateurish dabbling in psychoanalysis. The result is that not only the man but the music is misrepresented, albeit from the best of motives. An artist might well consider that it is as irritating to be fashionable for the wrong reasons as it is to be unfashionable for the right ones. The portrait of 'Mahler, a suitable case for treatment' has been overdone.

I would like to acknowledge a very special debt of gratitude to Mr Renaud C. Bruce, of New York, who went to immense trouble on my behalf in research of Mahler's years in New York, and to Miss Carlotta Wilsen, of the New York Philharmonic Society, for all the assistance she gave him. For help in various ways I thank Mr and Mrs Henry Raynor, Mr Deryck Cooke, Mrs H. F. Riley, Mr Kenneth Thompson, Mr C. E. Meek, Assistant Chief Librarian of the City of New York Fire Department, Dr Wolfgang Stresemann, Intendant of the Berlin Philharmonic, Dr N. Campbell Brown, Dr D. U. Bloor, and Mrs A. Wragg.

I gratefully acknowledge permission to quote from Mahler's letters as published by John Murray Ltd in Alma Mahler's *Gustav Mahler: Memories and Letters* (enlarged edition, 1968) and I thank Universal Edition for permission to reproduce extracts from Mahler's published scores. In assembling illustrations I acknowledge help from Miss Anna Mahler, the Mansell Collection, the Austrian National Library, the State Library, Berlin, and Mr H. J. Nieman, of the Dutch branch of the Internationale Gustav Mahler Gesellschaft.

February 1974   M.K.

Preface to the second edition

With the opportunity to revise this book, I have been able to draw on the vast amount of documentation about Mahler's life and career which has emerged since 1974. This includes more comprehensive editions and better translations of his letters. There is also the invaluable collection of source-material in the shape of reminiscences of Mahler by his contemporaries in Norman Lebrecht's *Mahler Remembered* and, of course, the continuing musicological research and analysis afforded in Donald Mitchell's massive study of the music. In this connection I gratefully acknowledge permission from Faber and Faber to print extracts from the *Selected Letters of Gustav Mahler*, edited by Knud Martner, and translations by Norman Lebrecht from *Mahler Remembered*.

In the past fifteen years, there has been no lessening of public interest in Mahler and his music. With the introduction of the compact disc even finer recordings of his works are now available. His time has truly come.

1989   M.K.

Note on the 2000 reprint

For this reprint, I have added an extra chapter to take account of some of the important and interesting research on Mahler which has emerged in the past decade. I have also made a few minor corrections and amendments.

M.K.

Contents

List of illustrations

1

The boy martyr

The music of Gustav Mahler is the bridge from the nineteenth century to the twentieth. His last seven major works were composed in the first decade of the twentieth century, which was also the last decade of his life; and while it is true that in his music we can hear the culmination of the Romantic tradition, it is equally true that in it we hear the music of the new epoch in composition which followed the overthrow of tonality. Nostalgia and prophecy, both are there, symbolic of Mahler as man and musician. Arnold Schoenberg summed it up in a letter he wrote to Mahler in 1909: 'I rank you with the classical composers; but as one who to me is still a *pioneer*.'

Of Mahler's great contemporaries – Richard Strauss, Jean Sibelius and Edward Elgar – none evoked from the succeeding generation of composers the kind of admiration which was accorded to Mahler by Schoenberg, Berg and Webern – not admiration based solely on 'liking' his music but on regarding him as a teacher, a source, a fellow radical. Nor was this true only of their generation. The *avant-garde* leader of a later day, Karlheinz Stockhausen, has acknowledged a debt to Mahler; and so have composers of more conservative outlook, Shostakovich and Britten. Likewise conductors. Bruno Walter, whose musical sympathies did not lie with the progressives, found in Mahler the heir of Schubert and Bruckner. Pierre Boulez, like Mahler a composer-conductor, is a devoted Mahlerian; and Sir John Barbirolli, for whom the music of Boulez and his followers held little appeal, found in the works of Mahler the novelty and adventure without which creative and executive artists become stagnant. Even more important, audiences throughout the world hear in Mahler's music a modern voice which speaks to them in terms they can understand. They recognize that it is a troubled voice, the voice of a man beset by doubts and fears which have always nagged at mankind's consciousness but which the dwellers in the second half of the twentieth century sometimes seem conceitedly to imagine are exclusively theirs. It is music of exultation and hope, of fatalism and

1

optimism, of anguished questioning and universal affirmation, of emotional intensity and intellectual detachment, worldly-wise and world-weary. This is the essence of Mahler; largely because of it – and notwithstanding Schoenberg, Stravinsky and Debussy – the proposition is tenable that it is Mahler who has had the most potent widespread influence on twentieth-century music.

Mahler's life and work must be viewed in the light of three of his own sayings:

'I am thrice homeless, as a native of Bohemia in Austria, as an Austrian among Germans and as a Jew throughout all the world. Everywhere an intruder, never welcomed.'

'My beliefs? I am a musician. That says everything.'

'The symphony is the world! The symphony must embrace everything.'

Although Mahler and his work have at last come into their own, both are still widely regarded as 'neurotic', 'self-indulgent' and 'decadent'. None of these epithets is accurate. None is deserved.

In the nineteenth century large Jewish colonies lived uneasily in Bohemia and Moravia, then crown lands in the Austrian Empire ruled by Franz Joseph I. At Kališt, Bohemia, in 1827 Bernhard Mahler was born. A coachman who became the proprietor of a small drink-shop or off-licence at No. 265 (later No. 4) Pirnitzergasse (renamed Znaimergasse), Bernhard married in 1857 Marie Hermann, the twenty-year-old daughter of a soap-maker. Marie married 'on the rebound'. She did not love Bernhard and indeed they were remarkably ill matched, he coarse, virile, uninhibited, ambitious and with intellectual pretensions, she lame from birth and conscious of having married 'beneath her'. Fourteen children were born from this misalliance. The first, a son, Isidor (b. 1858), died in early infancy from some mishap. In 1860 on 7th July Gustav was born. Of the twelve subsequent children, six died in childhood from diphtheria or similar scourges. Six others of whom we shall hear further were Ernst (b. 1861), Leopoldine (b. 1863), Alois (b. 1867), Justine (b. 1868), Otto (b. 1873) and Emma (b. 1875). Marie Mahler was forty-two when her fourteenth child, Konrad, was born in 1879. He lived twenty-one months.

The marks of his childhood stayed with Gustav all his life. Perhaps out of sympathetic imitation of his mother's limp, he manifested as a child the peculiar gait – a change of pace every three or four steps –

which was often the first thing people noticed about him, even in New York in his last years. This 'jerking foot' or tic is well described by the theatrical designer Alfred Roller, who worked closely with Mahler in Vienna and wrote one of the finest of all essays about him.[1] 'As a child,' Roller wrote,

> he was afflicted by involuntary movements of the extremities. These are commonly found in mentally advanced children and, if neglected, can develop into St Vitus dance. That ailment, however, disappears when the child's mind and body grow and are properly occupied. With Mahler, unfortunately, an involuntary twitch persisted in his right leg throughout his life. He never mentioned it to me, and I gather he was rather ashamed of it. When he was walking, one noticed that anything from one to three steps would sometimes fall out of the regular rhythm. Standing still, one foot would tap lightly on the ground, kicking the spot. With his incomparably powerful will, he usually managed to control the impulse . . . It is incorrect, as is often said, that the stamping reflected Mahler's impatience or annoyance. It would occur just as often and even more vigorously when he laughed. And Mahler laughed readily and heartily like a child, tears streaming from his eyes. He would then take off his glasses to wipe the lenses dry, and give a little dance of joy on the spot where he stood . . . In conversation, peacefully expounding his thoughts, the tic was never seen. Nor did it appear when he exerted his will as, for example, while conducting. But when walking alone, working out a musical idea before he entered it in his sketch-book, he regularly started striding along with one or two paces that were too short.

Mahler's wife Alma wrote[2] that he 'dreamed his way through family life and childhood. He saw nothing of the unending tortures his mother had to endure from the brutality of his father'. This is inaccurate. In August 1910 Mahler consulted Sigmund Freud, the psychoanalyst, and in the course of their talk related this incident, which was recounted by Freud in a letter to Marie Bonaparte in 1925:

> His father, apparently a brutal person, treated his wife very badly,

[1] A. Roller (ed.), *Die Bildnisse von Gustav Mahler* (Leipzig and Vienna, 1922), pp. 9–28. Reprinted in N. Lebrecht's *Mahler Remembered* (London, 1987), p. 153.

[2] Alma Mahler, *Gustav Mahler, Memories and Letters* (2nd ed., 1968), p. 7.

3

and when Mahler was a young boy there was a specially painful scene between them. It became quite unbearable to the boy, who rushed away from the house. At that moment, however, a hurdy-gurdy in the street was grinding out the popular Viennese air O, *du lieber Augustin*. In Mahler's opinion the conjunction of high tragedy and light amusement was from then on inextricably fixed in his mind, and the one mood inevitably brought the other with it.[3]

It would be wise not to be too ingenuous about this piece of Mahlerian self-analysis, especially the conclusion which Freud said Mahler drew from it. He 'suddenly said that now he understood why his music had always been prevented from achieving the highest rank through the noblest passages, those inspired by the most profound emotions, being spoilt by the intrusion of some commonplace melody'.[4] It is all too pat, like a film-scenario simplification of an interview between Freud and Mahler. Of course Freud diagnosed a mother-fixation (and a father-fixation in Alma) and of course Mahler dredged this incident from his memory. But one suspects an element of scepticism in Mahler's approach to the encounter. It is difficult to believe that he really thought the juxtaposition of pathos and bathos 'spoiled' his works: many of the finest and most effective passages in his symphonies are occasioned by it, as he must have known. His model in this respect could well have been Schubert's Octet.

The roots of Mahler's virtues and failings both as man and composer may be found in other aspects of his childhood background. First, the consciousness of being a Jew. Even though in the Austria of Mahler's youth the attitude to Jews was reasonably liberal, they were still left in little doubt that they were 'outsiders', subject to frequent outbursts of anti-Semitic prejudice, tolerated by some but openly derided by the German minority. When Mahler was born in 1860 there were still restrictions on their movements, although these were lifted during that year, enabling Bernhard Mahler to move his business in December to Iglau (Jihlava), where he described himself on his letterhead as 'manufacturer of liqueurs, rum, rosolio, punch, essences and vinegar'. The inevitable consequence of their treatment was that some members of the Jewish communities became aggressively self-assertive. Bernhard Mahler,

[3] Ernest Jones, *Sigmund Freud: Life and Work*, Vol. II (1955), p. 89.
[4] Ernest Jones, *Sigmund Freud*, op. cit.

who seems to have been a typical *petit bourgeois*, took a leading part in the life of the Jewish community, and Gustav received an orthodox Jewish education. In later life, as we shall see, he became a Roman Catholic for political reasons, but he never denied his Jewish origin (not that he could easily have done so, because his appearance betrayed him). He disliked jokes about Jews, but asked his wife to warn him when he gesticulated too much because he thought it 'ill bred'. In 1906 he wrote to the conductor Oskar Fried: 'And don't forget we can do nothing about our being Jewish, our chief mistake. We must merely try to moderate a little those superficial aspects of our nature which really *do* disturb.'[5]

Alfred Roller believed that Mahler derived 'no joy' from his Jewish origins.

> They were a spur and a goad towards even higher and loftier achievement. He once explained to me the effect of his background on his creative works. 'You know', he said, 'it's like a man who comes into the world with one arm shorter than the other. The other arm has to cope with so much more, and in the end perhaps manages to do things that two sound arms would never have achieved.' People who were trying to be pleasant to him would often say that because of the way he had developed, he was really no longer a Jew. That made him sad. 'People should listen to my work', he said, 'and see if it means anything to them, then either accept it or reject it. But as for their prejudices for or against a Jew, they should leave those at home. That much I demand as my right.' The main thing that bound him to Judaism was compassion ... He was not a card-carrying Jew and at times was more attacked for not being so than he was from the other side. 'It's a funny thing', he often said with amusement during his final period as Director in Vienna, 'but it seems to me that the anti-Semitic papers are the only ones who still have any respect for me.'[6]

The second important influence from childhood was *Des Knaben Wunderhorn* (*Youth's Magic Horn*). This famous anthology of German folk-poetry was published in two volumes between 1805 and 1808 by Achim von Arnim and Clemens Brentano. To an English mind it suggests an anachronistic mixture of Grimm fairy-tales and A. E. Housman – one might call it *A Salzkammergut Lad*. In these poems, dead soldiers answer a roll-call, girls try to lure

[5] *Mahler's Unknown Letters*, ed. H. Blaukopf (London, 1986), p. 55.
[6] *Die Bildnisse von Gustav Mahler*, op. cit.

sentries from their duty, St Anthony preaches to the fishes, drummer-boys go to the gallows, the cuckoo and the nightingale have a song contest with the donkey as judge. Always there are the symbols of night, of lost love, of the beauties of nature, of sudden death and trumpet-calls. It is sometimes said that Mahler discovered the *Wunderhorn* poems in his twenties, but Ida Dehmel, widow of the poet Richard Dehmel, recorded a conversation with Mahler in 1905 from which she learned that 'from earliest childhood his relationship to the book had been particularly close'.[7] Everything points to this being true. The book's spell would have been intensified in the boy's mind by the associations of its atmosphere with the reality of living near an army barracks and loitering there to listen to the bugles and the bands. From Slavonic servant girls he learned folk-tunes which, at the age of four, he could play on an accordion or concertina.

A childhood neighbour and schoolfriend of Mahler in Iglau and later at Vienna University, was Theodor Fischer, son of the choirmaster there. At a memorial meeting for Mahler in the town in March 1931, he gave his memories of those days, which were later printed in *Deutsche Heimat*. Fischer was by then chief magistrate of Iglau. His father taught Mahler harmony, and Mahler, in spite of his religion, sang in performances at St James's Church of Mozart's *Requiem*, Rossini's *Stabat Mater* and Beethoven's *Mount of Olives*. 'There was a children's maid in my family, Nanni', Fischer related,

who knew lots of fairy-tales. On rainy afternoons, when we could not go out, Gustav and I listened avidly to her tales. Among the stories was, I recall, *Des klagenden Lied* [*sic*] (The Song of Sorrow) which may have given rise to one of Mahler's subsequent compositions . . . His musical talent developed very soon; from earliest childhood he played by ear and with amazing skill and on the concertina all kinds of tunes and songs that he had heard from guests in his father's tavern. He had his first piano lesson at six years old from one of the players in the town orchestra, then from Kapellmeister Viktorin of the Iglau theatre, and eventually from piano teacher Brosch . . . An infantry regiment was permanently stationed at the Iglau garrison and we children would obviously always be there when the army marched out with fife and drum, staged exercises and played light music or at military funerals; we would blow childish imitations of signals . . .[8]

[7] See Alma Mahler's *Gustav Mahler*, op. cit., p. 93.
[8] T. Fischer, *Aus Gustav Mahlers Jugendzeit* (*Deutsche Heimat*, Vol. 7, 1931, pp. 264–8). Reprinted in *Mahler Remembered*, op. cit., pp. 15–20.

Another boy who lived in Iglau and was five years older than Mahler was Guido Adler, the musicologist. They became close friends when they were students in Vienna. He too remembered the bugle calls and drill motifs. The composer Ernst Křenek, whose uncle was born in Iglau at about the same time as Mahler, said that Iglau was not a garrison town and that the first soldiers to be stationed there were Prussians, after the defeat of Austria, in 1866. But this does not appear to contradict or disqualify Fischer's and Adler's recollection, or indeed Mahler's.

In the full version of her recollections of Mahler,[9] Natalie Bauer-Lechner recorded Mahler's own memories of his development as a musician:

> The first thing he composed on paper at the age of six was a polka, to which he added a funeral march as an introduction. [The child was father to the man!] . . . He produced this in response to a promise from his mother that he would receive two crowns. 'My second attempt [Mahler told her] was when my father gave me the task of setting a poem to music. Again a few crowns were promised as a reward – my various sallies into art were always for the sake of sordid gain . . . Later on I did become keener on composing of my own accord: a sonata for violin and piano, a nocturne for the cello: all sorts of things for piano, and finally an opera with a libretto that a schoolfriend wrote for me. It was on the basis of this fragment (because I never got round to finishing it) that I had the great misfortune to be accepted by Hellmesberger (that idiot) for the composition class at the Vienna Conservatory, missing out on the harmony and counterpoint classes . . . Apparently I was still a babe in arms when I copied little songs and sang them back. Then, when I must have been about three, I was given an accordion and by working out the notes of the things I had heard I was soon able to play them perfectly.
>
> One day when I was not yet four a funny thing happened. A military band – something I delighted in all my childhood – came marching past our house one morning. I no sooner heard it than I shot out of the living room. Wearing scarcely more than a chemise – they hadn't dressed me yet – I trailed after the soldiers with my little accordion until quite some time later a couple of ladies from near by discovered me at the market place . . .
>
> My first acquaintance with the piano was made on another visit to

[9] Owned by Henri-Louis de La Grange. Certain extracts were published for the first time in Lebrecht's *Mahler Remembered*, op. cit., pp. 7–14.

my grandparents in Ledeč. There was a battered old instrument in the attic which I came across by chance when we were clambering around and exploring the upper regions of the house. This jangling hulk excited my curiosity. I was still so small that I could only reach the keys with my hands held high above my head, but in this uncomfortable position and with my tiny fingers I plonked out all sorts of things I had heard, so recognizably that my parents and grandparents, who could hear down below – and then discovered that it came from me – were absolutely astonished. When Grandpa asked me whether I would enjoy having a big toy like that, I said yes with gusto, and the very next day, to my indescribable delight, the monstrosity arrived in Iglau, trundled over on an oxcart. They soon engaged a teacher for me and I know for a fact that, to please my mother who always sat near by when I was practising, I worked hard at the task . . .

Bernhard Mahler, impelled by desire for cultural improvement and by the not unworthy ambition that his children should succeed where he had failed, decided that Gustav's future lay in music. Within three years the boy had progressed so well that he could give pianoforte lessons to another boy. On 13th October 1870, when he was ten, he gave a public recital in Iglau. In the winter of 1870–1 he was sent by his father to study at the Gymnasium in Prague and to continue pianoforte lessons in the home of Moritz Grünfeld, a leather merchant with a family of eleven children. Here he was ill treated, his shoes and clothes were taken from him and others given to him to wear, his diet was near-starvation. Years later he told his wife: 'I accepted it as a matter of course.' All accounts of Mahler's boyhood mention his extreme passivity in the face of suffering and his dreaminess, as if he was oblivious of the anger and cruelty directed towards him, although the likely explanation is that he was deliberately suppressing their effect on him. Asked what he would like to be 'when he grew up', Gustav replied: 'A martyr.'

Eventually his father heard of the conditions at the Grünfeld house and fetched Gustav home, but not before the boy had witnessed, involuntarily, a crude love passage between one of the Grünfeld sons and a maidservant. Thinking the girl needed rescuing, he went across to her but was violently abused by both lovers. At home in Iglau Gustav's music lessons continued. He also read widely and deeply – where literature was concerned he was always an intellectual – and perhaps he had his father to thank for this too, for Bernhard boasted of having a library. In any case his taste for philosophical and religious controversy was typically Jewish. During 1874 he passed through the miserable experience of his thirteen-year-old brother Ernst's long fatal cardiac illness. 'For months he scarcely left his bedside and never tired of telling him stories,' Alma relates.[10] In the spring of 1875, on the prompting of an estate manager, who heard Gustav play Beethoven's *Les Adieux* sonata, Mahler's father took him to Vienna to play to Julius Epstein (1832–1926), professor of the pianoforte at the Conservatory. Epstein was 'struck by a remarkable look in the boy's face'. After hearing Gustav play for a few minutes he said: 'He is a born musician . . . I cannot possibly be wrong. This young man has spirit, but he will never take over his father's spirit factory!'[11]

10 Alma Mahler, *Gustav Mahler*, op. cit., p. 7.
11 Paul Stefan, *Gustav Mahler, a study of his personality and work* (1931), p. 13. Some accounts say that Mahler was first taken to Epstein on the recommendation of Gustav Schwarz, manager of the Morawan estate owned by the father of his friend Josef Steiner (1857–1913). Ignatz Steiner recognized Mahler's exceptional gifts and introduced him to Schwarz in 1874.

2

Bruckner's disciples

Mahler entered the Vienna Conservatory in September 1875. The director since 1851 had been Joseph Hellmesberger, violinist, leader of a celebrated string quartet, conductor, and anti-Semite. He was forty-seven. Mahler's teachers were Julius Epstein for pianoforte, Robert Fuchs (1847–1927) – who had only recently joined the staff – for harmony, and Franz Krenn (1816–97) for composition. Fuchs told Alma Mahler years afterwards: 'Mahler always played truant and yet there was nothing he couldn't do.' That he was already a composer of songs may be deduced from the fact that his fellow students spoke of him as 'another Schubert'. He also continued privately with his general education, for which he paid by giving pianoforte lessons.

Also in Vienna, attending the university, was his friend Theodor Fischer. He, Mahler, Emil Freund (later to be Mahler's lawyer), and the copper-engraver Gustav Frank formed a literary club. 'Our meetings', Fischer wrote,[1] 'would debate literary and current concerns and usually ended in us wandering half the night bewitched in the moonlight by the glorious buildings of Old Vienna and totally abandoned to romantic enthusiasms. Mahler lived in the fourth district, Margarethenstrasse 7, fourth floor, door 40. So far as I can recall he gave piano lessons and acted frequently as piano accompanist in solo concerts at the Bösendorfer Hall . . .'

Mahler's fellow students are of more interest than the professors, notably Hugo Wolf, Hans Rott, and Rudolf Krzyzanowski, who was Mahler's closest friend at this time. Together they shared poverty. Mahler was slightly more fortunate than the others: he had the income from his teaching (using some of it on one occasion to pay for the hire of Wolf's pianoforte) and his parents sent him parcels of food and clothing. Even so, he was very poor and in 1876 applied to the Conservatory, with Epstein's support, to be excused his fees.

[1] *Aus Gustav Mahlers Jugendzeit*, op. cit., p. 267.

Epstein, in fact paid a half fee for Mahler from 1876–7 onwards and found him pianoforte pupils, including his son Richard.

Mahler at this period has been described by Friedrich Eckstein (1861–1939), a pupil of Anton Bruckner, as

> shortish, betraying a certain irritability in his uneven gait. His small face, framed by a full brown beard, was intellectually alive and tense; he spoke wittily in a strong Austrian brogue. He always carried a bundle of books or scores under his arm and conversation with him was sporadic . . . Many years later Hugo Wolf told me that, when they were very young, he had met Mahler in the Herrengasse with a roll of music under his arm. Asked what it was, Mahler replied some songs he had just composed; could Wolf take a look? In the middle of the street, Wolf read the manuscript through and, beaming, declared: 'Very good! Excellent! I like them tremendously.' Mahler, delighted by his opinion, dropped his eyes, hesitated shyly and said: 'Well, I think we've got Mendelssohn licked!'[2]

Mahler's impulsive industriousness was evident even then and in 1880 it caused a rift with Wolf which foreshadowed the tragedy to follow. Wolf confided his wish to compose a fairy-tale opera and, in discussion with Mahler, chose *Rübezahl*. Mahler began work on the libretto and completed it within a few hours. He showed it to Wolf, who had also made a start. Wolf was so offended that he abandoned the scheme. Mahler's libretto still exists.

The friendship with Rott was significant. Two years older than Mahler, Rott was an organ pupil of Bruckner. He was an extremely gifted composer who died at the age of twenty-six. 'What music lost in him', Mahler wrote in 1898, 'is immeasurable . . . He was the founder of the New Symphony as I understand it'. Mahler wrote of their 'shared influences' and that they were 'like two fruits from the same tree, produced from the same soil, nourished by the same air'. The shared influences were Wagner – Rott went to the first Bayreuth Festival in 1876 – and Brahms. Rott composed a Symphony in E which was played through at the Vienna Conservatory in 1878 and condemned by the authorities there as 'too Wagnerian'. Presumably it was this work that was entered for the Conservatory's composition prize when a work by Mahler was adjudged first. When Mahler

[2] F. Eckstein, *Alte unnennbare Tage!* (Vienna, 1936) pp. 105–13. Reprinted in Lebrecht's *Mahler Remembered*, pp. 26–9.

proudly told his parents of his success, his mother, according to Alma Mahler's biography of Mahler,[3] 'wept tears of indignation and said: "All the same, Rott's work was better than yours".' Rott entered the symphony for the 1880 Beethoven Prize. Brahms was one of the judges and, when it was played to him, he remarked that Rott 'couldn't have produced it himself', having noted the similarity of one of its themes to the big tune in the finale of his own C minor Symphony.

In a letter to Emil Freund from Vienna on 1st November 1880, Mahler reported that 'my friend Hans Rott has become *insane!*' Rott was taken to an asylum, but was awarded a state stipendium in 1881. He died there of tuberculosis in 1884. Mahler did not forget his friend, nor did he forget the symphony. Its two inner movements, an *adagio* and a *Ländler*, are what we should now call Mahlerian, the *adagio* anticipating the *adagio* finale of Mahler's Third Symphony. Whether sub-consciously or as tributes to Rott's talent, Mahler 'borrowed' themes from Rott's symphony for his own Second and Fifth Symphonies and there are references, too, in his Third and Seventh Symphonies. In 1900, when Mahler was conductor of the Vienna Philharmonic Orchestra, he borrowed the manuscript with the intention of performing it. That he failed to do so may have been because he recognized that the symphony, for all its excitements, was not a fully developed work of art – 'it is like someone taking a run for the longest possible throw and not quite hitting the mark', he said –but more likely because of the severance of his connection with the orchestra in 1901.

There was another – and important – common factor binding these young men: their admiration for, leading to friendship with, Bruckner, who at this date was fifty-two. He went to concerts with them, preferring to stand in their company than to sit in the comfort of a box. Rott was a special favourite and it was probably through him that Mahler met Bruckner. One may imagine with what excitement the youths listened to his account of his journey to Bayreuth in 1876 for the first cycle of Wagner's *Der Ring*. Mahler enrolled for various courses at the university so that he could attend Bruckner's lectures, but instead of attending philosophy lectures he 'industriously visited the Vienna Woods'.

'I was never a pupil of Bruckner,' Mahler wrote.[4] 'Everyone thinks

---

[3] A. Mahler, *Gustav Mahler*, op. cit., p. 8.
[4] Gabriel Engel, *Gustav Mahler, Song-Symphonist* (New York, 1932), p. 21.

I studied with him because in my student days in Vienna I was so often in his company and was reckoned among his first disciples. Bruckner's happy disposition and his childlike, trusting nature made our relationship one of open friendship. Naturally the realization and understanding of his ideals which I then arrived at cannot have been without influence upon my development as artist and man.'

On 16th December 1877 the second version of Bruckner's Third Symphony was performed by the Vienna Philharmonic Orchestra, who had refused to play the first version three years earlier. The occasion was a disaster, but the unfortunate Bruckner was comforted by the enthusiasm of the two seventeen-year-olds, Mahler and Rudolf Krzyzanowski. To them he entrusted the task of making a pianoforte-duet arrangement of the symphony, under Epstein's supervision. This was published by Rättig in 1878, and Bruckner was so pleased that he gave his manuscript of the second version to Mahler. (This manuscript score, which lacked the finale, was bought by the Austrian Government from Alma Mahler in 1948.)

Mahler left the Conservatory, having gained his diploma, at the end of the summer term in July 1878. He had had a successful sojourn there: prizes for piano playing (Schubert's A minor sonata) in 1875–6 and 1876–7, and the composition prize in 1876–7 for the first movement of a pianoforte quintet. On his last day at the Conservatory the prize-winning *scherzo* of another Mahler pianoforte quintet was played. He had had frustrations too, including the refusal by Hellmesberger to continue rehearsing the students' orchestra in a symphony he had written[5] because 'your parts are full of mistakes'.

The Vienna of Mahler's impressionable youth had just emerged from the period in which it had become, both in appearance and in fact, a great administrative imperial capital. Its bourgeois atmosphere was a compound of sophistication and sentimentality. In its close-knit society, intrigues flourished and artists were worshipped or detested, such was the overriding interest in music, theatre and the graphic arts. The name and work of Richard Wagner still evoked passions and prejudices of the most violent, disproportionate and humourless kind, splitting families, affecting politics, determining lives. To the young he was a god; to the middle aged and elderly he was antichrist. No one could be neutral. In Mahler's first

[5] Presumed to be one of two symphonies of this period.

term at the Conservatory, in the winter of 1875, Wagner went to Vienna to supervise productions of *Tannhäuser* and *Lohengrin*. His visit was the major topic of conversation, and of course his antagonists, led by the critic Eduard Hanslick, went into action. The fanatical devotion to Wagner which these performances generated in Hugo Wolf is well known.[6] Mahler, too, was equally spellbound.

Yet we can also perceive what effect this sort of episode must have had on his sensitive and solitary nature. A Jew with his family background would inevitably feel isolated in Viennese society; add to this that he now saw what senseless and bitter hatred could be directed against creative geniuses like Wagner and Bruckner. After all, he had himself seen Hellmesberger, the Conservatory director, laughing and jeering at Bruckner's Third Symphony. He saw too with what simple faith Bruckner was able to combat the malevolence of his detractors and how his music remained unaffected by bitterness. He saw, with the fierce vision of adolescence, the depths of human suffering experienced within his own family: the deaths of Ernst and the other children, the unhinged behaviour of two of his brothers and of some of his friends, such as Rott, the misery of his parents. Imagine all these impressions crowding into a mind already striving to express itself in music and one has an epitome of the violent contrast in his spiritual outlook on mankind: regarding it in one light as squalid and base, in another as a doomed aspirant for redemption – perhaps for resurrection, even – infinitely deserving of compassion. What could he really believe? There is the crux of his lifelong inner conflict and tension, so obviously reflected in his music. No wonder that, like so many other doubters, he took comfort from the one unchanging element, the beauty of nature, a consolation for even the inescapable fact of one's own mortality. No wonder we find him, on the eve of his nineteenth birthday, writing to his friend Josef Steiner in these romanticized but significant terms:

A great deal has been going on since I last wrote. But I can't tell you about it. Only this: that I have become a different person; whether a better one, I don't know, anyway not a happier one. The greatest intensity of the most joyful vitality and the most consuming yearning for death dominate my heart in turn, very often alternate hour by hour – one thing I know: I can't go on like this much longer! When the abominable tyranny of our modern hypocrisy and mendacity has

[6] See Frank Walker, *Hugo Wolf* (London, 2nd ed, 1968), pp. 26–33.

driven me to the point of dishonouring myself, when the inextricable web of conditions in art and life has filled my heart with disgust for all that is sacred to me – art, love, religion – what way out is there but self-annihilation? Wildly I wrench at the bonds that chain me to the loathsome, insipid swamp of this life, and with all the strength of despair I cling to sorrow, my only consolation. – Then all at once the sun shines upon me – and gone is the ice that encased my heart, again I see the blue sky and the flowers swaying in the wind, and my mocking laughter dissolves into tears of love. Then I *needs must* love this world with all its deceit and frivolity and its eternal laughter . . . O earth, my beloved earth, when, ah, when will you give refuge to him who is forsaken, receiving him back into your womb? Behold! Mankind has cast him out, and he flees from its cold and heartless bosom, he flees to you, to you alone! O, take him in, eternal, all-embracing mother, give a resting-place to him who is without friend and without rest![7]

The forsaken one – the martyr! In that outburst is a forerunner of the poetic sentiments which were to inspire his masterpiece, *Das Lied von der Erde*, over twenty-five years later: 'Whither I go? . . . I seek rest for my lonely heart! . . . the dear earth everywhere grows green again.' To all this add, as a further facet of his complex personality, that Mahler was subject, like many creative artists, to periods of sudden melancholia. As he wrote to Emil Freund from Hamburg in 1891:

The past has caught up with me – all I have lost – the loneliness of the present – all sorts of things – you know these moods of mine from earlier years – when I would be overcome by sadness even while among my friends – when I was still all youth, vigour and stamina – so you can well imagine how I spend these long, *lonely* afternoons and evenings here. – *None* with whom I have anything in common – whether a share in the past or shared hopes for the future.

This is the characteristic complaint of the artist, yet another indication of the isolation he felt simply because he was a creator. Elgar, another poor boy who made good, whom Mahler resembles in several other respects, was also deeply conscious of this loneliness and complained strongly that 'no one wanted him'. But to interpret

[7] *Selected Letters of Gustav Mahler*, ed. Martner (London, 1979), pp. 54–6. Except where stated, all further quotations from Mahler's letters are from this source.

Mahler's adolescent letter to Steiner as symptomatic of a 'death-wish' is to go too far. It is easy to speak of men having a 'death-wish', but not easy to prove it. There is no doubt that Mahler, in common with the rest of mankind, thought a lot about death and was eventually forced to face the comparative brevity of his own life, but his music accepts death as a reality and is often filled with joyful affirmation of life and of the world's beauty.

Steiner, born in 1857, attended Iglau Gymnasium from 1867 to 1875, so was a fellow-pupil of Mahler. He read law at Vienna University from 1875 to 1879 where the friendship continued. He and Mahler spent summer holidays together in 1875 and 1876 at Ronow, a dairy farm near Caslau, Bohemia, about twenty-five miles from Iglau. (In one of his June 1879 letters to Steiner, Mahler mentions a memory evoked by the 'kindly name' of Ronow: 'I see gardens, and many people there, and a tree, with a name carved in its bark: Pauline. And a blue-eyed girl bends sideways, laughing, she breaks a bunch of grapes from the vine for me – memory causes my cheeks to flush for the second time – I see the two eyes that once made a thief of me – then once again it all recedes'.) During the 1875 holiday, Steiner wrote the libretto of an opera, *Herzog Ernst von Schwaben* and Mahler composed some of the music. Returning next year to continue their work, they found that Steiner's aunt, whose farm it was, had burned all the papers they had stored in the attic. They did not bother to start again, but thirty years later Steiner could remember enough of the music to play fragments of it to his wife. After 1879 he and Mahler lost touch as they pursued their different careers. One wonders if Mahler ever knew his friend's book of poetry, *Aus meinen Sommertagen*, published in Vienna in 1908.

After leaving the Conservatory in 1878 Mahler returned to Iglau in the late summer. He earned a precarious living by giving pianoforte lessons, but his preoccupation was with his compositions. While at the Conservatory he had composed part of a pianoforte quartet, and had written a violin sonata and a pianoforte quintet, both of which were played at Iglau on 12th September 1876. For his dramatic cantata, *Das klagende Lied*, he first wrote the poem himself, completing it in March 1878. After his holiday at home in 1878 he returned to Vienna in the autumn ostensibly to attend lectures at the university. He continued to earn from teaching the pianoforte.

In the summer of 1879, Mahler was engaged as piano-tutor to the children of Moritz Baumgarten at Puszta-Batta, near Budapest. It was from there, in mid-June, that he wrote his letters to Steiner from which quotation has been made above. He was bored and lonely there – hence his outpouring, no doubt – and wrote to Albert Spiegler: 'You cannot imagine, dear Albert, how I yearn to see human beings again, and how I long once again to hear the sound of the organ and the peal of bells'. In August he went to stay with Emil Freund at Seelau, twenty-eight miles from Iglau, and then spent some time at home, where he fell in love with Josephine Poisl, daughter of the postmaster. He returned to Vienna in September, sharing lodgings with Wolf and Rudolf Krzyzanowski at 23 Opernring. Later he rented a small villa in the suburb of Währing.

Writing to his friend Anton Krisper from Vienna on 22nd September 1879, Mahler said: 'A new name is now inscribed in my heart alongside yours – true, only whisperingly and blushingly, but no less powerfully'. This was Josephine. He wrote several poems about her and planned to set five of them to music. In February and March 1880 three songs were composed, *Im Lenz*, *Winterlied* and *Maitanz im Grunen*, but the other two were not written because the affair ended suddenly. He wrote to Anton Krisper in March 1880: 'I have just written some lines of poetry which I pass on to you because they will best reveal my inner thoughts to you'. The poem, headed *Vergessene Liebe* (Forgotten Love), contains lines like 'How desolate my heart, How empty the world . . .', 'My sweet love! For the last time?' and 'Ah, This torment indeed must burn in my heart for ever!'

Throughout this period he was at work on the music for *Das klagende Lied*. This typical piece of German fairy-tale romanticism was the first fruit of the influence of *Des Knaben Wunderhorn*. He completed the full score on 1st November 1880. On that day he wrote to Emil Freund: 'My fairy-tale is finished at long last – truly a child of sorrow, more than a whole year's labour. But it has turned out to be worth it. The next thing is to use all means at my disposal to get it performed.' In this aim he failed. He entered it in 1881 for the Beethoven Prize of 500 gulden instituted in 1875 by the Gesellschaft der Musikfreunde and open to present and past Conservatory students. The jury included Brahms, Hans Richter and Carl Goldmark, and they rejected Mahler's cantata.

3

Cassel, Leipzig, Budapest

Mahler said in later life that if he had won the Beethoven Prize he could have avoided 'this hellish life in the theatre', by which he meant conducting opera. He was romanticizing. He had begun his career as a conductor before he even finished *Das klagende Lied*. He had been given a post at the health resort of Hall, Upper Austria, in the summer of 1880 to conduct musical comedies and to perform such chores as tidying the pit after the performance. What remains unexplained is why he was advised to try conducting when he had hitherto shown no inclination in that direction. According to Paul Stefan,[1] the publisher Rättig advised Mahler to see an agent. Through this agent the Hall engagement was offered and accepted against the advice of Mahler's parents but on the advice of Epstein, his mentor and pianoforte teacher. Up to this point it might have been expected that Mahler would become a concert pianist. Accounts of his playing indicate that it was exceptionally compelling, especially of Beethoven and Bach. Friedrich (Fritz) Löhr, another member of Mahler's student circle in Vienna, spent a summer holiday with him at Löhr's home in Perchtoldsdorf in 1884 when Mahler played for many hours.

> Every technical problem was annulled, everything was disembodied, cerebral, passionately and spiritually intent on all that passed, without conscious contact, from the keys into himself . . . In Beethoven's Op. 111, the opening storm broke in a fearsome maestoso, shatteringly intense, with a ferocity wilder than I have ever heard; while the finale faded out luminously into the loveliest beauty, softly softer still, from earthliness into eternity.[2]

Yet after about 1880, except for chamber music for pleasure and

[1] P. Stefan, *Gustav Mahler*, op. cit., p. 20.
[2] A. M. Mahler (ed.), *Gustav Mahler Briefe, 1879–1911* (Berlin and Vienna, 1924), pp. 473–4.

playing through what he had written, he confined his playing to occasional appearances as accompanist in recitals of his songs. Otto Klemperer heard him in Berlin in 1906 as accompanist to the Dutch baritone Johannes Meschaert.[3]

The year 1880 is also notable for the evidence of another of the friendships which sustained Mahler during his youth. This was with Guido Adler, regarded as the true founder of musicology in Austria. He was born in 1855 and, as already related, spent part of his boyhood in Iglau. But he and Mahler did not meet until Mahler went to Vienna. A common interest in the music of Wagner may have brought them together. Several of Mahler's friendships at this time were the consequence of shared passions for Wagner or Dostoevsky, religion or vegetarianism. With Siegfried Lipiner, for example, religion as a moral force in art was the basis of their relationship.

Adler, with Felix Mottl, the conductor, and Karl Wolf formed in 1872 the *Wiener akademischer Wagner-verein*, to which Mahler belonged from 1877 to 1879, together with Krisper, Rott and Krzyzanowski. Another member of the society, later its chairman, was Franz Schaumann. From a letter from Schaumann to Adler, dated 10th April 1880, we learn that Adler must have suggested Mahler to Schaumann for the post of chorusmaster somewhere. Explaining that another individual was already being considered, Schaumann adds: 'Mahler, whose artistic aspiration is well known to me, would, with the exception of the direction of the concerts, hardly find a [suitable] sphere of activity; for in such positions it is less a matter of artistic ability than of a rather mechanical musician's experience. Just because of the friendly opinion that I cherish for Mahler's talents, I would advise against such a post, simply because of his competence; for he would certainly be disillusioned in the first weeks'.[4] From this, it can be deduced that Adler knew of Mahler's *conducting* ambitions.

After the summer at Hall – the theatre was a tiny wooden construction, seating about 200, unfit for use in wet weather – Mahler returned to Vienna and his pianoforte pupils. He finished *Das klagende Lied* and began an opera on the classical subject, *Die*

3 A Welte piano-roll recording, made in Germany, of Mahler playing the finale of his Fourth Symphony is included in Bernstein's box-set of the symphonies (CBS 77508).

4 E. R. Reilly, *Gustav Mahler and Guido Adler, Records of a Friendship* (Cambridge, 1982), pp. 82–3.

Argonauten. From September 1881 to April 1882 he was in Laibach (now Ljubljana) for a season at the Landestheater, conducting such operas as *Il Trovatore, Faust, Die Zauberflöte, Martha* and *Der Freischütz*. Back in Vienna he worked on another opera, never completed, *Rübezahl* (the cause of his rift with Wolf over the libretto), and on a *Nordic Symphony*. In 1882, on 19th September, his home town of Iglau saw him in action as a conductor when he conducted Suppé's operetta *Boccaccio* there. These early operatic experiences were invaluable. He learned how to cope with inadequacies and how to adapt.

From Iglau he returned to Vienna where he had a restless existence, as he told Anton Krisper early in January 1883: 'I have moved into new quarters every fortnight. I have now been in Vienna three months and, aside from various hotels, I am already at my fifth address. You can easily imagine that my work [on *Rübezahl*] has not been going particularly well; now that I ought to be in the best frame of mind, I am being disturbed by the screaming of a small child – thus I escape one vexation only to come up against another.'

This peripatetic existence had three weeks earlier evoked a delightful letter from his mother inviting him home for the Christmas holiday:

> You need not bring any luggage, of course. If need be I will help you out with laundry, though if you have any torn socks or shirts you can bring them with you in the coach in your travelling-bag and the journey will cost you next to nothing, then you can stay at home for a few days . . . Will you write now to let us know if you are coming? and when? so that I can warm your room . . . Why these endless changes of lodgings? I don't believe there can be a single person apart from you who changes his lodgings every fortnight. Are you going to end up changing your lodgings every time you change your linen? And won't you finally find yourself without any linen or clothes? I know you: you will forget something at each place – and will go on moving until you have nothing left. Am I not right? . . . One more thing, though: if you come home bring with you a bottle of *French brandy* . . .

In spite of all her tribulations, Marie Mahler sounds to have been rather fun.

For two months from 10th January to 18th March 1883 he conducted at the Royal Municipal Theatre in Olmütz (Olomouc), also in Moravia, where under primitive conditions he directed works by Meyerbeer, Verdi and Méhul (*Joseph*).

Jacques Manheit, a baritone in the Olmütz company (which comprised seventeen solo singers, a chorus of twenty-eight and an orchestra of twenty-four), has left an account[5] of Mahler's impact. Mahler was engaged in mid-season when the incumbent was dismissed. The director, Emmanuel Raoul, informed the company that 'he had found a young conductor, said to be a genius but also a very curious individual'. After Mahler's first chorus rehearsal, the singers emerged saying they were hoarse and could not work with him.

An hour later we soloists went into rehearsal. Mahler did not introduce himself to anyone. We regarded him with overt antipathy, but he did not respond to interruptions, merely demanded that we obey his instructions. And, curiously, no one dared contradict the young man . . .

Gradually the little provincial town became used to the peculiarities of the young conductor. He was not liked, but they learned to fear him. His manner of demanding and commanding was so decisive that no one dared oppose him, especially as performances had greatly improved under his direction. He hardly knew a single opera, learning each work as he went along. He did not mind that no one sought his company: all he demanded was that each did his duty. I considered myself lucky to see him often. I soon realized whose spiritual child he was.

The following episode is highly characteristic. One day I met Mahler in a coffee-house, utterly self-absorbed. When I sympathetically inquired why he was so sad, he replied that he had had bad news from home, his father was ill. Next morning on my way to the theatre I saw a very confused man running through the street, crying and groaning loudly. Only with difficulty did I discover it was Mahler. Remembering the previous day's events, I asked anxiously 'In heaven's name, has something happened to your father?' 'Disaster, disaster, a catastrophe', Mahler cried. 'The greatest disaster has happened. *Der Meister* is dead.'

This was 14th February 1883. Richard Wagner had died in Venice the previous day. Manheit added that it was impossible to deal with Mahler in the weeks following.

Mahler's feelings about his work in Olmütz were plainly expressed in a letter to Friedrich Löhr written on 12th February:

Since the moment I crossed the threshold of the theatre in Olmütz, I

[5] L. Karpath, 'Aus Gustav Mahlers Umfängen' (*Wiener Journal*, 5th February 1930). Reprinted in *Mahler Remembered*, op. cit., pp. 29–32.

have felt like a man about to face the Day of Judgement. Take a thoroughbred horse and yolk it to a cart with oxen — all it can do is pull and sweat along with them . . . I am more or less always alone — i.e. if I am not rehearsing — so far — thank God — what I have been conducting is almost exclusively Meyerbeer and Verdi. By dogged scheming I have succeeded in getting Wagner and Mozart out of the repertory — for I could not endure rattling off, say, *Lohengrin* or *Don Giovanni* in this place here. Tomorrow we are doing *Joseph in Aegypten* [Méhul]. An extremely charming work, with something of Mozart's grace. I really did get great enjoyment out of rehearsing it. And I must say — despite their incredible lack of sensibility, these people I have to work with here do now and then pull themselves together a bit for my sake, and this time they have tried somewhat harder — though I'm afraid it's only a way of showing they're sorry for the 'idealist' — a very contemptuous epithet, this — for the idea that an artist can become utterly absorbed in a work of art is quite beyond them . . .

On leaving Olmütz, Mahler returned to Vienna where from 31st March to 4th May 1883 he was chorus coach for a season of nine Italian operas which were performed at the Carltheater.

News of Mahler's success with Bizet's *Carmen*, which had first been produced only eight years earlier, reached Wilhelm Treiber, the principal conductor of opera at the Royal Prussian Court Theatre at Cassel. A stage director who had watched him at Olmütz commended his ability to obtain good results from poor material. An invitation followed to Mahler to become second conductor at Cassel in the autumn of 1883. Before taking up the post, he went in July to Bayreuth, where Hermann Levi was conducting *Parsifal*. From Iglau later in the month he wrote to Löhr, the closest of his friends at this period: 'When I walked out of the Festspielhaus, incapable of uttering a word, I knew I had come to understand all that is greatest and most painful and that I would bear it with me, inviolate, for the rest of my life. So I returned home, only to find those whom I love so poorly . . . my beloved parents – and I myself am so hard and cruel to them, yet I can't help it, and I go on tormenting them to the utmost.' In Cassel he quickly became disillusioned because Treiber insisted on confining him to comic operas by lesser composers. In January 1884 he wrote to Hans von Bülow asking if he could become personal assistant and pupil. Bülow sent the letter to Treiber.

Already the fanatical zeal which characterized his genius as a conductor was evident. He was, as we should now say, 'a natural'. To those who shared his ideals he seemed like the answer to their prayers; to the others – in his opinion fools, and he suffered them much less than gladly – he was the reverse. But, as Jacques Manheit recalled, he was not without a sense of humour :

> I persuaded Mahler to come to the café next door, where we played billiards. 'What exercises are you performing, my dear conductor?' I asked, as he waved his cue about in great circles. 'Carry on with your game', he replied, 'I am conducting the first act of *Les Huguenots*. Your colleagues are so tough with me that I have been practising giving them cues'.[6]

By now the pattern of Mahler's life was established – conductor and composer, one activity rivalling but fertilizing the other. He had one of those dual natures which need to be at full stretch, to be in perpetual conflict between one set of pressures and the other. To the scholar Guido Adler he analysed himself correctly: 'I need *practical* exercise for my musical ability to counterbalance the enormous creative activity that goes on within'. The warring elements in Mahler – the mystic and the man of action, the composer and the conductor – were the catalyst for his genius. Although he sometimes complained about his conducting 'crushing his soul', it became a necessity for him, if only because it enabled him to keep in intimate touch with the practical mechanics of his art.

At Cassel Mahler had another love affair – with a singer, Johanna Emma Richter. A native of Danzig, she was about twenty-two years old, an averagely competent dramatic soprano who specialized in coloratura roles. Mahler obliquely refers to the affair in a letter to Löhr dated 19th September 1883, a month after he took up his post: 'Of my own free will I have let myself be shackled, chain upon chain, and so have returned to that same disgraceful old condition of bondage. I mean to fight my way bravely through it . . .' Löhr, too, was in love and both men evidently found their affairs in crisis on Christmas Day 1883, for Mahler wrote to Löhr some months later: 'Heinrich [Krzyzanowski] told me, my dear Fritz, of the sorrows that befell you on Christmas Day. So I may as well tell you that I was afflicted in the same way on the same day, and that with that day there began a period of unceasing and intolerable struggle to which there is as yet no end in sight, a struggle I have to endure day in, day

[6] 'Aus Gustav Mahlers Umfängen', op. cit.

out, indeed hour by hour.'

The progress of this stormy love affair, until the time when Mahler knew that he was moving to another post, can be traced from references in letters to Löhr:

August 1884: I had scarcely set foot in the streets of Cassel when the same terrible old spell befell me, and I don't know how to regain my balance. I have seen her again, and she is as enigmatic as ever! All I can say is: God help me! You will have noticed, in the last days of the time we spent together [Löhr stayed with Mahler in Iglau in July 1884] how now and then some sombre forces took hold of me – it was my dread of the inevitable. I am going to see her this afternoon, 'I am going to call on her', after which my situation will at once take on definite shape.

1st January 1885: It was a strange way indeed that I spent the first minutes of this year. Yesterday evening I was alone with her, both of us awaiting the new year's arrival almost without exchanging a word. Her thoughts were not bent on the present, and when the bell chimed and tears gushed from her eyes, it overwhelmed me that I, I might not dry them. She went into the adjacent room and stood for a while in silence at the window, and when she returned, still weeping, the nameless grief had risen up between us like an everlasting partition-wall, and there was nothing I could do but press her hand and go . . . I have written a cycle of songs, six of them so far, all dedicated to her. She does not know them. What can they tell her but what she knows? I shall send with this the concluding song, although the inadequate words cannot render even a small part. – The idea of the songs as a whole is that a wayfaring man, who has been stricken by fate, now sets forth into the world, travelling wherever his road may lead him . . . I spent Christmas Eve alone, although she had invited me to her place. Dear Fritz! All that you know about her is mere misunderstanding. I have begged her forgiveness for everything, casting my pride and egoism from me. She is everything that is lovable in this world. I would shed every drop of my blood for her. But I do know that I must go away . . .

April 1885: I was near to the loveliest fulfilment and then at a stroke lost all – through no living being's fault. For a long time I did not know which way to turn – there was one sole sombre wish in me: to sleep – and not to dream!

28th May 1885: If I wrote to you recently that my relationship to 'her' had entered into a new and final stage, that was nothing but the ruse of a cunning theatre manager who announces a 'last performance' only to offer, the following day, a very last one. What was final has now given way to the definitely final. But since there are now only three weeks between me and our parting for ever, it doesn't seem very probable that there will be any 'widespread demand' leading up to yet another very – very last – But I cannot vouch for anything.

June 1885: All the jobs and prospects before me have helped me, sanguine type that I am, to get over many a bitter experience. I shall almost certainly leave her without so much as a word of farewell! For a whole month I haven't set eyes on her except at rehearsals. How it has come to this is something I may tell you about when we meet. Sometimes, when I start up out of my sleep, I simply cannot believe it.

A typical youthful love affair, which would be of little interest to us today were it not that the 'six songs' Mahler wrote for Johanna became a cycle of four, the *Lieder eines fahrenden Gesellen* (*Songs of a Wayfarer*), his first masterpiece. Johanna also left Cassel in 1885, joining a company in Rotterdam. She then worked in Cologne, Chemnitz and Königsberg before returning to Danzig in 1896. She retired in about 1904 and after 1906 was a teacher. She was last heard of in 1943 and it is presumed she never married.

In 1884 Mahler composed incidental music for a performance in Cassel on 23rd June of seven scenes selected from J.V. von Scheffel's narrative poem *Der Trompeter von Säkkingen*. 'I polished off this opus inside two days', he wrote to Löhr on 22nd June, 'and I must confess I am very pleased with it. As you can imagine, it has little in common with Scheffel's affectation, indeed leaves that author a long way behind.' There was one other performance of it a year later in Carlsruhe. As will be seen later, this was to be important in relation to the First Symphony, on which he also began to work at this time. On his way back to Cassel for his second season there, he stopped in Dresden on 23rd and 24th August to hear Ernst von Schuch conduct *Così fan tutte* and *Tristan und Isolde*. Schuch invited Mahler to meet him in the interval of *Tristan*. 'He was very amiable . . . He proposes coming to Cassel at some convenient time to watch me conduct. It is not inconceivable that I may still get a job in Dresden after all.' But nothing materialized. Instead, as he wrote to Albert Spiegler on 23rd January 1885: 'I have been appointed probably from the beginning of next summer (first) conductor at the Leipzig Stadttheater – together with Nikisch, with whom I rank exactly equal. The contract is for six years . . . But my ultimate goal is and must remain Vienna – there is nowhere else where I can feel at home.'

Mahler's contract at Cassel ended on 1st July 1885. He ended his time there by conducting Mendelssohn's oratorio *St Paul* at a choral festival at Münden. Mahler had conducted Haydn's *The Seasons* at Münden in February 1884, with Johanna among the soloists. It was so successful that the town decided to organize a festival and asked Mahler, in preference to Treiber, to conduct it. This caused an uproar in the press, including objections that a Jew was to conduct a Christian oratorio (composed by a Jew). The opera orchestra, loyal to Treiber, refused to take part. 'They can't forgive me my youth', Mahler wrote to Löhr, 'that goes especially for our profession. Our orchestra is on strike because the Herr Hofkapellmeister [Treiber] feels he has been made to look a fool.' The Intendant, Adolf von Gilsa, refused to allow the festival to be held in the court theatre, so the performance was given in a military drill hall in Münden, with an ad hoc orchestra. Rosa Papier was among the soloists. It was a triumph. Mahler reported to Löhr, 'honours and love have been simply showered upon me. A ring with a large diamond, a gold watch, a laurel wreath, an album etc . . . So in the end it did all turn out rather nicely, of course only after all the accumulated electricity on both sides had been discharged, myself naturally being the first from whom the sparks flew.'

Mahler had confided to Löhr that he was worried how to fill in the year before his Leipzig appointment. He planned to find piano pupils in Vienna, otherwise he would 'find it very difficult to escape landing in the debtors' prison'. But he had meanwhile applied to Angelo Neumann, a retired tenor who had recently been appointed director of the Deutsches Landestheater in Prague. Neumann was impressed by his letter, sent for Mahler and allocated him the performance of Cherubini's *Les deux Journées* on 18th August 1885. He did so well that Neumann offered him a year's contract as second conductor to Ludwig Slansky and entrusted to him *Rienzi*, *Die Meistersinger von Nürnberg*, *Das Rheingold* and *Die Walküre* and, in addition, *Don Giovanni*, *Der Freischütz*, *Fidelio* and *Iphigénie en Aulide*. As had happened in Cassel, so in Prague also he fell in love with a singer in the company, Betty Frank. He confessed to Löhr (28th November 1885): 'Oh, if you knew of all that has come over me again! . . . A thrashing's what I deserve! I keep on stumbling from one idiocy into another. In this short pause I have landed myself in something it will take a long time to get out of . . . Since I am doing "so well" here, playing first fiddle, as it were, whereas in Leipzig I shall have a jealous and very capable rival in Nikisch, I have moved heaven and earth to get out of it. Alas, it has all been of no avail and I shall just have to go.'

Betty Frank went one better than Johanna Richter in giving the first public performance of songs by Mahler. Accompanied by the composer, she sang five of his *Lieder* in Prague on 20th April 1886. Perhaps it was she, too, who was responsible for a change in his appearance. As he told Löhr in February 1886: 'I now wear a moustache only'. The affair drifted on after Mahler had left Prague. References in letters to Löhr chart its decline and end:

August 1886: Just think, poor F. has for a long time gone on struggling with her feelings and now, only a few days ago, she asked me point-blank whether my feelings for her amounted to anything more than friendship. I answered with equal sincerity, and now, brave and sensible as she is, she seems to have come to terms with it.

January 1887: Neumann continues to sigh mightily for my coming! F. ditto!

That was the last reference to her. She sang in opera companies in Zurich in 1893 and Berlin in 1894, but soon returned to Prague where, in 1893, she had married an insurance company director called Rückert.

While in Prague Mahler conducted (on 21st February 1886) Beethoven's Ninth Symphony and extracts from *Parsifal* from memory after one very short rehearsal. The performances created such a deep impression that the pathologist Philipp Knoll, political leader of the German community in Prague, presented Mahler with an address signed by all Knoll's German University colleagues, who included Guido Adler, then professor of musicology there.

Mahler's last weeks in Prague were clouded by worry about his family. His father had been ill and there was now concern about his mother, whom he and his sister Justine had persuaded to see a doctor in Prague. Marie Mahler wrote to her son on 10th June 1886:

I hope to come in a fortnight. By that time we think that dear Father will be able to travel . . . He is not even supposed to walk about in his room until the swellings on his feet go down. Really I am not sure at present whether it might not be better for us to go to Vienna to see Bamberger . . . I daren't make the journey on my own. Anyway, say what you think would be for the best, and whether you are still to conduct anything in Prague? I should like to see you conduct some time

27

— is that not a very modest wish? It will be quite impossible for me to come to Leipzig . . . Warmest regards and kisses from us *all*.

But six days later:

> It must have been written in the stars that I was not to see you conduct in Prague . . . I cannot risk the journey, having only last Friday had another violent attack of asthma . . . I am *very* glad that you, my dear son, will be coming home for a while, and I hope we shall have some happy days with you here. Dear Father too is very much looking forward to seeing you. Your being here will do him good.

Mahler stayed in Iglau from 16th to 24th July. Three months later he wrote to Löhr: 'Many, many thanks for all you have done for my father. You can imagine how distressing it all is for me. It is not given to me to have a relationship with my own people, and so I have to watch them going down without stirring a hand. At times I feel I am a solitary stranger everywhere! My whole life is one great homesickness.' He went direct to Leipzig from Iglau on 25th July. The Intendant there was Max Staegemann and the first conductor, since 1879, was Artur Nikisch, who was five years older than Mahler. Although he had wanted to introduce himself to the Leipzig audience with Wagner's *Tannhäuser*, Mahler made his first appearance at the Stadttheater on 3rd August with *Lohengrin*. The earlier opera followed and was the subject of a savage review, as was his performance of *Der Freischütz*. He wrote to Löhr during his first month in Leipzig:

> I quickly established my position – which at times is also an opposition, as you can see from one of the two enclosures . . . I am again as lonely as ever. If only I could have you here with me just for a few days . . . Tonight I am conducting *La Juive* [Halévy] – I am utterly fascinated by this wonderful, magnificent work, and rank it among the greatest ever created . . . Almost everywhere I have been welcomed in the most cordial way . . . There are a few excellent people among our men. Above all our leader, a truly warm-hearted young Dutchman by the name of Petri, who reads my baton's most cryptic indications and transforms them into music.

This was Henri Petri (1856–1914), whose son Egon was the great pianist. Mahler also enjoyed working with the baritones Otto Schelper and Karl Perron, the bass Paul Knupfer and the soprano

Josephine von Artner. A memory of Mahler in Leipzig – 'when Mahler conducted, every bar gained new interest' – is provided by Max Steinitzer,[7] who combined an academic musical and literary career with occasional appearances as conductor and pianist:

> Many people got off to a bad start with the glowering young Austrian. Only a few companions felt the full impact of a personality whose every word and gesture was absolutely precise and individual . . . He did his best to be polite, but whenever anybody uttered a stupid remark or banality – even though it may have been apt for the occasion – his facial expression made his feelings all too clear . . . Later, when I read in the Vienna newspapers of Mahler's authoritarianism, despotism, even satanism, I would smile and recall the affability, humour and good nature that characterized his private relations with us musicians.

Steinitzer relates an incident which shows how kind and understanding Mahler could be. At a social gathering, a young man played his piano piece 'In the Silent Valley' which, by reason of its *salon* nature, embarrassed the musicians present. It was received in silence, whereupon Mahler went smilingly to the unfortunate composer and shook his hand, saying: 'That's it exactly! I know that valley, at least I think I do. It's in Styria. Thank you so much.'

Mahler's optimistic belief that he would be 'equal' in status to Nikisch soon proved ill-founded. 'Often I am quite happy about him', he told Löhr in the autumn of 1886, 'and I can look forward to a performance with him conducting as confidently as if I were going to conduct myself – even though the greatest heights and the greatest depths are a closed book to him . . . There is no personal contact between us. He is cold and reserved towards me – whether out of vanity or out of mistrust, I really don't know! In short, we pass each other by without a word!'

Mahler had hoped to conduct *Der Ring des Nibelungen*, for which Staegemann had recently obtained from Bayreuth the rights to a production. When it became clear that Nikisch had exercised his own rights to conduct, Mahler on 27th November asked to be released from his contract. Staegemann, who liked Mahler, stalled. By Christmas, Mahler was in a strong position. He had had an offer of the Hamburg post from its Intendant, Bernhard Pollini, Neumann

[7] M. Steinitzer, 'Mahler in Leipzig' in P. Stefan (ed.) *Gustav Mahler, ein Bild seiner Persönlichkeit in Widmungen* (Munich, 1910), pp. 10–14. Reprinted in *Mahler Remembered*, op. cit., pp. 39–44.

wanted him back in Prague, and he was invited to succeed Mottl in Karlsruhe. In addition, he knew that Nikisch had been offered Budapest. 'If he leaves, I shall take his place as first conductor, with a completely free hand. If he stays, I shall go to Hamburg . . . having been offered really splendid terms . . . You can imagine I naturally wish to go to Hamburg – but I am not free to choose, because if Nikisch decides to go to Budapest, Direktor Staegemann will not release me from my contract'.

But Nikisch did not leave. In February 1887 he became seriously ill with inflammation of the lungs and Mahler took over the *Ring* operas. At the same time Mahler received an offer from New York to succeed Anton Seidl as conductor of the German Opera there. Nikisch was away for three months. Mahler told Löhr in April: 'I have gone up a good deal in the public's estimation . . . All this also means an increased prospect of my staying on here, since I really no longer have any reason to go away. This latest turn of events means that to all intents and purposes I am now on equal footing with Nikisch, and need have no qualms about fighting him for the upper hand, which I am certain to gain if only on grounds of physical superiority. I don't think Nikisch will stand the pace . . .' Not, perhaps, the most gracious attitude, but honest.

But to return to Mahler's first months in Leipzig. Löhr must have smiled ruefully when he read this passage later in the letter about Nikisch's coldness: 'I have met a beautiful person here in Leipzig –and let me tell you at once, the sort that tempts one to do foolish things. Do I make myself clear, *amice*? But this time I mean to be careful, or else I shall be in trouble again.' The 'beautiful person' was Marion Mathilde von Weber, wife of Captain Karl von Weber, grandson of the composer. Captain von Weber invited Mahler to inspect the fragmentary notes and sketches of Weber's comic opera *Die drei Pintos* and to try to complete or reconstruct it. Mahler agreed and thus came much into contact with Marion, four years his senior and Jewish by birth. They fell in love. By January 1887 Mahler was confessing to Löhr: 'I have remained pretty much my old self and am just on the point of once again committing a number of "follies".' Details of the affair are scanty and contradictory, but it is believed that Mahler and Marion planned to run away together. He waited for her to join him on a train, but she did not turn up. Mahler described her years later to Natalie Bauer-Lechner as 'a luminous being, entirely dedicated to Beauty and Good' and said she had given a 'new meaning' to his life.

The first night of *Die drei Pintos* was on 20th February 1888, having been postponed from the previous month. Mahler conducted, and the occasion was a triumph. Fifteen more performances were given in the Leipzig season. Later it was performed in nearly twenty other European opera houses, including Vienna, Berlin, Munich, Hamburg and Dresden. Mahler had completed work on the opera in October 1887. On the 17th of that month, the Symphony No. 2 in F minor by the 23-year-old Richard Strauss was conducted by the composer at the Leipzig Gewandhaus concerts. Mahler was there and the two men met. Strauss went to the opera; and Mahler invited him to his home to play him some of the *Pintos* score. As Strauss reported to his mentor Hans von Bülow a few days later: 'I made a new, very delightful acquaintance in Herr Mahler, who seemed a highly intelligent musician; one of the few modern conductors who knows about tempo modification, and generally held excellent views especially on Wagner's tempos (in contrast to those of the currently acknowledged Wagner conductors). Mahler's arrangement of Weber's *Drei Pintos* seems to me a masterpiece; the first act, which Mahler played to me, I found quite delightful . . .'

There is no indication that Mahler played to Strauss any of the composition on which he was at work, what we today know as the First Symphony, but then entitled simply Symphonic Poem. He told Löhr in January 1888: 'At least I can reveal that I have filled many a sheet of music-paper – and that everything in that quarter has turned out splendidly . . . Yes! It is all very beautiful and great!' Two months later: 'Well! My work is finished! Now I should like to have you by my piano and play it to you! . . . It has turned out so overwhelming it came gushing out of me like a mountain torrent! This summer you shall hear it! All of a sudden all the sluice-gates in me opened! Perhaps one of these days I shall tell you how it all happened! . . . I must get out and take deep breaths of fresh air. For the last six weeks I have seen nothing but my desk.'

Mahler told Max Marschalk in 1896 that the symphony had been inspired by a passionate love. 'The symphony begins where the love affair ends; it is based on the affair which preceded the symphony in the emotional life of the composer.' The use of themes from *Lieder eines fahrenden Gesellen* points to Johanna Richter as the inspiration of the work, although the song *Maitanz im Grünen* is the basis of the theme of the second movement and this was written for Josephine Poisl. Yet the impetus to compose the symphony came from the passion for Marion von Weber – on the last page of the manuscript of the later discarded *Blumine* movement, Mahler wrote 'An M. zum Geburtstage' (To M. on her birthday) – so it would be accurate to say that 'a state of being in love' is at the root of the symphony.

In May 1888 another crisis occurred for Mahler, this time over the production of a Spontini opera. He wrote to Albert Spiegler in Vienna on 2nd May 1888: 'Greetings to you in your quiet haven from one who is tossed on the high seas by all the storms that be. Though the sails are in tatters, the helm is still in one piece! I shall survive, salvaging many a precious possession from many a ship-wreck.' This refers to the disputes between Mahler and Albert Goldberg, stage director of the Stadttheater, which led, on 17th May, to Mahler sending in his resignation to Staegemann. It was accepted.

Again without a job, Mahler wrote to Frankfurt, which had offered him a post two months earlier, and sounded out Munich. He then went for a holiday with the Krzyzanowskis and finally to Iglau in July. Impresarios were now wary of him because of his reputation for amorous affairs. Nevertheless, he applied for the post of conductor of the Royal Hungarian Opera, Budapest. A few days later, the Czech cellist David Popper, professor of cello at Budapest Academy of Music, wrote to Mahler's friend Guido Adler on behalf of the composer Ödön von Mihalovich, Director of the Academy and chairman of a committee formed to select a new musical director for the Opera, inquiring about Mahler's credentials. Adler strongly recommended him. The committee were trying to sign Mottl, but Adler urged the claims of 'Mahler the human being'.

In the meantime rescue came from Neumann in Prague, who invited Mahler to conduct and prepare the production there of *Die drei Pintos* in August. This was a triumphant success at each of its five performances and he then began to rehearse Cornelius's *Der Barbier von Bagdad*. During rehearsals he had a violent quarrel with Neumann, who dismissed him on the spot. That same day he met David Popper, who had attended the previous evening's per-formance of *Die drei Pintos* and had been most impressed. They had lunch together and Popper took to him at once. Popper returned to Budapest to recommend him for the post. This led to a Vienna meeting between Mahler and a representative of Franz von Beniczky, Intendant of the Budapest Opera. On 28th September he signed a ten-year contract. He remained on good terms with Staegemann, sending him 'genuine Magyar specialities' for Christmas.

Mahler was given a free hand to reorganize the Budapest Opera and to rescue it from near-bankruptcy, both financial and artistic. This was his first chance really to display his genius not only as a conductor but as an administrator. He determined, although he could not speak Hungarian, to create a national company un-hampered by imported and expensive stars.

He succeeded, when in some physical pain and at a time of personal strain. Within three months he had staged *Das Rheingold* in Hungarian, quickly following it with *Die Walküre*, but his plan to complete *Der Ring des Nibelungen* failed. Word of his prowess spread, audiences increased and the company made a profit. (It should not be forgotten when there is discussion of Mahler's so-called 'unbalanced' nature that to run opera companies as he did in Budapest, Hamburg and Vienna requires exceptional administrative acumen.) On 18th February 1889 his father died at the age of sixty-one. Whatever his feelings, Mahler owed his musical education to Bernhard's encouragement, and not every young musician can say that. He had made no attempt to break with his family, returning regularly to Iglau for summer holidays even when he knew that his parents' unhappiness and increasing ill health would depress and aggravate him. It is possible that he was prepared to put up with this emotional stress for the sake of the walks in the countryside near his home. The necessity for regular contact with the beauties of nature was as strong for Mahler as it was for Beethoven, and a powerful stimulus to composition, as is obvious from his music, in which birdsong and the sound of village festivities are frequent features. When he was walking with his friend, the violinist Natalie Bauer-Lechner (1858–1921), they heard a medley of village sounds — fairground booths, merry-go-rounds, military marches. 'Do you hear it?' Mahler exclaimed. 'That is polyphony. That's where I get it from'.[8] His friendship with Löhr owed much to their mutual love of nature. As Löhr put it, when describing their walks: 'Orgiastic abandonment to nature, meditative absorption in the charms of old-world Austrian villages and the historical memories they evoked, and not least the sympathy of two hearts in accord.' In the glorious countryside around Iglau, they would walk for half a day every day;

[8] N. Bauer-Lechner, *Recollections of Gustav Mahler* (London, 1980), p. 155.

'and on Sunday afternoon there was an expedition to where authentic Bohemian musicians set lads and lasses dancing in the open air . . . The archaically earthy charms of nature and nature's children, which Mahler came to know in his youth, prepared the ground for his creative work and never ceased to vitalize his art.'

In July of 1889 Mahler had a painful operation for haemorrhoids. In 1889 too, on 11th October, his mother died, aged fifty-two. So Gustav was now head of the family, responsible for his surviving two sisters and two brothers. The next oldest to him, his sister Leopoldine, had also died in 1889 from a brain tumour. His ne'er-do-well brother Alois was now twenty-two. His sister Justine, who had nursed their dying mother, was nearly twenty-one, a neurotic girl with a vivid imagination. Otto, a talented composer and Mahler's favourite, was fifteen. The youngest, at thirteen, was Emma. Mahler sold his parents' business, gave his share of the proceeds to his sisters and ordered his brothers to do likewise, much to their chagrin. He took Justine to Budapest to keep house for him. From this time their particularly intense relationship developed. It was with all this on his mind that he conducted in Budapest on 20th November 1889 the first performance of what we know as the First Symphony but which was then described as a Symphonic Poem in five movements. It was coldly received.

Mahler later told Natalie Bauer-Lechner:[9] 'Naively, I imagined it would be child's play for performers and listeners, and would have such immediate appeal that I should be able to live on the profits and go on composing. How great was my surprise and disappointment when it turned out quite differently! In Budapest . . . my friends avoided me afterwards; no one dared to mention the performance or the work to me, and I went about like a leper or an outlaw. In the circumstances you can imagine what the reviews were like!'

Löhr and his wife Uda, most loyal of friends, helped Mahler by inviting his brothers and sisters to stay with them. Mahler spent the summer of 1890 with them near Vienna, but before that, in May, he took Justine to Italy, visiting Florence, Milan, Bologna and Genoa. 'We've been having a glorious time', he wrote to Uda Löhr. In Florence he did not even visit the most famous art galleries. 'Mahler lacked what is so important when travelling in Italy', Friedrich Löhr wrote, 'namely enthusiasm for the incomparable treasures of visual art to be found there. He understood only one artistic language, that

[9] *Recollections of Gustav Mahler*, op. cit., pp. 160–1.

of music . . . It was not that he was incapable of receiving impressions from works of painting and sculpture . . . but left to himself, when he visited new places, he sought out only the never-failing charms of nature, such as the flowery countryside around Florence and Fiesole or near Paris.'

Mahler soon realized that the favourable atmosphere at the Budapest Royal Opera House would not last and he began to put out feelers elsewhere, in particular to Hamburg. In December 1890 he conducted a *Don Giovanni* which Brahms declared to be the best he had heard; in the next month Beniczky resigned and was succeeded by the one-armed Count Zichy, a fanatical nationalist. Zichy clashed with Mahler by interfering where Beniczky had given a free hand. After an especially violent quarrel Mahler arrived at the opera house to find himself locked out. He was, in effect, dismissed, but insisted upon the large sum of 25,000 florins as compensation for the breaking of his contract. He formally resigned on 14th March and used some of the money for a large flat for his brothers and sisters in Vienna. Meanwhile he had received a telegram from Bernhard Pollini,[10] director of the Hamburg Municipal Theatre, offering him the post of chief conductor. He took up the post on 29th March and was to remain in it for six important years.

---

[10] Pollini was born Baruch Pohl and had been a tenor. He had been director at Hamburg since 1873. Wits called him 'Monopollini'.

4

Hamburg's Pygmalion

Hamburg has a long and honourable musical tradition. When Mahler arrived there the city's symphony concerts were in the charge of another great conductor, Hans von Bülow. Within the first few days of his régime Mahler conducted *Siegfried*. Bülow attended the performance and wrote to his daughter Daniela on 24th April 1891: 'Hamburg has now acquired a simply first-rate opera conductor in Mr Gustav Mahler ... who in my opinion equals the very best conductors (Mottl, Richter etc.) ... Recently I heard *Siegfried* under his direction ... Without an orchestral rehearsal, he compelled the musical rabble to dance to his tune.' Mahler quickly began to infuse into Hamburg the same zeal for artistic perfection which had marked his stay in Budapest. But now he had the advantage of an excellent orchestra and of gifted singers already under contract to the shrewd Pollini, among them the soprano Katharina Klafsky, a great Leonora in *Fidelio*, whose husband, Otto Lohse, was second conductor; the tenors Max Alvary and Julius Lieban, and the Czech contralto Ernestine Schumann-Heink.

In some memories of her Hamburg days quoted in her biography,[1] Schumann-Heink paid tribute to the help Mahler gave her:

the more interesting because he didn't like me as a woman ... He wanted and sought endlessly for perfection. He forgot that there is no perfection in this world. In his own mind and ideals, yes, but he forgot that when the orchestra was before him it was only eighty or a hundred men who were not geniuses like himself, but simply good workers. They often irritated him so terribly that he couldn't bear it; then he became a musical tyrant ... It was a tragedy for him, this attitude, for deep in his heart he had charity, and he was the most lovable and kindest creature you could imagine – except when he was conducting ... But he didn't bear malice. He was an idealist in every way. He enjoyed so every living thing. Why, the shining of the sun, a tree, even the smallest flower, could make ecstasy for him. But the people couldn't understand him, and so they condemned him.

The operas of Mozart and Wagner – and Beethoven's *Fidelio* – were the foundation of his work, but he lost no chance to introduce new works during his tenure – Puccini's *Manon Lescaut*, Verdi's *Falstaff*, Humperdinck's *Hänsel und Gretel* – and unfamiliar ones such as Tchaikovsky's *Eugene Onegin* (with the composer present), Smetana's *Dalibor* and *The Bartered Bride* and Bizet's *Djamileh*. One of the new operas he conducted was Mascagni's *L'Amico Fritz* which, he told his sister Justine, he considered 'a distinct improvement on *Cavalleria*'. He was convinced that 'our dear conductors have once again ruined the work, which due to its great subtleties is difficult to perform. You will easily understand the sympathy I feel for the ill-treated composer who failed with this work; I've put all the weight of my personality behind it to prove its worth to the rabble.' A Viennese opera director, who had heard Mascagni conduct the work in Vienna, told Mahler that at Hamburg 'he had thought that *Mascagni* was there on the rostrum – in such detail had I reproduced *his own* style. I can well understand that, since Mascagni and I have a *vast* amount in common.'[2] The public, he told his sister, 'adores me, but Pollini is "dumb as an ox" '.

In June and July 1892 Mahler visited London for the only time in his life. Sir Augustus Harris, manager of Covent Garden, planned to stage *Der Ring des Nibelungen* for the first time at the Royal Opera House[3] and through his friend Pollini engaged a German cast, the nucleus of which was the Hamburg company with the addition of two Bayreuth stars, Rosa Sucher (as Brünnhilde) and Theodor Reichmann, also noted for his Sachs. Harris wanted Richter, since 1877 a regular visitor to London, as conductor but he was busy in Vienna and Pollini urged Mahler instead. With typical thoroughness Mahler at once began to learn English, practising it on walks with a Hamburg friend, the physicist Arnold Berliner. From 69 Torrington Square he wrote to Berliner: 'I found the circumstances of orchestra here bader than thought and the cast better than hoped . . . I make greater progress in English as you can observe.'

[1] M. Lawton, *Schumann-Heink, the Last of the Titans* (New York, 1928), pp. 358–61. Reprinted in *Mahler Remembered*, op. cit., pp. 85–7.
[2] H. Blaukopf (ed.), *Mahler's Unknown Letters* (London, 1986), p. 108.
[3] The cycle had only once before been performed in London, in 1882 at Her Majesty's under Angelo Neumann. It was given under Mahler out of sequence, thus: *Siegfried* (3), *Das Rheingold* (1), *Die Walküre* (2), *Götterdämmerung* (4).

The performances of *Tristan und Isolde* and *Fidelio* – which were both staged at the Theatre Royal, Drury Lane – were a revelation to London audiences. Among those who heard *Tristan* was a twenty-two-year-old conductor at the beginning of his career, Henry J. Wood (he met Mahler), and a nineteen-year-old composition student at the Royal College of Music, Ralph Vaughan Williams, who was so moved that he told his teacher, Hubert Parry, he was unable to sleep for two nights. The critics were far from unanimous about *Fidelio* (its first performance in German in England), finding Mahler's reading 'unconventional'. Mahler wrote to Berliner: 'All the same, the public absolved me from my blasphemy with a regular *hurricane* of applause – in fact, they overwhelm me with rapturous signs of approval. I've got to go before the curtain literally after *every act* – the whole house yells "Mahler" till I appear.' By this time he performed the *Leonora No. 3* overture between the two scenes of Act II instead of between the acts. He first began this practice in Hamburg in April 1891, and continued it thereafter, although it is said to have been inaugurated by Mottl[4] at Carlsruhe. No doubt there are other and earlier candidates. Mahler delayed his return to Hamburg for the start of the season in September 1892 because of an outbreak of cholera in the city. Pollini fined him 12,000 marks for breach of contract. This was paid by a friend, but the incident led to the continuous and open hostility between Pollini and Mahler which lasted for four years until Mahler left for Vienna.

The transformation Mahler wrought at Hamburg can be gauged from the continuing admiration of Bülow. He sent Mahler a laurel wreath inscribed 'To the Pygmalion of the Hamburg Opera'. When Bülow's health failed Mahler deputized for him, the first occasion being on 12th December 1892. After Bülow's death in Cairo on 12th February 1894 Mahler succeeded him and thus became all-powerful in Hamburg. Bülow's admiration did not extend to Mahler's music. In September 1891 Mahler played to him the first movement of a symphony (No. 2) he had been writing for several years. Bülow did not like it – it made *Tristan* sound like a Haydn symphony by comparison, he said. This was the original version of the movement, *Totenfeier*, which differs in structure and scoring.)

[4] Felix Mottl (1856–1911) was conductor of the Carlsruhe Opera from 1881 to 1903, when he went to Munich. He was noted for his Wagner and Berlioz interpretations. He orchestrated Wagner's *Five Wesendonck Songs*.

Ironically, it was Bülow's funeral service which provided Mahler with the inspiration he was seeking to finish the Second Symphony. He was so impressed by Klopstock's hymn *Auferstehung* (Resurrection) that he incorporated it into the finale. The occasion was vividly recalled by one of Mahler's closest Hamburg friends, the Czech composer Josef Bohuslav Foerster, whose wife Berta Lauterer was a soprano at the Hamburg Opera under Mahler, where among other roles, she sang Eva in *Die Meistersinger von Nürnberg*. After Bülow's funeral service (29th March 1894), Foerster could not find Mahler. In the afternoon he

> hurried to his house . . . I opened the door and saw him sitting at the writing-desk, his head sunk low and his hand holding a quill over music paper. As I stood in the doorway, Mahler swung round and said: 'Dear friend, I've got it!' I understood. As if enlightened by a mysterious power, I retorted: 'Rise up, yea rise up from that brief sleep . . .' Mahler looked at me with an expression of extreme surprise. I had divined the secret that he had not yet divulged to anyone . . .[5]

Foerster has also left us a description of Mahler's living-room in Hamburg in which 'almost all the space was taken up by a piano, bookshelves and a table'. There was also a chair which had belonged to his father.

> On the walls, there was no sign of a beloved family portrait. Only a reproduction of Dürer's *Melancholy*, the photograph of a drawing unknown to me, *St Anthony's Sermon to the Fishes*, and finally Giorgione's *Monk*, the one with his hand on a keyboard and an expression of indescribable beauty on his face. (Mahler once told me: 'That picture I could compose for ever'.) [The painting, usually called *Concert*, is now attributed to Titian and hangs in the Galleria Palatina, Florence] . . . Johann Sebastian Bach was his hero. When I had seen the open score of a cantata on his piano top, I made some remark about the great Leipzig cantor. Mahler played a couple of marvellous pieces and voiced his amazement that Bach's cantatas were so seldom performed that they were almost unknown . . . 'Here in this Castalian spring, I rinse the grime of the theatre off me', he remarked once after Pollini, though aware of Mahler's opinions, placed a new opera in his hands, hands that touched it only with disgust.[6]

[5] J. B. Foerster, *Der Pilger* (Prague, 1955), pp. 404–5. Reprinted in *Mahler Remembered*, op. cit., p. 79.
[6] *Der Pilger*, op. cit., pp. 350–7.

It was at this period of Mahler's life, when the demands of running a profitable opera company and his increasing success as a concert-hall conductor intensified, that he began to concentrate his composing into the duration of a summer holiday. Wryly, he described himself as 'der Sommerkomponist', the 'summer-composer'. As he put it in a letter to the critic and composer Max Marschalk in December 1896:

> One who is chained in that galley, the opera house, cannot get as much music written as do the current matadors of the concert hall. He can only write on his 'day off'. But then his inner experience concentrates in *one* work. I cannot do anything but give myself *completely* to *each* new work.

From 1893 he spent his summers at Steinbach-am-Attersee, near Salzburg. At the inn there Mahler took five rooms for his family and his friend Natalie Bauer-Lechner. She had first met Mahler in 1878 at the Vienna Conservatory, where she was a violin student. Daughter of a bookshop owner, she came of a musical family and for a time played the viola in the all-female Soldat-Röger Quartet. She met Mahler again at a dinner party at the Löhrs' in Vienna after he had been appointed to Budapest. He invited her to visit him there, which she did about a year later, just after the break-up of her marriage. Obviously attracted to him, she appointed herself (to our immense gain) his 'Boswell', writing down details of their conversations. He seems to have been fond of her, if occasionally irritated by her, in a non-sexual way. 'Dear merry old Natalie' was one of his descriptions of her.

The fields surrounding the inn at Steinbach were full of flowers and for his second holiday there, in 1894, Mahler had a work-cabin built at the end of a field near the lake. It had one room, with double windows on three sides and a glassed door facing the inn and village. This door could be closed off at night by wooden shutters. There was a wood-burning stove, a table, chairs and a Bösendorfer baby grand. He worked in the cabin from about 7am until mid-afternoon or the evening. The rule was that if the door was shut, he was under no circumstances to be disturbed. The builder of the hut, Franz Lösch, wrote forty years later: 'Mahler would always say: the lake had its own language, the lake talked to him. From up at the inn he couldn't hear it, so he needed to have a little house right by the shore. When he heard the lake he composed more easily . . . I understood very well.'[7]

[7] *Mahler Remembered*, op. cit., pp. 71–2.

Justine described the régime at Steinbach:

> Mahler's diet had to be simple and light because he was susceptible to
> migraine, and by this could be utterly incapacitated from work. His
> beverage was pure fresh spring water. He smoked cigarettes modestly,
> with the occasional cigar as an indulgence. Mahler had a friend in
> Hamburg, the famous actor Kurt Wagner, who used to present him
> with a box of fine imported cigars on the occasion of Mahler's annual
> benefit performance. This box was taken along in the summer, and if
> Mahler was especially satisfied with his morning's work, he awarded
> himself one of these cigars. During lunch he would rise from the table,
> pick up a gold-wrapped cigar from the drawer, and with a pleased
> expression set it before him at the table. Everyone then knew that he
> was happy about something well done. This cigar was his ration for the
> day, however.[8]

During his first stay at Steinbach he revised the Symphonic Poem
which had been such a failure in Budapest and Hamburg. (In the
latter city, Mahler conducted it on 27th October 1893, together with
six of his *Wunderhorn* songs.) He now called it a symphony, with the
subtitle *Titan*, a homage to the novel by Jean Paul Richter. The
revised score was performed at the Weimar Festival on 29th June
1894. Mahler described the result to Arnold Berliner:

> My symphony was received with a mixture of furious disapproval and
> wildest applause. It is amusing to hear the clash of opinions in the street
> and in drawing-rooms. Well, when the dogs bark, we know we are in
> the saddle! 'Me top again'! (at least in my view, which will, however,
> scarcely be shared by more than a select few). . . . Performance, after
> utterly inadequate rehearsal, extremely shoddy. Orchestra retrospec-
> tively extremely satisfied with symphony as a result of barrel of free
> beer, also their affections won by my style of conducting. My brother
> was there . . .

Among those who read the hostile critical notices of this performance, especially of the movement called *Funeral March in the
manner of Callot*, was a Jewish musician of seventeen, Bruno
Schlesinger. He was fascinated by the idea of this work and
determined somehow to work under its composer. So, a few months
later, he obtained a post at Hamburg as coach and chorus-master.

[8] From Norman Lebrecht, *Mahler Remembered* (Faber, 1987), p. 70.

He is known to posterity by the name he adopted a few years later: Bruno Walter. Through Walter's eyes we see Mahler as he was then – midway through his Hamburg period and approaching his thirty-fifth birthday, with more than two-thirds of his life already lived:[9]

> Pale, thin, small of stature [not much over five feet], with longish features, the steep forehead framed by intensely black hair, remarkable eyes behind spectacles, lines of sorrow and of humour in the face which, when he spoke to others, would show the most astonishing change of expression – the very incarnation of that Kapellmeister Kreisler – interesting, demoniac, intimidating – as he would appear to the imagination of youthful readers of E. Th. A. Hoffman's fantastic tales.

Walter hero-worshipped Mahler thenceforward, but was not blind to his hero's faults or the manifestations of his autocratic behaviour.

> Never before had I seen such an intense person, never dreamed that a terse word, a commanding gesture, and a will directed solely towards a certain goal, could frighten and alarm others and force them into blind obedience . . . I was fascinated to observe how the same intensity, the same spiritual tenseness, that had previously filled his rehearsing, was now manifested in his conversation. The vehemence with which he objected when I said something that was unsatisfactory to him . . . his sudden submersion in pensive silence, the kind glance with which he would receive an understanding word on my part, an unexpected, convulsive expression of secret sorrow and, added to all this, the strange irregularity of his walk: his stamping of the feet, sudden halting, rushing ahead again – everything confirmed and strengthened the impression of demoniac obsession.

Walter mentions again in another passage this frequent sudden changing of Mahler's facial expression from cheerfulness to gloom 'as if he were reproaching himself for having thoughtlessly forgotten to remember something that was sad'. Alma mentions the same trait; and we can recognize its reflection in his music. In Mahler's symphonies, one may say, every silver lining has a cloud. He had a natural gaiety, but he attached importance to 'suffering'.

From Walter too we have a detailed account of Mahler's

[9] The quoted passages from Bruno Walter which follow are from his *Gustav Mahler*, trans. J. Galston (London, 1937) and his *Theme and Variations*, trans. J. Galston (London, 1947).

intellectual curiosity and literary tastes, and the brilliance of his conversation: he was also a good listener, except in uncongenial company, when he made no attempt to disguise his boredom, for he had cultivated few social graces. In Hamburg in 1891, as he told Freund, he had 'been reading something so remarkable and strange that it may very well have an *epoch-making* influence on my life'. This was Nietzsche. In 1894 his principal literary preoccupations were Dostoyevsky and Schopenhauer – one can readily imagine the appeal to Mahler of Schopenhauer's theory of a universal Will which generates suffering, so that the more we know the more we suffer. The novels of Jean Paul Richter, Sterne's *Tristram Shandy*, Cervantes's *Don Quixote*, the poetry of Hölderlin, Nietzsche's *Also sprach Zarathustra* and, of course, Goethe were among his favourites. ('Goethe and apples are two things he cannot live without', a friend said of him.) His interest in the natural sciences was also keen. Berliner had high praise for the acuteness of his understanding of physics. Walter recalls, too, happy evenings of music-making when Mahler and he played pianoforte works for four hands by Mozart, Schubert, Schumann and Dvořák, with Mahler inventing words to Schubert's march melodies and singing them while playing, then laughing uncontrollably and relapsing into 'gloom and silence which nobody dared to disturb'. It must have been unnerving. But everyone who has written personal memories of Mahler mentions his infectious and hearty laughter.

Mahler was at once touched and flattered by Walter's devotion and readiness to listen. 'Whence do we come? Whither does our road take us?' he said to his impressionable young disciple. 'Why am I made to feel that I am free while yet I am constrained within my personality as in a prison? What is the object of toil and sorrow? Will the meaning of life be revealed by death?' These fundamental questions were at the root of the enormous work, the Second ('Resurrection') Symphony for soloists, chorus and orchestra which he had completed at Steinbach on 25th July 1894. The three instrumental movements (Nos. 1, 2 and 3) were performed in Berlin by the Berlin Philharmonic Orchestra conducted by Mahler on 4th March 1895. The 1894–5 Berlin Philharmonic season was conducted by Richard Strauss, who was responsible for the inclusion of the Mahler movements. A month earlier Mahler had conducted the Prelude to Act I of Strauss's first opera, *Guntram*, in Hamburg. ('It sounded wonderful!' Mahler wrote to his colleague.) Later in the year, on 13th December, he conducted the symphony in full, again with the Berlin orchestra which, according to Walter, he engaged at his own expense in order to have sufficient rehearsals. The audience and performers were ecstatic about the work; the critics were divided. The performance might well have been disastrous because an attack of migraine prostrated him on the afternoon of the concert and only by a superhuman effort of will did he control those vast forces that evening. This is scarcely to be wondered at, since Pollini had refused to release Mahler from any of his Hamburg opera performances. During the rehearsal-period in Berlin, Mahler conducted an opera every night, took the night train to Berlin, rehearsed the symphony in the morning and then returned to Hamburg to conduct the opera that evening. He also fitted in Hamburg rehearsals for a performance of Beethoven's Ninth Symphony.

There was another reason why it is hardly surprising that there should have been a physical manifestation of the strain Mahler was under, not only because of the personal and practical stresses involved in bringing such a tremendous work to birth, but also because his much-loved brother Otto had shot himself on 6th February 1895. Otto was also a musician – 'more gifted than I', said Mahler, who paid for him to attend Vienna Conservatory for four years – but he lacked the application which distinguished his older brother. Mahler found him posts as choirmaster in provincial towns but Otto never stayed long. He left a suicide note saying that life no longer pleased him, so he 'handed back his ticket'. So now Mahler sold the Vienna flat, took Justine and Emma to Hamburg and left the hapless Alois to his own devices, although he was ever ready with money to help him out of trouble. In later years he was to say bitterly to his wife: 'You are lucky. You were born with a silver spoon in your mouth. You can go your flowery way – no grim past, no family round your neck – but I have had to stagger on all my life with clods of earth weighing down my feet.' Mahler was conscientiously devoted to his family.

Nor was all right with the world at the Hamburg opera. In the spring of this fated 1895 Klafsky and her husband Lohse, the second conductor, broke their contracts and went to America.[10] All the conducting now devolved upon Mahler. 'Just think', he wrote to

[10] Klafsky died suddenly at the age of forty-one in Germany in September 1896, just after returning to the Hamburg Opera.

Arnold Berliner when the new season began in September, 'Lohse has really left, *I* am the *sole* conductor, and Pollini has not made the slightest attempt to find a replacement for L. So I am actually conducting *every* day, since even the light operas, which indeed Pohlig [Karl Pohlig, second conductor] might very well conduct, are handed over to me. Cannot help wondering how long I shall be able to stand it.' Writing to Strauss the previous June from Steinbach, he had said: 'I have in the meantime fallen out completely with Pollini and tendered my resignation a few weeks ago.'

Pollini, we may be sure, was much less concerned about the conducting than he was about replacing Klafsky. He encouraged Mahler to promote Bruno Walter from coaching the chorus to conducting some operas and went off in search of a new leading soprano. He consulted Rosa Papier, the Wagnerian mezzo-soprano who was now a teacher at the Vienna Conservatory. She had a gifted twenty-two-year-old pupil, Anna von Mildenburg. Pollini heard her and engaged her to sing Brünnhilde, Elisabeth and Leonore in *Fidelio* in her first week in Hamburg. She later described her first piano rehearsal with Mahler:

> From the first his manner gave me a confidence that released me from all my doubts and anxieties. A boundless sense of security came over me in that first hour of being with him. The bustle of theatre life had amazed and frightened me. I was in a foreign country and felt utterly alone and abandoned. And then suddenly there was this man speaking to me with true human kindness – the very man I had most cause to fear, the chief conductor.

Mahler and Mildenburg became lovers and a rumour persists that they were at one time engaged. Most of his letters to her, deposited in the Austrian National Library, remain unpublished for copyright reasons, but they leave no doubt of the intensity of his feelings for her. It was a strong and passionate relationship. He was tender and violent, she was possessive and jealous. She was also indiscreet, so that the whole opera company knew of their relationship. His letters to her veer between ecstasy and unhappiness – 'My whole being is so full of you, my love, my love . . .' 'My God, Anna, what can I do? What has put you into such a state? . . .' 'You ask me if I miss you. How wicked of you! Can you doubt it? Do you think it is any different for me than for you? When one is accustomed to such a sweet "tormentor", when the time comes when one used to go to that horrible boarding-house in Magdalenstrasse, then enter a certain beloved room, take that usually unruly little head in my hands and cover it with . . . then of course one misses many things! Just wait: when you come here, I shall show you what I mean!'

Not only did he love her as a woman, he admired her as an artist – she was his creation, for he made her into a great singer. He also respected her intelligence and wrote to her about his own works and ambitions in a way he had hitherto reserved for male friends such as Löhr and Berliner. In her first Hamburg season she sang Aida, conducted by Walter. After the Nile Scene in Act 3, Mahler wrote to her:

> So glad, satisfied! None but myself (who draws every breath with you) noticed that you were labouring hard in your singing this evening. The voice was *always* beautiful – the *p* very beautiful, poise and appearance capital. You are maintaining the standard you have achieved . . . The fact that the end of the aria did not go according to *our* plan is entirely Walter's fault for taking the whole preceding aria too fast, *rushing* it, so that you never had time to *breathe*; otherwise you would have been first-rate. So don't take it to heart. Tonight has given me the *certainty* that you can do it . . . Sleep well! I am *very* satisfied with this evening.

A few weeks later, after her Ortrud in *Lohengrin*, he wrote:

> Enjoyed it very much tonight. In splendid voice: it sounded wonderful. Undoubtedly great success with audience! Tone and poise surprisingly good. Enunciation almost always *clear*, great progress. Often, unfortunately, quite incorrect . . . It was also too facile. We shall have a thorough go at it again before the next *Lohengrin*. The scene with Elsa was very good, but *too loud* . . . Appearance in Act II in first costume wonderful – but not so good in the second because of careless *posture*. For heaven's sake make the most of your imposing presence in such roles. The running up the steps in front of Elsa was not right either. What was best, almost good, was jumping up from the steps. All in all delighted to note still further *progress*. What a good omen for the New Year that begins tonight! Goodnight! See you soon! . . .

Writing about Mahler in 1921, Mildenburg said:

> Many had an eerie feeling at seeing him at the podium. They sensed an extraordinary power and backed away as if from something threatening, or stood and stared at him inquisitively with a pleasurable thrill.

46

And when one told them that this apparently ominous man could be as cheerful as a child, carefree and high-spirited like a boy on the first day of the summer holidays, they would smile incredulously and serve up examples of his terribleness. The victims of his sarcasm were the most unforgiving. He hurt many unintentionally with his humour.

Mahler conducted at Hamburg on twenty occasions in April 1896 and twenty-one in May, whereas Walter and Pohlig conducted only seven and nine times respectively. He wrote to Anna from his Steinbach holiday in July: 'I really dread returning to Hamburg. Perhaps even Pollini himself has no notion how things will turn out there. But the situation is bound to become pretty explosive, with all those conflicting interests. Will Pollini succeed in driving me into clearing out? I really don't yet know what I should do then, since there is nowhere a vacant post I could accept . . .' This was ingenuous. He had one goal, and one alone – Vienna. It is beyond doubt that Mahler schemed with all his skill for a post in Vienna, where Wilhelm Jahn had been director of the Imperial Court Opera since 1881 and Hans Richter principal conductor since 1875. In a letter to Löhr from Hamburg in 1894 he wrote: 'Several agents have in fact "proposed" that I should "accept" Richter's post – but that is so much hot air . . . The situation in the world being what it now is, the fact that I am Jewish prevents my getting taken on in any Court theatre. Neither Vienna, nor Berlin, nor Dresden, nor Munich is open to me. The same wind is now blowing everywhere.' But on 29th August 1895 he casually mentions to Löhr, 'I have heard nothing about Vienna since my conversation with Besetzny' (*sic*). This referred to a meeting with Dr Josef von Bezecny, the Intendant of the Vienna Court Opera. In the summer of 1896, when he was writing to Anna as above, he tried to renew contact with Count Albert Apponyi, one of his staunchest supporters in Budapest, who was staying in Attersee and whom Mahler knew had influence in Vienna. He also went to Ischl to see Brahms, as he did most years. 'He is a gnarled and sturdy tree', he told Anna, 'but bears sweet, ripe fruit . . . Admittedly we are not quite compatible, and the "friendship" is maintained only because, as a young man, still developing, I don't mind treating the grand old master with due consideration and forbearance, showing him only the side of myself that I think he finds agreeable.'

But there were still two main obstacles to his appointment: the intensifying anti-Semitism in Germany and Austria and the unwritten law that posts such as the Vienna directorship were not available to non-Catholics. Mahler had a Jewish upbringing in Iglau, but like many Jews who leave home and settle in a more cosmopolitan society, he ceased to observe any religious ritual when he went to Vienna in 1875. In 1880, Emil Freund told Mahler of the suicide of a young female relative of his, with whom Mahler had had a holiday flirtation in 1878. In reply Mahler referred to All Souls' Day 1880, the Roman Catholic holy day in memory of the dead, as 'the first I have ever known. Now for me too there is a grave on which to lay a wreath.' The previous year, in December 1879, in a letter to Anton Krisper, he had written 'Now the little Christ-child is here and should be bringing me something *really* lovely.' But when in 1895 he was setting Klopstock's hymn for the finale of his Second Symphony, he omitted the mention of Jesus.

On 21st December 1896 Mahler formally applied to Bezecny for the post of conductor at the Vienna Court Opera. A second letter, addressed to Eduard Wlassack, director of the secretariat of the Generalintendanz, carried a postscript: 'Perhaps I should tell you that quite a while ago in pursuance of a long-standing resolution, I entered the Catholic faith.' This was only partially true: he had, obviously, made the first moves towards conversion, but his official baptism into the church was on 23rd February 1897. He told Ludwig Karpath that he had taken this step 'from an instinct of self-preservation' and that it had cost him 'a great deal'. The theory, propounded by Leonard Bernstein, that Mahler was thereafter ravaged by guilt for betraying his Jewishness, cannot be substantiated and seems highly unlikely.

In the first month of 1897 Mahler rallied all the support he could find. First, he asked Pollini to release him from his contract in Hamburg before he left in March on a conducting tour of Russia and elsewhere. He was in any case becoming increasingly dissatisfied with the staging of the operas and complained bitterly to Pollini in December 1896 about the incompetence of the stage manager Franz Bittong. To Marschalk on 14th January 1897 he wrote: 'I have managed to get my resignation through here . . . They need a director in Vienna and have come to the conclusion that I am the right man for the job. But the great stumbling-block —my being a Jew — lies in the road . . .' The critic and composer Wilhelm Zinne, writing in 1925, summed up Mahler's work in Hamburg: 'He was often able to take the wind out of Pollini's sails who, contrary to Mahler, was no champion of sacred causes . . . And this purity, decisiveness, honesty, together with Mahler's all-embracing soul, has left behind a lasting legacy: a pure and radiant page of Hamburg opera history.'

Wlassack put out feelers: Vienna knew about Mahler's reputation as a tyrant where orchestral players were concerned. Mahler, who feared that the post might well go to Mottl, asked Lipiner to write to Wlassack about this question of his temperament: 'Mahler is a man of genius, of a passionate nature, that is true; but his passion is far removed from the impatience of superficial characters. To achieve as much as possible and to see that others do likewise: that is his aim.' Mihalovich and Beniczky from Budapest both supported their former conductor, the latter stressing that besides his artistic gifts, Mahler had 'a healthy regard for the commercial side of an artistic institution'. But the longest and warmest encomium came from Count Apponyi: 'In my fairly comprehensive acquaintance with distinguished conductors, I have not found his like . . . With all the works he produces he dominates the stage, the action, the expressions and movements of actors and chorus, with supreme control, so that a performance prepared and conducted by him attains artistic perfection in every dimension. His eye ranges over the entire production, the decor, the machinery, the lighting. I have never met such a well-balanced all-round artistic personality.' Also working in Vienna on Mahler's behalf was Rosa Papier, briefed no doubt by her ex-pupil Anna von Mildenburg and in an influential position as Wlassack's mistress.

Opposition to the appointment, when rumour began to circulate, was mobilized by Hans Richter and the second conductor, Nepomuk Fuchs. They found a staunch ally in Cosima Wagner, whose candidate was Mottl. (Mahler, one of the greatest Wagner conductors, was never invited to conduct at Bayreuth, although Cosima occasionally sought his views on individual singers and had the highest admiration for his conducting of Wagner.) But Bezecny was determined to capture Mahler, realizing that only a fanatic with up-to-date ideas and unswerving ideals could drag the Opera from its complacent torpor. Mahler was asked to be in Vienna at the beginning of April and on the 15th Jahn signed the contract whereby he was engaged as conductor for a year. But Mahler had already been told he would soon be director in the nearly-blind Jahn's place. He wrote to Marschalk on 20th April from Hamburg: 'I just do not know whether I did the right thing in accepting Vienna . . . For the time being all I ask of Providence is not to be kept from my 'vocation' [composing] for too long. You know of course that what I feared most was being made a director, which is precisely what has now happened. But: *vederemo!*' And to Berliner two days later: 'I have to reckon with bitterest opposition from unwilling or incapable elements (the two normally coincide). Hans Richter especially is said to be doing his best to make things hot for me.' Two days after his appointment was announced, two newspapers criticised the 'Jewification' of the Opera, and the *Reichspost* said it would refrain from comment on 'this unadulterated Jew' until 'Herr Mahler starts his Jew-boy antics on the podium'.

Anna von Mildenburg's attitude to Mahler's departure can be guessed. She asked a Dominican monk to her home to marry them, but the ploy failed. He wrote to her: 'Au revoir, my darling, my little Anna! . . . I am yours, my dear, and I shall remain faithful to you . . .' Mahler said farewell to Hamburg on 24th April with a performance of the *Eroica* Symphony, followed by *Fidelio*. The next day, as he was leaving, he received a letter of congratulations from Camilla von Stefanovic-Vilovska who as the violinist Milla von Ott had played Beethoven's *Kreutzer* Sonata with him at Iglau in August 1883. He replied immediately and delightedly: 'Just like yourself, I remember my youth and my youthful experiences fondly! . . . Do not fail to look me up when you come to Vienna. That would really please your old friend and 'colleague'. Perhaps we can *play* together again, as in old times. And I promise to bully you again as I always used to. Agreed?'

On 11th May 1897 Mahler made his Vienna opera debut conducting *Lohengrin*. Six days later he wrote to Anna von Mildenburg: 'There was a tremendous whirl of congratulations, visitors, etc! All my troubles are over now, thank God! The whole of Vienna hailed me with out-and-out enthusiasm! Next week we have *Walküre*, *Siegfried*, *Le Nozze di Figaro* and *Zauberflöte*. There can no longer be any doubt that I shall become director before long . . . Do tell me how things are with all of you in that theatre (that penitentiary) of yours!' For the first fortnight of June he conducted operas like *Lohengrin* and *Der fliegende Holländer* while suffering from the effects of having a tonsils abscess opened. (Another operation on his throat followed in August.) On 13th July he became deputy director to the ailing Jahn. On 8th October the announcement was made of his appointment as artistic director, with almost unlimited powers, a salary of 24,000 kroner a year, gratuities and a pension. Mahler wrote to Marschalk: 'I am as "swamped" as only a theatrical director can be. A dreadful, consuming life it is! All my senses and emotions are turned outward. I am becoming more and more of a stranger to myself. How will it all end? . . . Remember me as one usually remembers those who have died.'

As a conductor Mahler had now achieved the summit of his profession at the age of thirty-seven. Yet he of all people knew how the hour of triumph is often marred by sorrow or cruelty. His first weeks at the Vienna Opera were overshadowed by the tragic end of an old friendship. It is true that the coolness with Hugo Wolf had persisted since the *Rübezahl* libretto episode and that since that time they had met only once, at Bayreuth in 1883, and merely acknowledged each other curtly; nevertheless they shared old memories. Although each disliked the other's music, Wolf greatly admired Mahler's conducting. On 4th June 1897 Mahler undertook to consider producing Wolf's opera *Der Corregidor*. In September Wolf went to see Mahler at his office, where they had a violent argument when Mahler told him that the work would not be performed during the 1897–8 season. This was enough, alas, to unbalance Wolf's precarious mental stability. He announced to his friends that Mahler had been dismissed and that he was now director. It was the beginning of the end, which came on 22nd February 1903; a year later Mahler conducted *Der Corregidor* in both its revised and original versions. It was not a success.

There was no 'summer-composing' in 1897, but Mahler went to Vienna having completed his Third Symphony at Steinbach in the summer of 1896, the year in which he had conducted the First Symphony in Berlin, preceding it with the first performance of his song-cycle *Lieder eines fahrenden Gesellen*.

There was a new feature in the 1896 holiday – Mahler's bicycle. Cycling had become a popular sport in Germany in the late 1880s. Wilhelm Zinne taught Mahler to ride a 'velocipede' in the spring of 1895 (five years before Elgar, another keen bicyclist, learned). Mahler consulted Zinne about buying a bicycle – 'I have heard that *English* bicycles ('Premier', for ex.) only cost *250 marks* etc.' – and wrote to him, 'I'm admired by all and sundry on my bike! I really do seem to be a born cyclist . . . I'm at the stage when all horses get out of my way — it's only with *bell-ringing* that I have trouble: if this becomes necessary I often dismount (very smoothly) — I can't yet bring myself to run down a taximeter, although they deserve it, stationing themselves in the middle of the road with no consideration for the fact that every road is too narrow for such an energetic cyclist ... Yours most sincerely, Gustav Mahler, Bicy-Clerk and Road Hogger.' When he went to visit Brahms at Ischl in 1896, he cycled there.

At Steinbach that summer, amid the beauty of the Salzkammergut, he played the new six-movement symphony — 'A Summer Morning's Dream' — to Bruno Walter. 'I am afraid the whole thing is again sicklied o'er with the notorious spirit of my humour', he had written to him. It is his Pastoral Symphony, in which his affinity with nature is the prime element. 'I saw Pan within him,' Walter wrote; and indeed Mahler thought of calling the symphony *Pan*. 'It always strikes me as odd,' Mahler wrote to Richard Batka in November 1896, 'that most people when they speak of "nature", think only of flowers, little birds and the scent of the pine forest. No one knows the god Dionysus or great Pan. There now! You have a sort of programme — that is, a sample of how I make music. Everywhere and always, it is the very sound of nature!'[11] The second movement, the minuet — 'the fashionable flower piece' — was performed separately by Nikisch and Felix Weingartner in the winter of 1896. Mahler realized that, played out of context, this movement could give a false impression of the symphony but, he told Batka, 'if I want at long last to get a hearing I must not be finicky'.

Music was not merely a profession for Mahler; it was a sacred mission, to which everyone and everything took second place. Even Anna von Mildenburg found this hard to understand. Absorbed in his work in the summer of 1896, he had not written to her for some days and she rebuked him. 'But I did write and tell you I was engaged in a major work', he retorted on 18th July.

> Don't you realize it takes all a man has, and how one can be so deeply involved that one is almost dead to the outside world? ... I have often explained this to you before — and you must accept it if you really understand me. Look, everyone who has shared my life has had to learn this. At such times I am no longer my own master ... The composer of

[11] A. Mahler (ed.), *Gustav Mahler's Letters 1879–1911* (Berlin, 1924), pp. 214–15.

such a work has to suffer terrible birth-pangs, and before it all assumes order in his mind, building up, surging up, he is often preoccupied, self-immersed, dead to the outside world . . .

Those are almost exactly the words of his most famous song written five years later: 'Ich bin der Welt abhanden gekommen' ('I am lost to the world').

As he prepared for the arduous and consuming battles which awaited him in Vienna, he remembered what he had written to Friedrich Löhr in the spring of 1894 when he was first approached by Vienna:

How would I be treated in Vienna with my way of going about things? I should only need to try once to convey my interpretation of one of Beethoven's symphonies to the famous Philharmonic Orchestra, trained as it has been by the honest Hans, to be involved forthwith in the most repulsive dog-fight. Haven't I had the same experience here [Hamburg] where I hold undisputed sway by virtue of Brahms's and Bülow's utterly unqualified championship of me? . . . I have only one desire: to work amid simple, ingenuous people in some small town where there are no 'traditions' and no guardians of 'the eternal laws of beauty', to my own satisfaction and that of a small select circle who can follow me. If at all possible, no theatre and no 'repertoire'! But, of course, for as long as I must pant along after my precious brothers, always so daringly taking wing, and until my sisters are tolerably provided for, I have to continue my lucrative bread-winning artistic activity.

5

Vienna

When Mahler left Vienna in 1907 he described his decade at the Opera as 'ten war-years'. Arnold Schoenberg, in a letter to him in 1910, referred to 'our hated and beloved Vienna'. From his days at the Conservatory Mahler knew only too well how Vienna treated its great men, canonizing them when they were dead, often reviling them during their lifetime. The city repelled him yet fatally attracted him. It was, after all, the city of Haydn, Mozart, Beethoven, Schubert and Bruckner, the city of the Strauss waltz, of the coffee-houses, of the Prater and the Opernring. The city of light-hearted, easy-going, gracious living, of intrigue, callousness and spite where revolutionary ideas in art struggled for expression in a climate of conservative, sometimes reactionary, opinion. The years from 1897 to 1914 were Vienna's 'Edwardian' age, an almost exact parallel to the London of the same period. With hindsight, it seems that the life of Europe then was illuminated by a garish light shed by the sun as it gradually became obscured by the storm clouds. In Vienna the opera had a golden age under Mahler; the operettas of Lehár and Oscar Straus were on everyone's lips; science and medicine thrived; writers and painters abounded. But the Emperor was growing old; the political scene was seething; anti-Semitism grew fiercer and more open.

Mahler, as artistic director of the Royal and Imperial Opera, was responsible only to the Emperor's Lord Chamberlain of the Household, Alfred, Prince Montenuovo, who supported him through many crises. From the day he took up his post Mahler set musical Vienna by the ears. 'As a man I am willing to make every possible concession,' he said, 'but as a musician I make none. Other opera directors look after themselves and wear out the theatre. I wear myself out and look after the theatre.' Gossip columnists seized on every scrap of information about him, true or false. Anything he said at rehearsals was 'news'. Public and performers alike were disciplined. He re-introduced Wagner's custom of dimming the house lights before the curtain rose. Latecomers were shut out until Act I was over. More and stricter rehearsals were held and no excuses for absence were accepted, however luminous the star concerned. The orchestral players' custom of sending deputies was outlawed. Wagner's operas were given complete. He eliminated spurious top notes and cadenzas inserted into Mozart by some singers.

The Viennese music critic Max Graf has related[1] how Mahler's personality pervaded stage, orchestra and auditorium in Vienna.

When the house grew dark, the small man with sharply chiselled features, pale and ascetic-looking, literally rushed to the conductor's desk. His conducting was striking enough in his first years of activity in Vienna. He would let his baton shoot forward suddenly, like the tongue of a poisonous serpent. With his right hand, he seemed to pull the music out of the orchestra as out of the bottom of a chest of drawers. He would let his stinging glance loose upon a musician who was seated far away from him, and the man would quail. Giving a cue, he would look in one direction, at the same time pointing his baton in another. He would stare at the stage and make imploring gestures at the singers. He would leap from the conductor's chair as if he had been stung. Mahler was always in full movement like a blazing flame. Later he became calmer.

Mahler supervised every detail of the operas (the very idea of an independent producer would have horrified him). Lighting, costumes, décor, acting – all these he rigorously controlled, in pursuit of his ideal of opera as an art form in which music, drama, ballet and design played equal parts. In 1903 he had hydraulic equipment installed so that the orchestra pit could be lowered by one and a half metres for Wagner. But his first task in his early years was to impose his musical standards on the singers. He found he could not work with some of the 'old guard'; they found him tyrannical, overbearing and rude. So they left, and he built up a new company of his own choice, among them Marie Gutheil-Schoder, Selma Kurz, Erik Schmedes, Leo Slezak, Leopold Demuth, Friedrich Weidemann and Richard Mayr. (And in those days, of course, they stayed in Vienna – they did not gad about the world in jet aircraft.) He constantly gave young singers chances in major rôles; as frequently he dropped them if he realized he had misjudged their potential.

[1] M. Graf, *Legends of a Musical City* (New York, 1945), pp. 204–8. Reprinted in *Mahler Remembered*, op. cit., pp. 102–3.

A first-hand portrait of Mahler in Vienna was provided by the composer Franz Schmidt, who was a cellist in the opera orchestra from 1896. 'Mahler burst over the Vienna Opera like an elemental catastrophe', he wrote.[2]

> An earthquake of unprecedented intensity and duration shook the entire building from the foundation pillars to the gables. Anything that wasn't very strong had to give way and perish. In a short time the largest part of the singers fled (Van Dyck, Marie Renard, Reichmann, Winkelmann), conductors (Hans Richter!), two-thirds of the orchestra. In the orchestra in particular Mahler dismissed and pensioned off so many people in his rage that although I was the youngest [23] in 1897, in 1900 I was already the longest-serving active cellist.

One singer above all he wanted in his Vienna company – Anna von Mildenburg. But he did not bring her there at first. When news of her engagement there was announced, one newspaper said that it was Mahler who had arranged for his 'girl friend' to follow him. The likelihood is that Rosa Papier pressed for her to come. One opponent of Anna's transfer was Mahler's sister Justine, who was jealous of her influence and also realized that she herself could provide the feminine care her brother needed without the emotional complication of being his wife or mistress. But Justine could not sing. Mahler offered Anna some guest engagements and in February 1898 she joined the company. She had a long interview with him in the director's room. No one knows what was said, but it seems likely that Mahler re-emphasized that their former intimacy could not continue. Her indiscreet gossip had caused him trouble in Hamburg. Writing to her in July 1897, Mahler said that if she accepted an offer from Vienna it was essential that

> we restrict our personal relations to an absolute minimum in order not to make life intolerable for one another again. The entire opera personnel is on the alert because of the gossip from Hamburg, and the news of your engagement will burst like a bomb. If, therefore, we were to give the slightest reason for further gossip, *my own position* could rapidly become untenable, and I'd have to pack my bags again, as I did in Hamburg . . . And so I ask you, dearest Anna: have you the strength to work with me in Vienna and – at least for the first year – to renounce

[2] F. Schmidt, *Autobiographical Sketch* in H. Truscott's *The Music of Franz Schmidt*, Vol. I (London, 1984), pp. 175–9.

any private relationship and any form of favour from myself? I hope you realize it will be *no less difficult for me* than for you . . .[3]

Anna kept her side of the bargain, if with difficulty, and became the mistress of both Siegfried Lipiner and Ludwig Karpath before marrying Hermann Bahr in 1909.

Mahler was criticized because he sometimes preferred less-than-perfect singers with outstanding acting ability to those who had only 'a lovely voice' (a parallel with Verdi, who advised impresarios to engage Victor Maurel for Iago even if he could only speak the part, because he acted it so superbly). As reported by Natalie Bauer-Lechner, he pointed out to a friend:

Do you imagine, for example, that Mildenburg, whom you now admire as the greatest truly classic dramatic actress, was always so? You should have seen her as a beginner; how clumsy and awkward she was then! Much in the same way as I drilled her musically, I told her to study every expression and gesture of her music and to act in front of a mirror. So that she should acquire a quiet, poised stance, I made her go out walking in the streets without umbrella and muff – nothing in her hands – with a regular and upright gait, and do exercises at home morning and evening . . . I showed her every step, every attitude and movement, rehearsing it in the greatest detail in relation to the singing. That was how I rehearsed the Wagner roles with her, from beginning to end . . . At first, she even walked so awkwardly that she stumbled over her long dresses . . . Only when, on Justine's advice, she started to wear long trailing gowns at home did she accustom herself to them for the stage as well.

Mahler said that he had never found anyone else so ready to learn, except perhaps Marie Gutheil-Schoder – later to be the first Vienna Elektra and Oktavian in *Der Rosenkavalier*. He told Bauer-Lechner: 'It is always the way, that I encounter the highest and best achievement in *women*. Schoder and Mildenburg tower high above all the rest; they reassure one that there is still natural talent on the stage, not only affectation, grease-paint and pretence.' Of Schoder he added: 'There again you have the mystery of personality, in which all one's potential lies concealed. Look at this woman, unimpressive at first sight, with her average voice and its quite unsympathetic middle

[3] Undated letter quoted in Kurt Blaukopf, *Gustav Mahler oder der Zeitgenosse der Zukunft* (Vienna, 1969), p. 213.

range! – yet every note is from the heart and every expression, every movement is a revelation of the character she is trying to get inside, and whose every feature she reproduces from within . . .'

Gutheil-Schoder had been coached by Strauss at Weimar and made her Vienna debut as Carmen in 1900. When she had a baby in 1902 Mahler was beside himself, 'regarding her happiness as a calamity for our opera-house'. For her part, she wrote of Mahler:

> He showed me that every opera is a stylized work of art and everything must arrive at the style that the music and text demanded . . . He would reorganize a scene as many as twenty times, making changes even at the final orchestral rehearsal . . . His suggestive power was unbelievable. I became aware of it in seemingly minor details in recitatives in the new production of the Mozart cycle, which he accompanied from the harpsichord: when he struck a chord, one knew immediately how to sing and act what followed . . .[4]

It is clear that Mahler was a great opera producer as well as conductor.

His *tempi* in Wagner, so different from Richter's, aroused controversy. Told that such things were traditional, he replied: 'What you theatre folk call your tradition is really nothing but your comfort and your laziness.' His refusal to join any cliques, inability to dissemble, to conceal his contempt for the second-rate, or to learn tact, made him enemies even among those who approved of what he was trying to achieve. There were no half-measures on either side. Cheers and boos mingled to greet his arrival at the desk. His enlightened policy of staging new works, while acclaimed by the minority of progressives, enraged and estranged the multitude. Some of the older singers, of course, acknowledged his worth. Theodor Reichmann, a great Sachs and Wotan, who privately called Mahler 'the Jewish monkey' because of the way he would leap from the rostrum and scramble through the double basses on to the stage at rehearsals, nevertheless wrote in his diary: 'The inspiration that radiates from the little man is fantastic. He makes you give more than you ever had.' Within a year the Emperor had personally congratulated Mahler on 'making himself the master of conditions at the Opera'. Mahler even scored over the royal household. Told that one

[4] M. Gutheil-Schoder, *Mahlers Opernregie* in P. Stefan (ed.), *Gustav Mahler: Ein Bild seiner Persönlichkeit in Widmungen*, op. cit., pp. 34–7.

of the royal family wanted the Hofoper to perform an opera by his Budapest adversary Count Zichy, Mahler said to Montenuovo: 'Very well, but I will state in the programme that it is staged "by imperial command".' This was reported to Franz Joseph, who said: 'I will certainly not *command* such a thing.' Mahler was incorruptible, and he even tried to abolish the *claque*, though the singers defeated him.

His relationship with Richter, as could be expected, was cool.[5] It is always said that Mahler drove him out; while this may be partially true, because Mahler took over the Wagner operas (and gave *Der Ring des Nibelungen* without cuts), it should be remembered that Richter had been formally offered the conductorship of the Hallé Orchestra of Manchester in November 1895, two years before Mahler took up his Vienna post. He procrastinated for nearly four years on the grounds that he was re-negotiating his Vienna pension. But from the first he said he wanted to go to the Hallé, so we need not shed too many tears for him. As his assistant conductors Mahler engaged Franz Schalk, from 1900, and Bruno Walter, from 1901.

Strangely enough, in the spring of 1898 Mahler seriously contemplated leaving his Vienna post. He told his friend the soprano Lilli Lehmann (who sang Isolde for him on 22nd May 1898) that he had received an offer from New York to succeed Anton Seidl, who had died while plans (later abandoned) were being made to form an orchestra run by the Orchestra Society of New York. He was also offered the directorship of the National Conservatory of Music, which Dvořák had held from 1892 to 1895. 'I see from your letter that I have you to thank for the offer', he told Lehmann. 'I am requested to state my fee! Let me know the sum you think I should demand.' The offer was not taken up. Mahler considered it because his supporter Bezecny had retired in February 1898 and he could not get on with the bureaucrat who succeeded him, August Plappart von Leenheer. Later he negotiated a working agreement with Plappart.

Among the contemporary operas produced in Vienna during Mahler's tenure (not all of them conducted by him) were Puccini's *Madama Butterfly* and *La Bohème* (with Caruso as Rodolfo);

---

[5] Richter said to Busoni in London in June 1899: 'I have heard that Mahler gave you a lesson in the rehearsal [for a Vienna Philharmonic concert]. That is the limit! He doesn't like soloists because he has no routine and cannot conduct at sight' F. Busoni, *Letters to His Wife*, (London, 1938), p. 31).

Leoncavallo's *La Bohème* and *Pagliacci*; Mascagni's *Cavalleria Rusticana*; Richard Strauss's *Feuersnot*; Siegfried Wagner's *Bärenhäuter*; Zemlinsky's *Es war einmal*; Reznićek's *Donna Diana*; Charpentier's *Louise* and Hans Pfitzner's *Die Rose vom Liebesgarten*. Reznićek, Mahler's compatriot and contemporary, paid high tribute in his memoirs to Mahler's attitude when *Donna Diana* was performed in Vienna in December 1898. 'Mahler was almost the ideal conductor for a composer. During the stage rehearsals he turned to me a hundred times and asked me "Is that how it should be?" And whenever I replied "Excellent, fantastic", he was not at all pleased. "You must say if it doesn't sound exactly as you conceived it" etc. He performed the miracle of making the whole work sound as though I had conducted it myself.' Mahler suggested changes in the final scene, with which Reznićek gladly complied, providing extra music.

But it was in the revivals (in many cases this was the *mot juste*) of the great classics that his most significant work was done, in three works in particular: *Don Giovanni*, *Fidelio* and *Tristan und Isolde*. Bruno Walter and Erwin Stein have fortunately left us vivid recollections of Mahler's greatest achievements. Stein describes[6] his *Tristan* as 'feverish and even delirious'. It was in three central moods: 'unrelieved yearning, white-hot passion and violent suffering'. The climaxes were 'shattering indeed. To him they were not only a means of expression, but also a means of architecture'. Mildenburg's Isolde was a great tragic performance. The Tristan was Erik Schmedes. (It was to him that Mahler said: 'Well, my dear Schmedes, don't forget: before the love potion you are a baritone, after it a tenor', a remark of even more point when one knows that Schmedes had started his career as a baritone.) Under Mahler *Die Walküre* 'became a singers', almost a *bel canto*, opera. The huge *Ring* orchestra had to play with chamber-music delicacy ... He gave every phrase the utmost intensity of expression'.

The *Tristan* production, 21st February 1903 (to mark the twentieth anniversary of Wagner's death), was the beginning of Mahler's collaboration with the stage-designer Alfred Roller (1864–1935), a man as dedicated, uncompromising and pioneering as Mahler himself. He was a friend of Gustav Klimt, leader of the

[6] The ensuing quotations are from E. Stein, *Mahler and the Vienna Opera* in *The Opera Bedside Book*, ed. H. Rosenthal (London, 1965), pp. 296–317, and from Walter's *Gustav Mahler*, op. cit.

60

Sezession group of artists at whose exhibition in May 1902 Mahler had conducted the *Ode to Joy* from the finale of Beethoven's Ninth Symphony with the accompaniment arranged for wind only. Roller and Mahler discovered that they shared ideas on how to revitalize opera production. In *Tristan* Roller made use of kaleidoscopic light and colour effects and bathed Act II in violet to symbolize night. Mahler, before he met Roller, had replaced the pantomime spookery of the Wolf's Glen scene in *Der Freischütz* by an impressionistic display of light and shade and clouds.[7] Five Mozart operas were re-staged in 1906 to mark the 150th anniversary of the composer's birth. In *Don Giovanni* the famous 'Roller towers' were first used. These were two massive grey structures on either side of the stage and served as the Commendatore's house, Elvira's balcony, the Don's house, and tombstones, thus revolutionizing quick scene-changing. In Beethoven's *Fidelio* (1904) the first scene was restored to Rocco's lodge as in the 1806 version. The prisoners realistically came groping from a dark hole, with the guards lurking in the shadows: the darkness of Roller's sets was a regular target for critics.

The 1906 revivals of *Die Entführung aus dem Serail* and of *Così fan tutte* were box-office failures (as was Verdi's *Falstaff* in 1904). In *Don Giovanni* and *Figaro* Mahler restored the *secco* recitatives, which he accompanied himself. He ended the former after the Don's descent into Hell, omitting the final sextet. 'Mahler', said Stein, 'was the ideal Mozart performer. He was capable of the exceedingly subtle rubato that is implied in Mozart's melodies . . . There was always time for the music to sound and for the singer to sing.' In *Figaro* 'it was the leisure of even the quickest *tempi* that brought the points of music and play across . . . The last finale . . . was built up as a great Nocturne, beginning in an atmosphere of curious suspense'. In order to make Marcellina's lawsuit clearer, he inserted the trial scene from Beaumarchais in *secco* recitative 'composed' for the production from Mozartian works.

The Mahler-Roller *Fidelio* (first produced 7th October 1904) was one of their finest achievements, distinguished by Mildenburg's legendary Leonora. Mahler 'did not try to smooth . . . Beethoven's occasional oddities and abruptnesses, but made the music sound as strange as it is conceived'. He considered the 1907 *Iphigénie en*

---

[7] See Prawy's *The Vienna Opera* (London, 1969) for a detailed account of these productions.

Aulide, in Wagner's version of Gluck, 'the best that Roller and I have achieved so far'. Earlier triumphs included Tchaikovsky's *Queen of Spades*, of which he was very fond, Weber's *Euryanthe*, Goetz's *The Taming of the Shrew*, and Offenbach's *Tales of Hoffmann*. And on New Year's Eve he would conduct *Die Fledermaus* in aid of the staff's pension fund, with some of the stars of the casts of other operas singing in the chorus and champagne in the glasses.

Bruno Walter marvellously summed up Mahler's genius as a conductor of opera:

> He lived in everything and everything lived in him. And no matter how foreign a sentiment might be to him, how contrary to his character, his imagination would enable him to place himself inside the most opposite person and in the strangest of situations. Thus, Mahler's heart was on the stage when he sat at the desk. He conducted or, rather, he produced the music in accordance with the drama.

Walter has also left us an account of the physical aspects of Mahler's conducting:

> Boehler's excellent silhouette caricatures [see p. 2 of plates] show the violent and drastic nature of his gestures during his first years in Vienna . . . His agility at that time and also previously, in Hamburg, was astonishing. . . . As time went on, his attitude and gestures became quieter . . . In his last years his conducting presented a picture of almost uncanny quiet, although the intensity of expression did not suffer by it.

This is corroborated by Richard Aldrich of the *New York Times*, reviewing a Mahler concert on 30th November 1908: 'He has absolutely none of the poses or ornate and unnecessary gestures of the "prima donna" conductor as he stands upon the platform, short in stature, without distinction of figure or manner, with the left hand occasionally thrust into his pocket.'

After a year or two in Vienna, and in spite of violent anti-Semitic attacks on him in some newspapers, Mahler was reckoned to be the most famous man in the city after the Emperor. Cab-drivers stopped when they saw him, pointing out to their hirers: 'Der Mahler!' When he walked from his house to the Opera, patrons of the coffee-houses ran to the windows to watch him pass. He himself went into the coffee-houses, where his circle of friends included Gerhart Hauptmann, Hugo von Hofmannsthal, Felix Salten, Arthur

Schnitzler, Stefan Zweig, William Ritter, Ernst Decsey, Richard Specht and many others, headed of course by Löhr, Lipiner, Freund and Adler, the friends of his youth. (Very few of those who made Vienna great at the turn of the century could have remained there after March 1938.) At his flat, a telephone was installed and the management put a car at his disposal. Just as he had become an enthusiastic cyclist, so now he became a keen motorist.

On Richter's resignation, the Vienna Philharmonic, a self-governing body, elected Mahler as his successor. (The same players constituted the opera orchestra.) From the start, in September 1898, there was tension between them. They resented his intolerance of slovenly performance and his habit of stamping his feet and pointing his baton at recalcitrant players. There was also an element of anti-Semitism. When a player remarked that Richter had been much tougher with them, his companion replied: 'Yes, but Richter's one of us. We can take it from him.' Mahler's programmes were always interesting, including Bruckner symphonies and his own First and Second Symphonies.

Maria Komorn, who attended the performance of the First Symphony (18th November 1900), recalled in an article in the *Neues Wiener Journal* in 1930, how 'the malicious haters of genius' were 'on hand with all their weapons' and that

> there was a regular first-night riot, with hissing, whistling, enraged shouting and fisticuffs – a so-called flop. But even then it was already evident that this filthy torrent of hostility was directed not so much at what must at the time have been quite a difficult work, but rather at the personality which bore the name of Gustav Mahler. Only the youngest listeners stood amid the thunderous noise, overwhelmed by the power of that serious, bespectacled figure, and clapped and shouted themselves hoarse . . . Their impassioned and unshakable feelings told them: this is the pure confession of a great man . . . We rushed to the rostrum with the others and called Mahler out again and again in wild ecstasy while the Antis behind us roared their insults, and we can never forget the pain in the smile with which Mahler acknowledged our applause . . .

The orchestra resented the violent criticisms provoked by his re-orchestration of several classic scores – Beethoven's Seventh and Ninth Symphonies, for example, his arrangement of Beethoven's Op. 95 string quartet for full strings (while in Hamburg he had arranged Schubert's 'Death and the Maiden' quartet in this way), and his extensive amendments to the Schumann symphonies, all directed towards clarity of sound, Mahler's ideal.[8] Relations worsened after Mahler took the orchestra to give five concerts in Paris in June 1900, at the time of the World Exhibition. These were unsuccessful with some of the press and public, one of them coinciding with a fearful migraine which nearly prostrated Mahler.[9] He was invited to attend a performance at the Paris Opéra and was shown round by the directors. Asked for his opinion about the theatre, he bluntly replied: 'Very dirty'. As a result, a general cleaning was ordered in the course of which more than a ton of dust was removed.[10]

On 24th February 1901 in Vienna Mahler conducted a Philharmonic concert in the afternoon and *Die Zauberflöte* at the Opera in the evening. Afterwards he collapsed with a near-fatal haemorrhage from haemorrhoids which necessitated an immediate operation, his third for this ailment. While he was convalescing at Abbazia on the Adriatic the Philharmonic gave two concerts, one conducted by the mediocre Joseph Hellmesberger, son of the former director of the Conservatory, the other by Franz Schalk. The critics were pointedly extravagant in their praise. On his return, Mahler withdrew his candidacy for re-election to the conductorship.

At one of his concerts with the Philharmonic, in February 1899, Mahler had conducted the first complete performance of Bruckner's Sixth Symphony – two movements only had been performed sixteen years earlier – even though the work was heavily cut. At this point it is worth glancing at Mahler's attitude to the music of some of his great contemporaries, bearing in mind that he was a creature of impulse, prone to swift and sudden changes of mind. Discussing Bruckner with his brother Otto in 1893, Mahler (according to Natalie Bauer-Lechner, who noted the conversation[11]) spoke of being 'carried away by the magnificence and wealth of Bruckner's inventiveness, but at the same time you are repeatedly disturbed . . . by its fragmentary character.' He acknowledged Brahms as the greater, viewing their work as a whole. Yet, eleven years later,

[8] See Appendix E.
[9] His programmes included Berlioz's *Symphonie Fantastique* and the Scherzo of Bruckner's Fourth Symphony.
[10] Obituary of Mahler in *The Times*, 20th May 1911.
[11] N. Bauer-Lechner, *Recollections of Gustav Mahler*, op. cit., p. 37.

writing to Alma he described Brahms and Bruckner as 'an odd pair of second-raters', Brahms being (musically) 'a puny little dwarf with a rather narrow chest . . . It is very seldom he can make anything of his themes, beautiful as they often are'. Yet his deeds were better than his words in Bruckner's case, and he kept faith with the promise he made in a letter to the composer in 1886 'to help your glorious art to the triumph it deserves'. He conducted the *Te Deum* twice in Hamburg (1892 and 1893), the Mass in D Minor (1893) and the Third Symphony (1895). With the Vienna Philharmonic he also conducted the Fourth and Fifth Symphonies, but cut them.

Mahler's relationship with Richard Strauss, four years his junior, is a complex study in opposites, as Mahler himself acknowledged when he told Alma that 'Strauss and I are digging our tunnels from different sides of the mountain. We shall surely meet some day.' They were totally different personalities, the one obsessively introspective, the other almost phlegmatic. Where Mahler had had to struggle for recognition from a comparatively poor background, Strauss had had a relatively comfortable ride to early success. Both were great composer-conductors. Mahler's rise to eminence as an opera conductor was quicker than Strauss's, but Strauss's early compositions were acclaimed sooner (and played more often) than Mahler's. It would have been unnatural if there had not been a tinge of jealousy in Mahler's attitude. But his respect for Strauss's ability was unstinted. J. B. Foerster, writing about Mahler in Hamburg, said that 'I noticed that Mahler saw in Strauss his only rival; he got hold of each of his scores . . . immersed himself in them, talked about them and made a number of pertinent criticisms, which were always well-founded and without a trace of denigration'. Both were eager to conduct each other's music: Strauss on one occasion in their correspondence referred to himself as 'the first "Mahlerian" '. Mahler wrote to Arthur Seidl on 17th February 1897:

I shall never cease to be thankful to *Strauss* for getting things going, and in what a truly high-minded way! Let no one suggest that I might regard myself as a 'rival' . . . I number it among my greatest joys that I found among my contemporaries such a comrade-in-arms, such a comrade in creation . . . When you refer to us, in a way so flattering to me, as the 'opposite poles' of the new magnetic field, you express a view I have for a long time held in secret . . .

Once Alma came on the scene, Mahler became more ambivalent about Strauss. Neither of them much cared for Pauline Strauss and both – again perhaps enviously – professed to be offended by Strauss's attitude to the commercial side of music such as royalties and percentages. But several of the derogatory stories about Strauss recounted by Alma in her book are fictions. In his annotated copy of her biography of Mahler, Strauss showed himself almost mystified by her attitude, writing against one distorted or invented episode: 'I don't pretend to understand such things'.

But Alma or no, Mahler continued to admire Strauss's music. He regarded *Salome* as 'emphatically a work of genius . . . one of the greatest masterpieces of our time' and fought a long battle with the censor from 1905, when his proposed production of the opera was forbidden. During 1906, Mahler even considered making the *Salome* issue a question of confidence in him as director of the Opera. Strauss implored him not to do so: 'We need an artist of your determination, your genius and your outlook in such a position too badly for you to put anything at stake on *Salome*'s account. In the end we shall attain our ends without this.'

Of Puccini Mahler held a poor opinion – 'nowadays any bungler orchestrates to perfection', he said of *Tosca* – nor did he think much of Reger and Pfitzner. His famous remark about Hugo Wolf's songs was made to Oskar Fried in 1910: 'Of Wolf's one thousand songs I know only 344. Those 344 I do not like.' His 'gods' were Beethoven and Wagner, 'and after them, nobody'.

After the enormous effort involved in composing the Second and Third Symphonies and in putting the Opera on its feet, Mahler lay fallow during 1897 and 1898. He prepared the Second Symphony and *Lieder eines fahrenden Gesellen* for publication in 1897 and the often-revised First Symphony was published in 1899. In 1899 also he worked on a minor revision of his early cantata *Das klagende Lied* preparatory to publication in 1902. In 1899 he bought a plot of land at Maiernigg on the Wörthersee in Carinthia and began to build a chalet. That summer he spent at Alt-Aussee, Styria, where in August he began what was to be his happiest, least spectre-ridden symphony, the Fourth. He completed it on 5th August of the following summer, 1900. On 17th February 1901 Mahler conducted *Das klagende Lied* – 'the first work in which I really came into my own as "Mahler" ' – in Vienna. That summer at Maiernigg he began work on the Fifth Symphony, and on settings of poems by Friedrich

Rückert. But the most significant event of 1901 for him was a dinner party on 7th November, at the Vienna home of the Zuckerkandls, when he met the beautiful 22-year-old Alma Maria Schindler.[12] Eighteen days later, in Munich, he conducted the first performance of the Fourth Symphony. Two days afterwards, he proposed to Alma. Their engagement was disclosed in a newspaper on 27th December. In January 1902 Natalie Bauer-Lechner, who had seen all his compositions grow on the summer holidays since 1893, wrote this last comment in her memories of those years: 'Mahler became engaged to Alma Schindler six weeks ago. If I were to discuss this event, I would find myself in the position of a doctor obliged to treat, in life and death, the person he loves most in the world. May the outcome rest with the Supreme and Eternal Master.'

Alma – a Roman Catholic who described herself at this time as 'sceptical' – was the daughter of the landscape painter Emil J. Schindler, who died in 1892. Five years later her mother married Carl Moll, one of the founders of the *Sezession* group of young artists and architects.[13] Alma was a musician and became the pupil of Alexander von Zemlinsky. A fellow pupil was Arnold Schoenberg. To Alma in 1901 Mahler, besides being nineteen years her senior, was known as the all-powerful conductor who was the prey of every young woman with operatic ambitions, and as a composer whose First Symphony she had disliked and rejected. Her first impression was of a man who talked as if he was addressing a meeting. 'He had wielded power so long, encountering only abject submission on every hand, that his isolation had become loneliness.' Within five months, on 9th March 1902, they were married in the Karlskirche.

12 Born 31st August 1879.
13 Moll in later years became an ardent Nazi. With his daughter and son-in-law, who had influenced his views, he committed suicide at the age of eighty-four in 1945 when the Russians entered Vienna.

6

Alma

Alma Mahler wrote two remarkable books: *Gustav Mahler* and her autobiography *And the Bridge is Love*.[1] After Mahler's death she became the mistress of Oskar Kokoschka, the painter, and married the architect Walter Gropius, founder of the Bauhaus, in 1915. Soon they parted and were divorced. By Gropius she had a daughter, Manon, whose death from polio at the age of eighteen is commemorated in Berg's Violin Concerto, with its dedication 'to the memory of an angel'. In 1929 she married the writer Franz Werfel and eventually settled in the United States, where she died in 1964. Although she lived to the hilt for fifty-three years after his death, one senses from her writing that Gustav Mahler, even when she reacted against his music, dominated her existence. Their marriage was, on the face of it, doomed to failure, yet despite storms and stresses it held (just) because of Mahler's intensive love for her. They were Hans Sachs and Eva personified. Her books are often fearfully inaccurate, they may have offended individuals, but by their frankness and tactlessness as an unlikeable self-portrait they give an unrivalled, if distorted, picture not only of Mahler but of a whole artistic circle. The letters Mahler wrote to her for ten years are a moving and vivid revelation of his real personality, belying the superficial impression of him as a neurotic megalomaniac teetering on the brink of madness, a misrepresentation for which Alma is largely responsible. She lays candid stress on his egocentricity, his intolerance, his incredible *gaucherie* in some personal dealings, but through her pages and through his letters shines a man with a keen sense of observation, a philosophical acceptance of human frailties, a sardonic sense of humour, an astute business mind and a touching capacity for real affection. He could laugh at himself. Writing to Alma in 1910 he admitted he had lost his temper at a rehearsal of the Eighth Symphony but later: 'I came out of my corner like a sulky boy.' It is also clear that, despite her pretensions, he was by miles her

[1] Hutchinson (London, 1959).

intellectual superior. He was not 'self-centred' in the narrow meaning: he was centred on his religion, which was music. No doubt Alma resented this omnipotent rival, more seductive than any mistress.

The world can never repay her for her influence on Mahler's compositions. From 1880 to 1901 he had written four symphonies, a cantata and songs: no mean output for a busy conductor. Yet between 1902 and 1907 while in charge of the Vienna Opera and in increasing demand as a conductor of his own and others' symphonic work, he wrote four enormous symphonies and the *Kinder-totenlieder*. In the last three years of his life he wrote three symphonies. A month after their meeting he wrote to her from Berlin, where he conducted the Fourth Symphony on 16th December: 'I should like now to have success, recognition, and all those other really quite meaningless things people talk of. I want to do you honour.' Their rapid engagement, as can easily be imagined, was the talk of Vienna. It can also easily be imagined in what a vulnerable position Alma found herself, the target for all who wished to try through her to influence the director of the Opera. He, too, was pathetically easy prey for 'friends' who took him every piece of café tittle-tattle about his fiancée. No wonder she intensely disliked some of those who had known him since before she was born.

It would be an intolerable slight on Mahler's memory if he were to be judged for evermore by the picture of him committed to paper by Alma. She represents him as so self-centred that he was incapable of real love for anyone else. His long and frequent letters to her when they were apart show that he was always deeply concerned about her health and happiness. It is he who has to complain time after time that he has not heard from her or received only a short note. Alma was a born seductress glorying, as such women do, in their powers. Her first *amour* had been Klimt. When she met Mahler she was passionately in love with Zemlinsky and ready to lose her virginity to him, even if it meant pregnancy. In her diary[2] she wrote of her doubts: 'Could I ever love Mahler as he deserves? . . . I don't know my own heart . . . Would Mahler encourage me to work? Would he stand by my art? Would he love me for it, as Alex does?' She chose Mahler because he was 'the purest, the greatest genius' she had met.

---

[2] Quoted by Henri-Louis de la Grange in 'Mistakes about Mahler', *Music and Musicians*, October 1972, pp. 16–22.

She hoped he would 'raise her to his level'. Yet she admitted to herself that she was 'incapable of warmth of feeling. Everything about me is calculation, cold, cold calculation.' Mahler was under no illusion about the nature of her character: while they were engaged he reproved her for her constant flirting with other men and asked her to give up everything, including her composing, if she was to be his wife. She agreed. This was a cruel imposition by Mahler, for Alma's songs, settings of Heine, Rilke and Dehmel among others, are of considerable interest and worth. 'I buried my dream then', she wrote years later. 'It left a nagging wound which never completely healed.' But, as will be seen, the sentence was not for life.

Alma implies that Mahler was totally inexperienced with women until she met her. While his affairs were often platonic, others were not (Mildenburg in Hamburg, for instance), but he worried about marrying a beautiful and passionate woman nineteen years his junior. In the early days of 1902, however, they made love and Alma was pregnant when they married on 9th March 1902. The next day Mahler's sister Justine married Arnold Rosé, the leader of the Vienna Philharmonic, with whom she had been having a clandestine affair for some time, a circumstance which in itself had a deleterious effect on the orchestra's relationship with their conductor. The Mahlers spent their honeymoon in Russia, where Mahler conducted three concerts in St Petersburg. For the first time Alma sat behind the orchestra to watch him: 'His exaltation when he was conducting was always intense and the sight of his face on these occasions, uplifted and open-mouthed, was so inexpressibly moving.'

Home in Vienna, at a flat in the Auenbruggergasse, Alma found that her husband was deeply in debt, largely because of Justine's improvident housekeeping. It took Alma five years to get matters under control. She accompanied him to Crefeld for the first performance of the Third Symphony on 9th June. (None of his symphonies had first performances in Vienna in his lifetime. He was scrupulous, as opera director, in refusing to promote his works there.) Alma shrewdly summed up the contemporary attitude to Mahler as 'the Great Director of the Opera who to please himself had composed a monstrous symphony'. But this performance was a triumph and was the beginning of a genuine enthusiasm for Mahler's works, at any rate outside Vienna. Elated, Mahler and Alma went to Maiernigg for their first summer together. He in his oldest clothes, they went for long walks. They rowed, swam and sunbathed. He was anxious to complete the Fifth Symphony, so he worked in his hut in a wood, and she sat in the house making a fair copy of his score. 'His life during the summer months,' she wrote, 'was stripped of all dross, almost inhuman in its purity.' By autumn the symphony was completed in short score; he orchestrated it fully during the winter, working before breakfast. During this 1902 summer holiday, he also composed the Rückert song, *Liebst du um Schönheit*, for Alma: 'If you love for love's sake, yes, then love me'.

Their first child, a daughter, was born on 3rd November 1902; although known always by the affectionate pet name 'Putzi', she was christened Maria, after Mahler's mother. According to Freud, Mahler had wanted Alma to use her second name, Maria,[3] and to look 'more stricken', reflecting justifiable distrust of her youth and beauty and of the attention paid to her by Hans Pfitzner and other young men in her artistic circle. He tyrannized her in the sense that he insisted on their life's subservience to music. Nothing must disturb that. It was a severe burden to lay on a young woman but, to her credit, she saw the cause of it — in retrospect, at any rate: 'Work, exaltation, self-denial and the never-ending quest were his whole life on and on and for ever. . . . He noticed nothing of all it cost me. He was utterly self-centred by nature, and yet he never thought of himself. His work was all in all.'

And his work, quite apart from the Opera, increased during 1903. A happy experience awaited him in October when he first conducted the Concertgebouw Orchestra of Amsterdam, whose conductor Willem Mengelberg was a devout Mahlerian. He fell in love with the orchestra ('glorious') and they with him; and with the Dutch countryside: 'Enchanting roads, paved, and lined with trees . . . and the long undeviating canals, converging from every quarter, shining like streaks of silver, and the little green-washed houses; and, above it all, the grey-blue, cloudy sky and flocks of birds. So lovely.' After the Third Symphony 'the tumult of applause was almost daunting. Everyone said nothing like it could be remembered. Strauss, who is much in vogue here, has been beaten handsomely.'

---

[3] Again I feel the need for a pinch of salt. Mahler never used 'Maria' in his letters; in fact he seemed to derive pleasure from concocting numerous affectionate diminutives of Alma. And to name one's daughter after one's mother (and then call her by a nickname anyway) is surely a pretty compliment rather than an indication of an obsession.

That 1903 summer in Maiernigg saw the completion of two movements of the Sixth Symphony. On his return to Vienna in September, Mahler told Arthur Seidl that Nikisch wanted to give the first performance of the Fifth Symphony in Berlin, 'but I do not wish to take the risk because of the unfavourable attitude the press there have adopted towards me, as you know. After all, I should not care to let the same thing happen to me with this work as happened to the First, Second and Fourth, all three of which at their first performance there were slaughtered in the bloodthirstiest way, as a result of which they have not been in demand anywhere else.' Nevertheless, in 1904 there were more performances of his symphonies, notably the Third, throughout Germany. 'In your new toilette you're well up to my Third, well performed,' he wrote to Alma. From him that was a compliment. On 15th June 1904 their second daughter, Anna, nicknamed Guckerl, was born in Vienna. When they went with Putzi and the baby to Maiernigg, he completed the Sixth Symphony, made some sketches for the Seventh, and added two settings to three composed in 1901 of Rückert's poems mourning the death of children, *Kindertotenlieder*. Alma was horrified by the idea of these songs. 'For heaven's sake, don't tempt Providence,' she told him. But the deaths of children had been a regular feature of Mahler's youth. As Cardus wrote, a coffin must have been a familiar item of furniture. He played her the completed symphony. 'We both wept that day' – so deeply were they affected by the personal nature of the music and especially by the three 'hammer-blows' in the finale. ' "It is the hero, on whom fall three blows of fate, the last of which fells him as a tree is felled." Those were his words.' Mahler, as we shall see, was to suffer three fatal blows in 1907. But the Sixth, prophetic as it may have been, was completed three years before these events occurred. Alma's remarks are the result of hindsight and should be treated cautiously. The Sixth ends in tragedy, but the first three movements and much of the finale are not overtly tragic – and whatever superstitions Mahler entertained when he conducted No. 6, they had not prevented his composing the mainly joyous and optimistic Seventh Symphony in 1904–5. Although the load of debt and the anguish of sexual jealousies were eroding their marriage at this time, Mahler was at his peak. 'I don't know anybody who can do more than I can,' he boasted. He went straight from this holiday to launch his wonderful *Fidelio* production.

During 1904 the Philharmonic played through the Fifth

Symphony with Mahler. Alma, who had copied it and knew it by heart, was mortified to hear that he had overscored the percussion so strongly that the themes were obscured. He agreed with her and made some revisions, the first of many. Because of illness she could not go with him to Cologne for the first performance on 18th October. He saw at his first rehearsal what difficulties he had created:

> The Scherzo is the very devil of a movement. I see it is in for a peck of troubles! Conductors for the next fifty years will all take it too fast and make nonsense of it; and the public – oh, heavens, what are they to make of this chaos of which new worlds are for ever being engendered: . . . What are they to say to this primeval music, this foaming, roaring, raging sea of sound? . . . Oh that I had been born a commercial traveller and engaged as baritone at the Opera![4] Oh that I might give my symphony its first performance fifty years after my death!

And after the performance: 'The Fifth is an accursed work. No one understands it.'

He received pleasure from the friendliness shown to him by many of the orchestras he conducted, in contrast to the tensions of Vienna. At Leipzig, for instance: 'Yesterday and today I pitched into them for four hours at a stretch, and instead of taking it in bad part they bade me an enthusiastic farewell at the end of it.' He was beginning to realize too that the younger generation admired him. After the first performance of the Fourth Symphony in 1901 a sixteen-year-old boy, Alban Berg, stormed his dressing-room and carried off his baton as a memento. And Alma's friend Schoenberg, thirty years old in 1904, who had begun by disliking Mahler's music and had had many an argument with Mahler, wrote to him in December after hearing the Third Symphony in Vienna:

> I saw your very soul naked, stark naked. . . . I felt your symphony. I shared in the battling for illusion; I suffered the pangs of disillusionment; I saw the forces of good and evil wrestling with each other; I saw a man in torment struggling towards inward harmony. . . . Forgive me, I cannot feel by halves.

If this language seems extravagant, it conveys the impact this music made when it was new. Mahler for his part was to

---

[4] A reference to Leopold Demuth.

demonstrate his belief in Schoenberg's music, even if he did not fully understand it. At the first performance of the Chamber Symphony No. 1, on 8th February 1907, he angrily silenced those who noisily pushed their chairs back during the performance; and at the end he stood applauding until everyone had left.

The year 1905 began for Mahler with the first performances, in Vienna, of *Kindertotenlieder* (29th January and the 3rd February). During the year he conducted several performances of the Fifth Symphony and, at Maiernigg, completed the full sketch of the Seventh Symphony. He had composed the two *Andante* movements (Nos. 2 and 4) the previous summer, and in a letter written in May 1910 he gave Alma a vivid description of how the rest of the work was written in 1905:

> In art as in life I am at the mercy of spontaneity. If I had to compose, not a note would come. . . . I made up my mind to finish the Seventh, both Andantes of which were then on my table. I plagued myself for two weeks until I sank into gloom. . . . then I tore off to the Dolomites. There I was led the same dance, and at last gave it up and returned home. . . . I got into the boat to be rowed across. At the first stroke of the oars the theme (or rather the rhythm and character) of the introduction to the first movement came into my head – and in four weeks, the first, third and fifth movements were done.

In those weeks when inspiration would not come, Mahler displayed his immense physical strength and energy – climbing, rowing, walking in the rain for five hours singing aloud as he composed – an alarming sight to come upon unawares, as a child named Rudolf Bing did.[5] To Alma, who had been urged by a Dr Rosthorn to ask him to rest, he contemptuously replied: 'Your Rosthorns have not the dimmest notion of an entelechy such as mine. . . . They cannot imagine the evil effects on me of not sticking to my work.' Alma has depicted Mahler as a weakly hypochondriac. Yet he was very tough and, apart from migraines and ominously recurrent sore throats, was hardly ever ill; in fact he regarded illness with scorn. He was a frugal eater and moderate drinker: he trained like an athlete for his work.

The most detailed verbal picture of the physical Mahler was written by Alfred Roller in 1921. He described his careless mode of

[5] Sir Rudolf Bing, *5000 Nights at the Opera* (London, 1972), p. 8.

dress except for what Mahler called his 'working clothes', his tails. These were impeccably maintained. He also always had good shoes, because he was such a keen walker.

While Mahler was sunbathing . . . I had the opportunity to study his naked body closely. It was very tidily formed and very masculine in its proportions. His shoulders were broader than one would imagine from seeing him in clothes, and perfectly symmetrical. His hips were very narrow and his legs, which were by no means short, had beautifully formed and regularly spaced axes, firm, clearly developed muscles and just a light covering of hair. There was no sign of any prominent veins. His feet were small with a high instep and short, regularly spaced toes, without a blemish. His chest stood out strongly with very little hair and well-defined musculature. His belly, like the rest of his body, bore no traces of excess fat, the central line of muscle was plainly visible and the outline of the other muscles as clear as on an anatomical model. In the course of my profession, I have seen a great many naked bodies of all types and can testify that at the age of forty Mahler had the perfect male torso, strong, slim, beautifully made . . . The most beautifully developed part of him, quite an outstanding sight because it was so well delineated, was the musculature of his back. I could never set eyes on this superbly modelled, sun-tanned back without being reminded of a racehorse in peak condition . . .

So long as he believed his heart was sound (that is, up to 1907), he was not only an avid walker but an outstanding swimmer, a powerful oarsman and an agile cyclist. At Maiernigg, by the Wörthersee, his summer residence for several years, he would rise at 5.30, take his first swim alone, then hasten through secret paths to his small composing-house deep in the woods . . . Then followed seven hours of uninter-rupted work . . . His swim usually began with a high dive. Then he swam under water and did not reappear until he was far out in the lake, bobbing about comfortably like a seal . . . Mahler at that time gave the impression of being utterly healthy. He slept splendidly, relished his cigar and in the evening enjoyed a glass of beer. Spirits he abstained from completely. Wine he drank only on special occasions, preferring Mosel, Chianti or Asti . . . You never saw him do anything in excess. He abhorred drunkenness, as much as obscenity or indecency . . .

Mahler's voice functioned in two separate registers, one directly above the other. A very sonorous baritone when he was speaking in a relaxed manner and a ringing tenor that came into play when his excitement began to grow. His voice could be raised to a very high volume without losing its deeper tones . . . I learned to recognize by the sound of his voice whether he was putting it on or whether he was really angry. In the latter case his voice would suddenly soar into the highest register with a kind of break: it would happen whether his excitement was of joy or anger or whether it sprang from intense involvement in a subject of conversation. After 1907 his higher voice was to be heard less and less. His increasing melancholy caused the lower register to predominate more and more.[6]

In March 1906 Mahler was again in Amsterdam to conduct performances of the Fifth Symphony, *Das klagende Lied* and *Kindertotenlieder*. Asking for extra rehearsals with the Concertgebouw Orchestra, he told Mengelberg: 'The Fifth is *very*, *very* difficult.' 'Mengelberg is a man you can rely on,' he told Alma. 'I have true friends here.' On his return he played through the Sixth Symphony with the Vienna Philharmonic, but the first performance was to be at a festival at Essen on 27th May. Mahler had a week of rehearsals, which went well and were brightened further by his meeting with the Russian pianist and conductor, Ossip Gabrilovitch, then aged twenty-eight. Alma joined him for the dress rehearsal. 'You are in for a treat,' he told her. The twenty-three-year-old conductor Klaus Pringsheim was at the Essen rehearsal and recalled how Mahler was 'above all concerned with the achievement of maximum clarity'. Strauss was there, too, and 'remarked casually that he considered the symphony to be partly over-instrumented'. After his experience with the Fifth Symphony and coming from Strauss, this remark worried Mahler, for he still valued Strauss's opinion higher than anyone's. 'Isn't it remarkable', he said, 'that Strauss could manage with a few rehearsals, and yet it always sounded good?'[7] To Richard Specht he wrote: 'My Sixth will pose conundrums that only a generation that has absorbed and digested my first five symphonies may hope to solve.' That forecast has been fulfilled. He was greatly affected by his own music. For instance, he wrote to Alma after conducting the First Symphony: 'Sometimes it sent shivers down my spine. Damn it all, where do people keep their ears and their hearts if they can't hear *that*!' As late as 1906, when Eduard Colonne was planning to perform some of Mahler's music in Paris, Mahler said: 'On no account would I advise the First; it is very hard to understand. Even the Sixth or Fifth would be preferable.'

[6] *Die Bildnisse von Gustave Mahler*, op. cit., pp. 9–28.
[7] K. Pringsheim, 'Erinnerung an Gustav Mahler', *Neue Zürcher Zeitung*, 7th July 1960. Reprinted in *Mahler Remembered*, op. cit., pp. 187–196.

At Maiernigg that summer, on the first day of the holiday, he 'went up to the hut with the firm resolution of idling the holiday away (I needed to so much that year) and recruiting my strength. On the threshold of my old workshop the *Spiritus Creator* took hold of me and shook me and drove me on for the next eight weeks until my greatest work was done.' Obviously, as Donald Mitchell has shown,[8] there was more to the beginning of the Eighth Symphony than that. A sheet of manuscript, on which Mahler wrote 'Aug. 1906. The first inspiration, preserved for my Amschl', was described in a Vienna newspaper in June 1933. This shows that the symphony was originally planned in four movements: I *Veni Creator*. II *Caritas*. III *Scherzo*. Christmas Games with the Christ Child. IV *Hymn*. Creation through Eros. On the sketch were two bars which might have been intended for *Caritas*, the slow movement. The rest of the page contained a draft of the symphony's opening theme, but in F sharp and without any words. It was at this point, presumably, that the '*Spiritus Creator* took hold'. Another surviving sketch contains two texts from *Des Knaben Wunderhorn* that would probably have been included as two songs in the 'Christmas Games' movement. At some point during those eight weeks, the contemplated hymn to Love gave way to the same idea as enshrined in the closing scene of Part II of Goethe's *Faust*, with its salvation through *das Ewige-Weibliche* (the eternal womanhead). This preoccupation with love, combined with the dedication of the symphony to Alma, is sure proof that the origins of the work were autobiographical.

He interrupted its composition to conduct *Le Nozze di Figaro* at the Salzburg Festival, where the critic Julius Korngold noticed that 'a much-thumbed volume [of *Faust*] protruded from his coat pocket'. He completed the sketch on 18th August and elatedly wrote that day to Mengelberg: 'It is the grandest thing I have done yet . . . Try to imagine the whole universe beginning to ring and resound. These are no longer human voices, but planets and suns revolving'.

The climactic year of 1907[9] began for Mahler with a gloom which was to increase. From Frankfurt in January he wrote to Alma: 'I am a hunted stag, hounds in full cry . . . What is the good of being pelted with mud time after time. The curs obviously take me for a lamp-

---

[8] D. Mitchell, *Gustav Mahler, Vol. III: Songs and Symphonies of Love and Death* (London, 1985), pp. 529–32.

[9] Alma Mahler's account of the last four years of their lives together has several inaccuracies and inconsistencies and its chronology is suspect.

post.' This outburst followed a savaging of his Third Symphony by the Berlin critics. 'I cannot even orchestrate, it seems.' But other clouds were gathering. 'All the newspapers [in Frankfurt] have reports from Vienna of my resignation. Does it mean there is another outcry because of my prolonged absence? The newspapers . . . say that I have piled up an enormous deficit, that I have become impossible, etc. etc.'

A crisis at the Opera had been brewing for some time. It was true that expenditure had risen – largely because of Roller's designs – and box-office takings had fallen. Mahler's enemies were ever ready to strike, to attack him direct or through his protégé, Bruno Walter. Increasing anti-Semitism was the background to this intensified campaign. Writing in his diary in January 1906, Hermann Bahr had noted: 'Once again Mahler is being hounded, hounded, hounded! Why do they hate him so? Well, why do they hate Klimt so? They hate everyone who tries to be "true" to himself. That is what they cannot bear . . . They cannot bear someone to have an opinion or a will of his own.' Prince Montenuovo had hitherto supported Mahler, but even between them relations began to cool. Mahler, out of loyalty, had taken Roller's side in a dispute between Montenuovo and Roller when Roller was flagrantly in the wrong. This gave the Chamberlain an opening for further protests about Mahler's absences to conduct elsewhere. The Prince had some cause to complain. Ida Dehmel, in her diary for March 1905, records Mahler as saying: 'I should like best to live only for my compositions and, to tell the truth, I am beginning to neglect my operatic duties.' He explained that bad performances of his Fifth Symphony under other conductors had reinforced his view that 'a musical score is a book with seven seals . . . There must be a tradition and no one can create it but I'.

In February and March he conducted remarkable performances in Vienna of *Die Walküre* and, with Gutheil-Schoder in the title-role, *Iphigénie en Aulide* – Lilli Lehmann called the Gluck 'the pinnacle of all his productions' – and then left to conduct in Rome, Brno and St Petersburg. While he was in Italy the *Deutsche Zeitung*, always his enemy, wrote: 'Direktor Mahler, having amassed a huge income which can only be called exorbitant in view of his pernicious behaviour, is now away "travelling in symphonies" – peddling his own products – and in the meantime everything is going to rack and ruin in the Court Opera.'

On 31st March 1907, Mahler handed Montenuovo his resignation. Although he knew he could have won yet another battle, he had had enough. Talking to Bruno Walter, he shook the legs of a chair and said: 'You see, that's what they are now doing to me: if I were to want to remain seated, all I would have to do is to lean back firmly and I could hold my own. But I am not offering any resistance, and so I shall finally slide down.' In a conversation with Natalie Bauer-Lechner in 1906 he had spoken of his determination to resign in 1907 because he was tired of repertory opera. He added:

All things have their day and I have had mine and so has my work as the local opera director. I am no longer 'news' as far as Vienna is concerned. So I want to go at a point when I can still expect that, at a later date, the Viennese will learn to appreciate what I did for their theatre.

Efforts to find a successor were not immediately fruitful, and Montenuovo tried to persuade Mahler to change his mind. But he had by now, as will be seen, secured his future in New York and he gave an interview, printed in the *Neues Wiener Tagblatt* of 5th June in which he said:

It is completely untrue to say that any 'intrigues' have brought me down. I have not been brought down at all. I am leaving of my own accord because I wish to have complete independence. And also – and this is the prime reason – because I have come to realize that the operatic stage is of its very nature an institution which cannot be maintained indefinitely. No theatre in the world can be kept at a level where one performance is equal to another. But this is exactly what repels me in the theatre, for of course I wanted . . . to attain an ideal which is unattainable.

He denied that the Opera deficit had increased and that this was why he was obliged to resign. Writing a few days later to Arnold Berliner he said: 'I am going because I can no longer endure the rabble.' On 10th August Montenuovo wrote to say that Weingartner would take up the post on 1st January 1908 and that the Emperor had granted Mahler a pension more than double that to which he was entitled, a large compensatory payment and a promise that Alma, after his death, would be 'entitled to the pension of the widow of a Privy Councillor (although you did not rank as such)'. He was handsomely treated. Montenuovo's letter ended: 'Conried need now delay no longer making your engagement public.' This referred to Heinrich Conried, director of the Metropolitan Opera, New York, since 1903, who had approached Mahler earlier in the year with an offer of a four-year contract. Mahler wanted one for only one year. On 5th June in Berlin they clinched an engagement for the first four months of 1908 at a salary of $20,000.

Overshadowing these negotiations was Mahler's health. Most accounts of this year in Mahler's life seem to telescope events which were in fact considerably spread out, as the documents show. It would seem that he had first consulted their family doctor Blumenthal early in January 1907 before he went to conduct the Third Symphony in Berlin and the Fourth in Frankfurt. In a letter to Alma from Frankfurt on 17th January 1907 occur the lines: 'You see, Almschili, one does not die of it – look at Mama with her heart – one goes full speed ahead and then suddenly comes the crash.' Both Bruno Walter and Roller saw him suddenly stand still while he was on stage directing the chorus in a rehearsal of *Lohengrin* in March, turn white as a sheet and clutch at his heart. Writing to Alma on 30th March, while she was convalescing from a throat operation, he said:

> I had myself inoculated yesterday by Dr Hamperl, who examined me too at the same time. He found a *slight* valvular defect, which is entirely compensated, and he makes nothing of the whole affair. He tells me I can certainly carry on with my work just as I did before and in general live a normal life, apart from avoiding over-fatigue. It is funny that in subst: ..ce he said just what Blumenthal said, but his whole way of saying it was somehow reassuring. Also I find I have no fear of conducting now.

This valve lesion was the tell-tale sign of the legacy of infection from recurrent 'bad throats', later to terminate in the fatal subacute bacterial endocarditis.

Determined on resignation from Vienna and with his visit to New York settled, Mahler took Alma and the children to Maiernigg in the middle of June. On the third day of the holiday their elder daughter Maria ('Putzi') developed scarlet fever and diphtheria. After a fortnight's struggle and an unsuccessful tracheotomy she died on 5th July, aged four and a half. Mahler was stricken. He had adored this beautiful child. 'Each morning', Alma wrote, 'Putzi would go into Mahler's study where they had long talks. Nobody has ever known what about . . . By the time Mahler brought her back she was usually smeared with jam from top to toe . . . They were so happy together.' Alma collapsed from exhaustion and Blumenthal, after examining her, again checked Mahler's heart. He advised him to consult Professor Kovacs in Vienna. Kovacs, it appears, told him the condition was serious and that he must shepherd his strength if it was not to prove rapidly fatal. It is unlikely that he pronounced a death-sentence in so many words, but Mahler drew the inevitable conclusion. He and Alma spent the next few weeks at Schluderbach in the Tyrol.

In the middle of August he returned to supervise his last productions at the Opera, where he was 'welcomed respectfully and cordially by all'. His final performance, *Fidelio*, was on 15th October. It was thinly attended. In early November he went to St Petersburg, revising his Fifth Symphony on the journey. Among those who heard and liked it there was the young Stravinsky. In Helsinki Mahler heard the music of Sibelius — 'hackneyed clichés' — and met the composer — 'extremely sympathetic'. It was then that they had their famous discussion on the symphony. Sibelius emphasized '[my] admiration for strictness and style in a symphony and the deep logic which unites all the themes by an inner bond. This was in accordance with my own creative experience. Mahler took a completely opposite view: "No, the symphony must be like the world. It must embrace everything".'[10]

Perhaps it was on this journey that he first read *Die chinesische Flöte* (*The Chinese Flute*), an anthology by Hans Bethge based on ancient Chinese poems, which a friend gave to him shortly after its publication in October 1907 (by Leipzig-Insel-Verlag) with the suggestion that some of the poems might be made into songs. Back in Vienna Mahler said farewell to his public at a special performance of his Second Symphony on 24th November by the Court Opera Orchestra and choral society. There was a 'hurricane of applause' which moved him to tears.

On 7th December he issued a farewell message to the Opera: 'Instead of a complete great work, such as I dreamed of, I am leaving only bits and pieces, for this is in man's nature . . . I meant well and aimed high . . . I have always given my all . . . In the crush of the struggle, in the heat of the moment, wounds were sustained, errors

10 K. Ekman, *Jean Sibelius* (Helsinki, 1935), pp. 185–6.

committed, by you as well as by me.' It was pinned to the notice-board. Next day it was ripped down and torn into pieces. This was symbolic of the manner in which Mahler was treated by Vienna, and indeed by the other cities in which he worked, where his single-minded dedication made him enemies, especially among upholders of the 'traditions' he renovated. (Yet Hanslick, to his credit, was one of his strongest supporters in Vienna and had urged his appointment.) No wonder Mahler referred to opera as 'shameless prostitution, reducing noble material to dirt' when he met opposition to all his reforms. The virulent and personally hostile press criticism of Mahler throughout his career has to be read to be believed. Much of it was directed against his racial origin. 'The Jewish dwarf', someone called him, little knowing of Mahler's sense of humour in that respect. For in 1898, criticizing a tenor who had caricatured the Jewish traits of the dwarf, Mime, in *Siegfried*, he had written self-revealingly to Natalie Bauer-Lechner: 'I know of only one Mime, and that is me . . . You wouldn't believe what there is in that part nor what I could make of it!'

There was one other letter to write on 7th December 1907, to Anna von Mildenburg. 'Dear old friend', he began. 'I have just composed a screed to the "dear members", which will be put up on the notice-board. But while I was writing it, it occurred to me that you were not among those addressed and that for me you are a being *quite* apart. I have kept on hoping to set eyes on you during these days. But there it is, you are at the Semmering (where it is of course much nicer to be). And so on leaving the Opera, not Vienna, where I shall go on living, I can only send you these few heartfelt words and press your hand in spirit. I shall always watch your progress with affection and sympathy, and I hope calmer times will bring us together again. In any case, you know that even from afar I shall remain a friend on whom you can rely. I write this in the midst of frightful turmoil. May all go well with you. And be of good heart. Your old friend. Gustav Mahler.'

Leaving their daughter Anna with Alma's mother, Mahler and Alma left Vienna for Cherbourg on 9th December. Schoenberg, Walter, Roller, Zemlinsky, Justine and Arnold Rosé, Klimt, Marie Gutheil-Schoder and Erik Schmedes were among those who went to the Westbahnhof station to wish them *bon voyage*. As the train moved off, Gustav Klimt said aloud: 'It's over!' ('Vorbei!'). The playwright Gerhart Hauptmann telegraphed to Mahler: 'Europe . . . needs men like you as it does its daily bread.'

7

New York

They arrived in New York the week before Christmas. With Anna in Vienna, the loss of Putzi was even more poignantly felt by them both. But for Mahler there was the Metropolitan Opera.

His impact on the New York scene was awaited apprehensively. An article in the *New York Mail* of 23rd September 1907 speculated about happenings at the Metropolitan under one who 'is no respecter of anything but his art. The "stars" may be compelled to drop from their height and take rehearsals like ordinary mortals . . . and they may be compelled to accept comments not in harmony with their opinion of themselves.' This publication also printed a candid description of Mahler by a young American conductor, Walter Rothwell, who had seen him in Europe:

> Where all others end he begins . . . He has many peculiarities which cannot in any way be explained. As example, innumerable times I have seen men in his orchestra lay down their instruments absolutely like paralysed, unable to sound a note, the only cause being the look in his eyes. I have heard them say 'I cannot play a note until you take your eyes off me'. He can secure almost any effect he desires through those wonderful eyes. Not by reason of his personality, because I do not think that anyone would call it agreeable . . . His most distinguishing feature is his wonderful power of becoming two men – a Mozart conductor and a Wagner conductor.

Mahler's first opera at the Metropolitan was *Tristan und Isolde* on 1st January 1908, with Olive Fremstad singing her first Isolde and Heinrich Knote as Tristan. 'The influence of the new conductor was felt and heard in the whole spirit of the performance,' Richard Aldrich wrote in the *New York Times*. 'Through it all went the pulse of dramatic beauty.'

Mahler was elated by the quality of the singers available; he seemed easier-going than in Vienna and made all the usual cuts in Wagner (perhaps to spare himself). The cast for his first *Don*

Giovanni on 23rd January was Antonio Scotti (Don Giovanni), Feodor Chaliapin (Leporello), Alessandro Bonci (Don Ottavio), Emma Eames (Donna Anna), Johanna Gadski (Donna Elvira) and Marcella Sembrich (Zerlina). At a later performance Geraldine Farrar sang Zerlina. On 7th February he conducted *Die Walküre*, with Gadski as Brünnhilde, Alois Burgstaller as Siegmund, Anton van Rooy as Wotan, Louise Kirkby-Lunn as Fricka and Fremstad as Sieglinde. In *Siegfried*, 19th February, Fremstad sang Brünnhilde. *Fidelio* was given on 20th March with a replica of Roller's sets. Berta Morena sang Leonora and Carl Burrian was Florestan.

Mahler hoped at first that he could obtain a post for Roller in New York. The two men had always been good friends since that first *Tristan* in Vienna, when Mahler had written to him that 'we are similar in one respect: in our completely unselfish devotion to art, even if we approach it by different roads'. In a letter written on 20 January 1908 from the Hotel Majestic, Mahler informed Roller of the bleak situation he had discovered at the Metropolitan:

> Conried has long been quite discredited here . . . The management (i.e. the millionaire board) has sacked him. At the same time it was planned to appoint me in his place – this even before I arrived . . . As you have guessed, I quite decisively refused . . . In these circumstances, I have little influence on future developments. The management plan, first of all, to appoint the present director of La Scala [Gatti-Casazza] manager of the Metropolitan Opera and to appoint Toscanini, a very well-thought-of conductor, to take charge of Italian opera, and hand, as it were, German opera over to me. But this is all still in the air . . .
>
> I have proved to the management (or rather, to one of them, the prime mover) beyond doubt that it is *above all* the *stage* here that needs a new master and that I know only one man with the artistic and personal ability to clear up the mess. At the same time I assured them (and I am still working on these lines) of the necessity of handing over the stage, and everything to do with it, lock, stock and barrel to this man. Rather the way I always saw our position in Vienna . . . Seize the opportunity, my dear fellow, if you receive an offer and if there is nothing to detain you in Vienna. The people here are tremendously unspoilt – all the crudeness and ignorance are teething troubles. Spite and hypocrisy are to be found only among our dear immigrant compatriots. Here the dollar does not reign supreme – it's merely easy to earn. Only one thing is respected here: ability and drive! . . . I almost forgot something important. You have been given a bad name by those dubious gentry who guessed I was going to propose you. They say you

'squander millions' and there would not be enough for you in New York. I explained to the management that you spent great sums of money in the *right place*, which in fact meant you were *very economical*. The (*very munificent*) board found this entirely plausible.

Nothing came of these plans, and a year later, when Roller resigned from the Vienna Opera, Mahler commented: 'Knowing you to be in that wilderness had been a constant worry to me since my departure, and I have been incessantly worrying about how you could free yourself from that web . . .'

Mahler had told Roller, in the first flush of his enchantment with New York, that there were 'no intrigues, no red tape' at the Metropolitan. He was soon to discover he was wrong. Desperate to withstand competition from Oscar Hammerstein's Manhattan Opera House, which opened on 3rd November 1907, Conried had engaged Mahler as one of his 'last throws', but even at the time of their Berlin meeting Otto H. Kahn, one of the Metropolitan leading backers, was in Paris persuading Giulio Gatti-Casazza, director of the Scala, Milan, to go to New York on the assumption that ill health would soon compel Conried's resignation, as it did.[1] If Gatti went to New York it meant that he would take Arturo Toscanini with him; hence Mahler's presence was an embarrassment to the Metropolitan board. Opera politics were not Vienna's copyright. When Kahn made a formal offer to Gatti and Toscanini in 1908 he asked for assurances that Toscanini would accept the Mahler situation. 'I hold Mahler in great esteem', was the reply. But Mahler was suspicious of Toscanini, as he had every right to be, and his fears were confirmed when the Italian insisted that *Tristan* should be ceded to him. In a letter to Andreas Dippel, associate director of the Metropolitan, before the 1908–9 season, Mahler wrote:

It is inconceivable to me that a new production of *Tristan* should be put on without my being consulted in any way and I cannot give my consent . . . If recently – out of consideration for the wishes of my colleague [Toscanini] – I gave a free hand to the new director, it was with the express exception of *Tristan*. I took very special pains with *Tristan* last season and can well maintain that the form in which this work now appears in New York is my spiritual property.

[1] He died on 27th April 1909.

For one season his wishes prevailed. Yet Toscanini opened the season on 16th November 1908 with *Aida* (Emmy Destinn as Aida, Caruso as Radames). Mahler returned on 13th January 1909 with Mozart's *Marriage of Figaro*, after twenty rehearsals. The cast included Eames, Sembrich and Farrar, with Scotti as the Count and Adamo Didur (a bass) as Figaro. On 19th February he conducted Smetana's *The Bartered Bride*, with Destinn as Marie and dancers imported from Prague. Then on 12th March came *Tristan*, with Fremstad and Burrian. A critic wrote that 'Mr Mahler turned loose such a torrent of vital sound as he had never before let us hear'. It was after this performance that he said to Alma: 'The stars were kind. I have never known a performance of *Tristan* to equal this.' He never conducted it again; and he conducted only one more opera – Tchaikovsky's *Pique-Dame* on 5th March 1910, with Leo Slezak as Hermann and Destinn as Lisa, its first performance in the United States. Slezak had been one of Mahler's principals in Vienna, a jovial Czech who originated the witticism 'What time does the next swan leave?' when his swan in *Lohengrin* departed before he had time to join it. He could be undisciplined, but although he sometimes clashed with Mahler – who didn't? – they liked each other. In New York he found his old chief 'a tired and ailing man . . . At the rehearsals it was usually he and I alone. The others did not turn up. He rarely had the whole company together. He sat there with me, resigned: a changed man. I looked in vain for the fiery genius of yesteryear. He had become mild and sad . . . Several weeks after that I met him in Central Park. He looked dreadful. We talked for a long time. It was the last time. He was like a shadow walking along.'[2] Alma describes Mahler in 1909 as 'in the best of health' after the critical summer of 1908 (see next chapter). She even persuaded him to accompany her to some dinner parties (not his favourite recreation) in the homes of the eccentric rich who financed the city's music-making.

During his second visit Mahler conducted three concerts by Walter Damrosch's New York Symphony Society on 30th November, 8th December and 13th December 1908. For the second concert the Oratorio Society joined the orchestra for his Second Symphony, its first New York performance. Mahler was dissatisfied with the artistic standard and lackadaisical attitude of the orchestra

---

[2] L. Slezak, *Mein sämtlichen Werke* (Berlin, 1937), pp. 158–65. Reprinted in *Mahler Remembered*, op. cit., pp. 118–23.

and vowed to have no more to do with it. A few days later he was approached by four women supporters of the sixty-six-year-old New York Philharmonic Society which had been in the doldrums for some time. The society's orchestra had lost many of its best players to the Metropolitan, which had formed two orchestras so that it could play in two cities on the same evening and thus out-trump Hammerstein's Manhattan Opera. The Philharmonic directors wanted an orchestra at least the equal of Boston's. To achieve this, and to combat the lure of the three opera orchestras, they realized they must offer the players permanent engagements under an outstanding conductor. This entailed abandoning the co-operative scheme, by which society members elected the conductor, and replacing it by a board of directors who managed the society and gave absolute artistic powers to the conductor. They raised a guarantee fund of over 80,000 dollars for three years and Mahler agreed to replace Wassily Safonoff and to train a reorganized Philharmonic.

Elated by their capture of such a notable quarry on a three-year contract, the Philharmonic arranged two special concerts, on 31st March and 6th April 1909, to 'introduce' Mahler. He chose routine programmes,[3] but although the critics were impressed by the drive and élan of the playing, he himself was under no illusion about the task which faced him and the need for new players – especially among the woodwind, who failed abysmally in the *Siegfried Idyll*. (A few months later he conducted it with the Concertgebouw and wrote to Alma: 'Balm after the experience in New York'.) The performance of Beethoven's Ninth Symphony at the second concert evidently surprised all the critics by its impassioned grandeur and by the unaccustomed violence of the timpani in the scherzo. A writer in the *New York Press* for 5th April 1909 proved to be the shrewdest student of his city, however, when he wrote:

> Evidently Mahler is not used to dealing with rough material. His interpretations, lucid, exquisitely balanced in dynamics, finely elaborated in every detail, require a well-nigh perfect instrument . . . Let us hope that those persons who have the power of supporting a permanent orchestra and of engaging so priceless a conductor as Mahler will fully appreciate the value of a reorganised Philharmonic Society and the

[3] 31st March: *Manfred*, Schumann; 7th Symphony, Beethoven; *Siegfried Idyll*, Wagner; Overture to *Tannhäuser*, Wagner; 6th April: Overture to *Egmont*, 9th Symphony, Beethoven.

genius of the man in charge. Unfortunately, however, there are many wealthy and generous persons who can see no difference in the conducting of a Damrosch and a Mahler.

One ominous fact was that Mahler left a sick-bed against doctor's orders to conduct the first of these concerts. He was reported as having influenza, but it is clear that this was an attack of the fever associated with the streptococcal infection that was to kill him.

Mahler opened the Philharmonic's sixty-eighth season on 4th November 1909. The new orchestra had ninety-five players, under a new leader, Theodore Spiering. The woodwind were strengthened and there were fewer strings but in better proportion: eight double basses, for example, instead of fourteen. In addition to the regular Thursday evening and Friday afternoon concerts (with the same programme) the season was expanded to include Sunday concerts, a Beethoven cycle and an historical cycle, forty-six in all. A special series was arranged for Brooklyn, and Mahler took the orchestra on its first tour: to New Haven, Springfield, Providence, Philadelphia and Boston, with Berlioz's *Fantastic Symphony* as the showpiece.

It is worth looking in detail at the programmes of Mahler's two Philharmonic seasons. They were designed to train the orchestra and, although they included 'novelties', these were by no means of such an enterprising kind as had distinguished the Symphony Society's programmes for several years in spite of critical discouragement. Safonoff had tried to brighten the Philharmonic programmes by introducing new Russian composers such as Skriabin, but had been taken to task by the critics. In 1909–10 Mahler's novelties included Dukas's *L'Apprenti Sorcier*, Debussy's *Nocturnes*, Busoni's *Turandot* suite ('With what love and unerring instinct this man rehearsed!' Busoni wrote to his wife[4]), Bruckner's Fourth Symphony[5] (30th March 1910), Pfitzner's *Christelflein* overture,

---

[4] *Letters to His Wife*, op. cit., p. 161.
[5] Alma Mahler's statement, repeated in other books, that Mahler conducted all Bruckner's symphonies in New York is nonsense. The Fourth was the sole performance. Bruckner did not lack champions in the United States. First performances of the symphonies in New York were: No. 3, 5th December 1885 (W. Damrosch); No. 4, 16th March 1888 (Seidl); No. 5, 14th December 1911 (Stransky); No. 7, 13th November 1886 (T. Thomas, after an earlier Chicago performance); No. 8, 6th December 1906 (Boston Symphony Orchestra, Karl Muck); No. 9, 7th November 1907 (Boston and Muck).

Dvořák's *Scherzo Capriccioso*, Rakhmaninov's D minor concerto (with the composer as soloist, 16th January 1910), and an evening of Bach, Handel, Haydn, Rameau and Grétry. Among soloists were Kreisler in the Brahms and Beethoven concertos, Josef Lhévinne in Tchaikovsky's First Piano Concerto and Busoni in Beethoven's Fifth Piano Concerto. He conducted his own First Symphony on 16th and 17th December 1909, and *Kindertotenlieder* on 26th and 28th January (the latter at Brooklyn) with Ludwig Wüllner as soloist ('in singularly poor voice,' said the *New York Times* critic).

The 1910–11 season, when he conducted forty of a contracted fifty-five programmes, included Strauss's *Also sprach Zarathustra* and *Ein Heldenleben*; the ballet music from Mozart's *Idomeneo*; Debussy's *Rondes de printemps*; Schumann's Second Symphony; Elgar's *Enigma Variations* and *Sea Pictures* (excluding 'The Swimmer'; the soloist was Kirkby-Lunn); Tchaikovsky's Second Symphony; a French programme including Debussy's *Ibéria*, Bizet's *L'Arlésienne* Suite No. 1 (with chorus), Chabrier's *España* and works by Massenet and Lalo; three excerpts from Berlioz's *Roméo et Juliette*; Stanford's *Irish Symphony*; MacDowell's D minor Piano Concerto; and many Wagner items. Of his own music there was only *Ging heut' Morgen* and *Rheinlegendchen* (22nd and 25th November 1910, sung by Alma Gluck)[6] and the Fourth Symphony (17th and 20th January 1911, soprano Bella Alten).[7] During the season Mahler took the orchestra to Pittsburgh and Buffalo. This gave him and Alma the opportunity to visit Niagara Falls. 'Fortissimo at last!' was his comment. His last concert on 21st February 1911 was an Italian programme with works by Sinigaglia, Martucci, Bossi and Busoni. The remainder of the season, while he was ill, was conducted by Spiering, the leader. Among the works Mahler had scheduled but did not conduct was Sibelius's Violin Concerto. It it known too that he intended in his third season to include the Third Symphony by Charles Ives.

Although Alma glosses over the facts, perhaps because she eventually made America her home, Mahler's short spell with the

[6] The concerts this season were on Tuesdays and Fridays.
[7] Apart from the three symphonies Mahler himself conducted in New York, No. 4 had previously been given in New York by the Symphony Society (W. Damrosch) on 6th November 1904 and No. 5 by the Boston Symphony Orchestra (Wilhelm Gericke) on 15th February 1906. The first American performance of the Fifth was by the Cincinnati Orchestra (Frank van der Stucken) on 24th March 1905.

Philharmonic was a failure. After his death the *New York Tribune* wrote: 'He was looked upon as a great artist, and possibly he was one, but he failed to convince the people of New York of the fact and, therefore, his New York career was not a success.' Why not? As with the Vienna Philharmonic, he aroused the dislike of many of the players. There is no doubt that he would pick on and persecute a weak instrumentalist. He foolishly made friends with one particular player, T. E. Johner, a second violinist, who told him all the tittle-tattle and exacerbated Mahler's dislike of some other members of the orchestra, which he realized needed much severe training. Not all the orchestra 'hated him', as Alma has said. Some of the survivors from those days whose reminiscences can be heard on a fascinating recording[8] make it clear that those who shared his ideals loved him too. His beat was hard to follow – a 'bad beat', some say – but the expressiveness of his hands and eyes conveyed his meaning. He aimed especially for flexibility and constant subtle variations of *tempo*; he wanted a lot of *portamento* and *vibrato* from the strings and constantly sang to the orchestra to illustrate the phrasing he sought. Whatever the work, one player said in a telling comparison, Toscanini always remained Toscanini, but Mahler entered into the spirit of each composer. The finest tribute to him at this period in his life was paid in a letter from Busoni, who was soloist at several concerts with him: 'Being with you has a sort of purifying effect. One has only to come near you to feel young again.'

Mahler soon discovered that he was a prisoner of that fearful matriarchy which has blighted so much of New York's musical life and blasted the hopes of other conductors since his day. The ladies of the committee soon found – as the Viennese had – that Mahler could not be bent to their will nor would he attend social gatherings, and if he did he was liable to be outspoken. He would not popularize the programmes as they wished. To Bruno Walter in December 1909 he wrote:

My orchestra here is the true American orchestra. Untalented and phlegmatic. One fights a losing battle. I find it very dispiriting to have to start all over again as a conductor. The only pleasure I get from it all is rehearsing a work I haven't done before. Simply making music is still tremendous fun for me. If only my musicians were a bit better . . . There are disgusting difficulties with the union here . . . The audiences are

[8] 'Gustav Mahler remembered', CBS-SBRG 72624 (1967).

very lovable and relatively far better mannered than in Vienna . . . The superiors [his word for critics] are the same as anywhere else. I don't read any of them . . . In the near future I hope to be starting work on [the full score of] my Ninth.

But Maurice Baumfeld, Vienna-born director of the German-speaking Irving Place Theatre in New York, said that although Mahler often had sharp words for the city's philistines and snobs, he was not blind to its special character. 'He felt quite passionately about the New York sun. From the corner window of his living-room at the Hotel Savoy, he had a broad view over the greenery of Central Park and could sit for hours entranced, staring out over its vibrant life. "Wherever I am, the longing for this blue sky, this sun, this pulsating activity goes with me".'[9]

Alma said that he was not criticized in New York as he had been in Vienna. This is untrue. His own music was attacked – 'painfully cacophonous din' was a phrase used about the First Symphony by H. E. Krehbiel in the *World* – and there was severe complaint about his 'tampering' with other composers' scores. To quote Krehbiel again: 'Mahler was willing wantonly to insult the people's intelligence and taste by such things as multiplying the voices in a Beethoven symphony (additional kettledrums in the *Pastoral*, for example), by cutting down the strings and doubling the flutes in Mozart's G minor.'[10] Mahler, like many conductors of that day and since, did not regard the letter of the score as sacrosanct. He added an E flat clarinet to the *Eroica* finale, telling the orchestra that it was a Hungarian tune and it ought to sound like gipsy music; he added instruments to Strauss's *Don Juan*, explaining that 'Strauss was a young man when he wrote it; he would score it differently now'. He liked double woodwind in Beethoven and Brahms.

In the middle of February 1911 Mahler was summoned to a full committee meeting, accused of various transgressions and informed of a severe limitation of his powers. His informant in the orchestra was dismissed. On 20th February he had a recurrence of a throat ailment which had afflicted him before Christmas. The next day, although a fever had developed, he insisted on conducting, and despite utter exhaustion completed the whole concert (at which

[9] M. Baumfeld, *Erinnerungen an Gustav Mahler* (*New Yorker Staatszeitung*, 21st May 1911). Reprinted in *Mahler Remembered*, op. cit., pp. 296–302.
[10] *New York Times*, 19th May 1911.

Toscanini was present). It was his last. After his return to Europe an American journalist interviewed Alma on 4th May. She told him that she attributed Mahler's illness 'to nervous prostration and its consequences caused by his unfortunate relations with the Philharmonic Society of New York. You cannot imagine what he suffered . . . In New York, to his amazement, he had ten women ordering him about like a puppet'. This is at least indicative of the emotional atmosphere in New York, though a nonsensical medical diagnosis. Busoni, the first performance of whose *Berceuse élégiaque* Mahler had conducted at his last concert, wrote revealingly to his wife[11] on 30th March 1911:

> Mahler has not conducted since 21st February. Spiering took his place on the 24th . . . and will remain until the end of the season. It was very creditable that an averagely good violinist should show so much *présence d'esprit* and was able to carry through the performance fairly well. But – ! The behaviour of the New York audience and the critics over the matter will remain in my memory as one of my most painful experiences. The sensation made by a leader of an orchestra being able to conduct unprepared has made a greater impression on them than Mahler's whole personality was ever able to do! Spiering has been exalted to the position of one of the greatest conductors, and they have spoken quite seriously about his continuing to fill the post. *Not one word of regret has fallen about Mahler's absence!!* One reads of such things happening in history, but when it is a personal experience, one is filled with despair.

When the Philharmonic gave a memorial concert for their late conductor on 23rd November 1911, they represented his genius as a composer by the first movement of the Fifth Symphony, nothing more. That too fills one with despair even now. His arrival in New York coincided with the beginning of its obsession with Toscanini. So the Metropolitan venture failed. He became involved with the Philharmonic, at a time of crisis and reorganization. Being the artist he was, he strove for perfection, as he had in Vienna, but his method of striving created enemies all too easily, and New York, with its notoriously shallow and sensation-seeking approach to music, added him to its roll of sacrificial victims.

[11] *Letters to His Wife*, op. cit., p. 194.

8

'Abschied'

Mahler spent only parts of 1908–11 in New York. We must therefore go back to May 1908, when he returned to Europe to conduct his First Symphony at Wiesbaden. He had composed nothing in 1907 and there was no question of returning to Maiernigg with its painful memories. Alma found them a farmhouse at Alt-Schluderbach outside the village of Toblach in the Dolomites, a region of unspoilt natural beauty. There in June he set to work again.

But now, perhaps for the first time, he fully realized the implications of his heart ailment. He wrote to Bruno Walter from Toblach:

> . . . It is not only a change of place but also a change of my whole way of life. You can imagine how hard the latter comes to me. For many years I have been used to constant and vigorous exercise – roaming about in the mountains and woods, and then, like a kind of jaunty bandit, bearing home my drafts. I used to go to my desk only as a peasant goes into his barn, to work up my sketches. Even spiritual indisposition used to disappear after a good trudge (mostly uphill). Now I am told to avoid any exertion, keep a constant eye on myself, and not walk much. At the same time the solitude, in which my attention is more turned inward, makes me feel all the more distinctly everything that is not right with me physically. Perhaps I am being too gloomy – but since I have been in the country I have been feeling worse than I did in town, where all the distractions helped to take my mind off things . . . For the first time in my life I am wishing my holidays were over . . . At the same time, I am noticing a strange thing. I can do nothing but work . . .

Alma described this as 'the saddest summer' they spent together:

> We were afraid of everything. He was always stopping on a walk to feel his pulse and he often asked me to listen to his heart and see whether the beat was clear or rapid or calm. I had often implored him to give up his long bicycle rides, his climbing and swimming under water, to which he was so passionately attached. There was nothing of that now. On the contrary he had a pedometer in his pocket. His steps and pulse-beats

were numbered and his life a torment. Every excursion, every attempt at distraction was a failure.[1]

Walter evidently suggested some psychological reason for Mahler's despondency. He received a dusty answer:

> What is all this about the soul? And its sickness? And where should I find a remedy? . . . It is only here, in solitude, that I might come to myself and become conscious of myself. For since that panic fear which overcame me that time, all I have tried has been to avert my eyes and close my ears. If I am to find the way back to myself again, I must surrender to the horrors of loneliness. But fundamentally I am only speaking in riddles, for you do not know what has been and is still going on within me; but it is certainly not that hypochondriac fear of death, as you suppose. I had already realized that I shall have to die . . . I'll just tell you that at a blow I have simply lost all the clarity and quietude I ever achieved; and that I stood *vis-à-vis de rien*, and now at the end of life am again a beginner who must find his feet . . . Where my 'work' is concerned, it is rather depressing to have to begin learning one's job all over again. I cannot work at my desk. My mental activity must be complemented by physical activity. The advice you pass on from doctors is of no use to me. An ordinary, moderate walk gives me such a rapid pulse and such palpitations that I never achieve the purpose of walking – to forget one's body . . . Now imagine Beethoven having to have his legs amputated after an accident. If you know his mode of life, do you believe he could then have drafted even one movement of a quartet? And that can hardly be compared with my situation. I confess that, superficial though it may seem, this is the greatest calamity that has ever befallen me. What it amounts to is that I have to start a new life . . . But I want to assure you that I have succeeded relatively well in discovering how to enjoy myself and life. Also that physically, on the whole, I am not doing too badly. It is wonderful here! . . . Make the most of a beautiful summer and do go for walks (for me too!). You don't realize how wonderful that is.

His salvation, in the end, was more-than-usual absorption in the Bethge songs he had begun in the previous year. *Die chinesische Flöte* was one more manifestation of the fashion for orientalism which spread throughout the arts of this period (Busoni's *Turandot* and Puccini's *Madama Butterfly* are two musical examples). The poems entranced him and matched his mood. He had intended to call the

[1] A. Mahler, *Gustav Mahler*, op. cit.

new song-cycle *Die Flöte aus Jade* (*The Jade Flute*) but he changed it
to *Das Lied von Jammer der Erde* (*The Song of Earth's Sorrow*).
Finally, he extended it by insertion of orchestral interludes into a new
kind of work, a song-symphony which he eventually entitled *Das
Lied von der Erde* (*Song of the Earth*). By 1st September the sixth
song was completed in short score. His visitors found him an altered
man: he had regained his calm and found a new delight in nature. To
Walter he wrote: 'I have been hard at work (from which you can tell
that I am more or less "acclimatized") . . . I think it is the most
personal thing I have done so far.'

The summer ended with a visit to Prague to conduct the first
performance of the Seventh Symphony on 19th September. Many
young musicians went there to hear the rehearsals, among them
Alban Berg, Otto Klemperer, Gabrilovitch and Bodanzky. Mahler
was 'torn by doubts' about the work and spent hours revising the
orchestration and himself altering all the orchestral parts – it was,
after all, three years since he had completed it. It was during a
rehearsal for woodwind and brass alone that a remark was made
which enabled Mahler, writing to Alma on 10th September, to make
a famous analogy:

> One of the trumpeters asked Bodanzky in despair: 'I'd just like to
> know what's beautiful about blowing away at a trumpet stopped up to
> high C sharp.' This made me think deeply about the lot of man, who
> also cannot understand why he must endure being 'stopped' to the
> piercing agony of his own existence, cannot see what it's for, and how
> his screech is to be attuned to the great harmony of the universal
> symphony of all creation.

Always the philosopher! The symphony had a respectful, puzzled
reception. Mahler enjoyed the adulation of the younger musicians,
whom he was always ready to help, often with money. His letters are
full of references to his efforts to obtain conducting posts for Rudolf
Krzyzanowski, his friend from student days; he encouraged Oskar
Fried, and when Klemperer was out of a job in 1909 and contacted
Mahler in New York, Mahler cabled to the Intendant at Hamburg:
'Grab Klemperer'.

Returning from New York in the spring of 1909, Mahler sat for
Rodin in Paris for a bust. At Toblach, in June, he was on his own, for
Alma was ill, her nerves 'in a critical state'. She had had a miscarriage
(not her first) in New York in March. Much is said about Mahler's

neuroses, but the reader of Alma's memoirs cannot fail to notice the hypertension of her own personality, the constant references to her fainting-fits and 'heart attacks'. She cannot have been easy to live with. Mahler at this time was taking pains to 'make peace' with people with whom he had quarrelled. 'It gives me the deepest satisfaction . . . to love as long as I still can love', he told Alma. She went to Levico and Mahler stayed with friends at Göding. He was at work on the Ninth Symphony:

> I feel marvellous here! To be able to sit working by the open window, and breathing the air, the trees and flowers all the time – this is a delight I have never known till now. I see now how perverse my life in summer has always been. I feel myself getting better every minute. I shudder when I think of my various 'workshops'; although I have spent the happiest hours of my life in them, it has probably been at the price of my health.

This mood of optimism had developed while he was in New York earlier in the year, when he had written to Walter:

> I am experiencing so infinitely much now (in the last eighteen months), I can hardly talk about it. How should I attempt to describe such a tremendous crisis! I see everything in such a new light – am in such a state of flux, sometimes I should hardly be surprised to find myself in a new body. (Like Faust in the last scene.) I am thirstier for life than ever before and find the 'habit of existence' sweeter than ever . . . How absurd it is to let oneself be submerged in the brutal whirlpool of life! . . Strange! when I hear music – even while I am conducting – I hear quite specific answers to all my questions – and am completely clear and certain. Or rather, I feel quite distinctly that they are not questions at all.

He was elated by the performances of his Seventh Symphony by the Concertgebouw of Amsterdam (3rd and 7th October) which he conducted before sailing to New York. 'The orchestra . . . said they wanted so much to learn Beethoven and Wagner from me. . . . When you have to work really hard, it is living.' There is no suggestion here, or in the music he was writing, of a man cringeing under the shadow of death. They returned to Europe in the spring of 1910 and again went to Paris, where Mahler conducted his Second Symphony. Debussy, Dukas and Pierné left during the second movement. Too Schubertian, they are said to have explained. But the public and critics liked it. Thence to Rome, where Mahler, alerted to the incompetence of the orchestra by Mengelberg, violently abused the players who walked out of rehearsal and adopted a policy of non-co-operation at the concert.

Mahler and Alma then returned to Vienna and to Toblach for their summer routine. But this time it was to be different. Since the dreadful month of July 1907 Alma had been far from well. The strain of coping with Mahler's new régime of life drove her to the brink of a breakdown, in which there was a strong element of sexual frustration. She went in May for a rest-cure to a sanatorium at Tobeldad where the doctor, worried by her despondency, prescribed dancing. Thus she met a handsome architect four years her junior, Walter Gropius, who soon declared his love for her and hoped for its reciprocation. Mahler was working on his Tenth Symphony and was also preoccupied with preliminary rehearsals for the vast undertaking of the first performance of the Eighth Symphony, scheduled for Munich in September. His letters are full of illuminating comments on the difficulties involved. When he visited Alma at Tobeldad he was struck by her radiance: 'When I told you how nice you looked, it was the expression of a spontaneous delight,' he solemnly wrote. 'I live only for you and Gucki.' Gropius wrote to Alma in July saying he could not live without her and inviting her to leave Mahler and go to him. By accident, so he later maintained, he addressed the envelope to 'Herr Direktor Mahler'. In what followed Alma at last told Mahler of all she had sacrificed for him.

At this point, Alma says, Mahler realized his own guilt. She was thirty and beautiful, still rejoicing in her attractiveness to men. Gabrilovitch, for example, had declared his love before they first sailed for America. Mahler's idea of a happy family evening was for Alma to read Eschenbach's *Parsifal* aloud or Lange's *Geschichte des Materialismus*, and to discuss lectures on astronomy which she had attended at his behest. 'You have an abstraction for a husband,' a friend told her. Not only were her sexual needs unfulfilled, she was starved of fun too. Now, in this crisis, she still kept something back: 'I knew that my marriage was no marriage and that my own life was utterly unfulfilled. I concealed all this from him, and although he knew it as well as I did we played out the comedy to the end.'

The bedroom intimacies of a marriage concern only the people involved, but Alma throughout her books drops hints like someone laying a paper trail. Whatever Mahler's weaknesses of the flesh, she did not intend that they should perish with him in 1911. If she means us to believe that he was intermittently impotent, then her book suggests she feared that his physical powers would be restored every time his old flame Anna von Mildenburg visited them. Whereas Alma, by her own admission, was highly sexed, it is likely that Mahler was one of those men for whom intellectual creative work, in his case composing and conducting, reduces and sublimates sexual drive. On the other hand, there is Ida Dehmel's impression of him in 1905: 'He is the first Jew except my father to impress me as a man – one who doesn't, to put it crudely, strike me as impotent.'[2] No doubt the crisis of 1908 when he became obsessed with the need to conserve his physical energies, affected him sexually. Perhaps by 1910 he was so disinclined for intercourse that Alma was ripe for the attentions of Gropius.

Gropius followed her to Toblach in July. Mahler insisted she should meet him and himself brought Gropius to the house, ordering her to choose between them. 'Almschili,' he wrote to her some weeks later, 'if you had left me that time, I should simply have gone out like a torch deprived of air.' She wrote in her book on Mahler:

> I could never have imagined life without him . . . least of all could I have imagined life with another man. I had often thought of going away somewhere alone to start life afresh, but never with any thought of another person. Mahler was the hub of my existence.

'He loved humanity but he often forgot man,' Walter said of him. Woman too. But during this time he found Alma's compositions, which she had kept since they were married. 'What have I done?' he said, and encouraged her to revise them. That was one frustration eased. He initiated publication of five of her songs by Universal Edition of Vienna with whom he had just signed an exclusive contract. One of his last letters from New York, in February 1911, to his beloved mother-in-law Anna Moll, said that 'Almschi is really blossoming, is keeping to a splendid diet and has *entirely* given up alcohol, looking younger every day . . . She has written a few delightful new songs that mark great progress. Her published songs are causing a furore here.' He became as devoted and submissive to her as he had formerly been tyrannical. (And it is distasteful, reading between the lines of Alma's book, to realize that she relished the

[2] Quoted in A. Mahler, *Gustav Mahler*, op. cit.

sense of power, at any rate for a time. One suspects she enjoyed crises.) He wrote loving notes to her while she slept and left them by her bed. His guilt sent him to a neurologist, who sent him to Freud in August. Whether Freud was of any help or whether he further distressed Mahler is arguable. Klaus Pringsheim recalled a conversation in the late summer of 1907 when Freud's name cropped up. 'Mahler's reaction was immediate silence. The subject of psychoanalysis did not interest him, and he made only a concluding remark, accompanied by a deprecatory gesture. "Freud, he tries to cure or solve everything from a certain aspect." He did not name it. Apparently he was reluctant, in the presence of his wife, to use the appropriate word.' It would be fair to surmise that he gained more in 1910 from his reconciliation with Lipiner and their subsequent long philosophical discussions.

This painfully intimate episode has been fully related, not only because it led directly to Mahler's consultation with Freud but because we have further visible evidence of his agony of mind during the crisis in the messages to Alma which he wrote on the manuscript of the Tenth Symphony. 'Farewell my lyre. . . . you alone know the meaning of this. . . . Almschili, to live for you, to die for you. . . . Have mercy, O Lord, why hast thou forsaken me?' The man was in a private hell, near to delirium. During this summer he reached his fiftieth birthday. 'I know if you were in Vienna now, you would be so warmly wrapped in honour that you might forget all your earlier and fully justified resentments,' Schoenberg wrote. A month later Mahler lent a large sum to Schoenberg, who was in financial distress. He also agreed to forgo profits on the publication of his first four symphonies so that Universal Edition could take over Bruckner's works.

The first performance of the Eighth Symphony meant even more to Mahler now for, as a thanksgiving, he had dedicated it to Alma. 'Does it not make the impression of a betrothal?' he wrote to her in one of the many passionate and almost painfully moving love-letters which poured from him, the last of them containing these poignant words: 'For the first time for eight weeks – in my whole life, for that matter – I feel the blissful happiness love gives to one who, loving with all his soul, knows he is loved in return. After all, my dream has come true: "I lost the world, but found my harbour!" ' A few days before the performance he developed a septic throat and high temperature, but recovered in time for the final rehearsal – 'Every note addressed to you' – and the performances on 12th and 13th September.

Preparation for the performances, in the Neue Musikfesthalle in the Munich Exhibition grounds, had begun early in 1910. The choirs were drawn from Vienna, Leipzig and Munich. Bruno Walter selected and prepared the soloists. The music festival at the exhibition was organized by the concert agent Emil Gutmann, who had promoted a performance of Mahler's Seventh Symphony in Munich on 27th October 1908. In March 1910 Mahler was worrying him about whether the choirs would learn the Eighth in good time for September and jibbed at 'your Barnum and Bailey methods' in publicizing the work as the 'Symphony of a Thousand'. There was a row with the Munich Philharmonic Orchestra, who objected to Mahler replacing their leader with Rosé for the occasion and walked out. Yet, while Mahler was coping with matters of this kind and rehearsing the symphony, Alma, its dedicatee, was spending her afternoons in bed with Gropius in a Munich hotel room.

But the performances were the greatest triumphs Mahler ever had. 'When he finally appeared on the podium', Maurice Baumfeld recalled, 'the entire audience, as if responding to a secret signal, rose to its feet, initially in silence. Only when Mahler, visibly surprised, gestured his gratitude did a cheering erupt of a kind that is seldom heard at such an event.' After the performance, to quote Bruno Walter, 'when the last note had died away and the storm of enthusiasm roared out to him, Mahler climbed the steps of the platform, at the top of which the children's chorus was stationed, cheering with all their might, and he shook every hand that was held out to him, walking right along the row.'

At last he received the acclaim owing to him. Royalty headed the audience, which included Strauss, Thomas Mann, Stefan Zweig, Schoenberg, Webern, Leopold Stokowski, Max Reinhardt, Arnold Berliner, Siegfried Wagner, Roller, Clemenceau, Anna von Mildenburg, and many more. Lilli Lehmann was shocked by how much Mahler had aged. 'His work ... sounded as from *one* instrument, from *one* throat ... I only know that for the whole of the second part I gave way to emotion which I could not control.' He never conducted in Europe again.

After Munich, Mahler went to Vienna, where he called on Prince Montenuovo, with whom he remained on excellent terms. Montenuovo told him what a failure Felix Weingartner had been as his successor at the Vienna Opera and that he would shortly be leaving. He asked Mahler if he could be induced to return to his old post. It is almost certain that if he had lived, Mahler would have left New York to become director for the second time. It is significant that in November 1910 he bought some land at Breitenstein am Semmering, outside Vienna, where he intended to build a house for Alma and himself.

The septic throat and accompanying fever returned in New York at Christmas and in February, when he was compelled to abandon the last part of his Philharmonic season. Joseph Fränkel, their New York doctor, realized the fatal nature of the illness and ordered blood tests which showed a streptococcal infection. Mahler's malady of subacute bacterial endocarditis occurs in hearts which have a congenital or acquired valvular lesion. In his case it was almost certainly acquired; this can be caused by rheumatic fever or syphilis or repeated streptococcal sore throats. There is no evidence of the first two where Mahler was concerned, but plenty of the last. Today penicillin would have saved him.

His condition fluctuated from day to day. He could still joke with Alma: 'You will be in great demand when I am gone. Now who shall it be?' He named the candidates. 'It'll be better, after all, if I stay with you.' Fränkel advised his return to Paris to see a bacteriologist: Paris at that time was the centre for the study of bacteria serums following Pasteur's discoveries. They sailed early in April. A passenger in the ship was Stefan Zweig, who watched the disembarkation at Cherbourg. 'I finally saw him: he lay there, deathly pale, motionless, his eyelids shut. The wind had blown his greying hair to one side, his rounded brow stood out clear and bold and beneath it the hard chin, showing the vigour of his will. The skeletal hands lay folded wearily on the blanket. For the first time I saw him, the pillar of fire, in his frailty'.[3] In Paris he saw André Chantemesse, of the Pasteur Institute. He grew weaker, rallied feverishly, relapsed. He read philosophy – Hartmann's *The Problem of Life* – as he had always done. He planned a holiday in Egypt when he was better. He told a reporter he wanted to conduct Cornelius's *Der Barbier von Bagdad* in Vienna and denied that his illness was caused by overwork in America. But he did not compose. When his condition worsened Alma sent for the Viennese blood specialist, Franz Chvostek, who ordered him to a

[3] S. Zweig, *Gustav Mahlers Wiederkehr* (Neue Freie Presse, 25th April 1915). Reprinted in *Mahler Remembered*, op. cit., p. 306.

Vienna sanatorium. There he lay, surrounded by flowers, sometimes lucid, sometimes delirious. Hundreds of people gathered outside. He saw old friends like Walter and Berliner. Walter found him gloomy, forbidding and pessimistic in mood, showing annoyance at the mention of what was going on in Vienna's musical life but anxious to hear about old friends. He entrusted the sketches of his Tenth Symphony to Alma's care and discretion. As uraemia set in and he passed from consciousness he said, again and again, 'My Almschi,' and sometimes, 'Mozart'. He asked: 'Who'll take care of Schoenberg now?' On 18th May 1911 he died, like Beethoven, during a thunderstorm. He was aged fifty years and forty-six weeks. 'No doubt he will now become a great man in Vienna too,' said Richard Strauss.[4] As he had wished, he was buried beside his daughter Putzi in the Vienna suburb of Grinzing. He had asked too for nothing but the name 'Gustav Mahler' on the headstone. 'Any who come to look for me will know who I was, and the rest do not need to know.'

[4] Letter to Hofmannsthal, 20th May 1911.

9

Characteristics

The tendency for discussion of Mahler's music to move into realms of philosophical and psychological verbiage is perhaps familiar to readers. His music lends itself easily to extra-musical analysis, indeed it is among the most autobiographical music ever written, and to pretend that it exists only in terms of musical procedures is to miss an element which Mahler explicitly commanded us to take into account. Each of his symphonies is an extension of his personality, an exploration of himself, and in his case, as in Elgar's and Berlioz's, it is not possible – in fact it is wrong – to separate the music from the life of its composer as though it was an isolated activity. At the same time one must guard against a too-literal association of life and music and make due allowance for the creative imagination.

Because of the tragi-romantic course of Mahler's life, in particular the shadow hanging over it from 1907 to its end, too much emphasis has been laid on the obsession with death and the long farewell. The picture of Mahler as doom-laden, neurotically introspective, temperamentally unbalanced, while not a total misrepresentation, is a distortion of the reality. True, his music derives its greatness from the conflicts and contradictions of his personality: the man of action (as he was) and the man who needed, as he told Alma, to be 'often and intensely alone'; the philosopher and quasi-scientist and the simple-hearted child of nature. The music does not bear out an interpretation of Mahler as a gloomy life-denier: he was positive, affirmatory. Most of the symphonies are joyous and life-giving, whatever struggles they may record. Only the Sixth ends in the minor.

We should beware, too, of the fashion for relating Mahler's music to such vague but imposing concepts as 'a microcosm of the decay of Western society'. It is tempting to be wise after the event and find hints and portents of impending dissolution and destruction in this music, even spurious relevances to the events of today. But it is Gustav Mahler who is in these symphonies in microcosm, not

Western society and its political evolution and revolution. The Left are naturally anxious to claim him for their own – a man of the people, bringing the music of the people into his own art. Of course he did: most great creative artists are humanitarians. In 1905, Alma records, he met a workers' May Day procession in the Ring in Vienna and accompanied it for some distance. 'They had all looked at him in so brotherly a way – they *were* his brothers – and they were the future!' If some of these brothers had turned up next day in the Vienna Opera chorus, they would soon have discovered how far Mahler's fraternal instincts went in practice. But it is true to say that he democratized the symphony, or rather that he gave it back its Beethovenian democracy. (It is also true that he belonged to a Vienna Socialist-vegetarian group in 1880.)

The use in his symphonies of waltzes, *Ländler*, marches and snatches of song was his practical means of fulfilling his creed that 'the symphony is the world, it must embrace everything'. For a man of his philosophical cast of mind the symphony was the obvious medium. Restricted to a few months' composing in a year, Mahler had no time for concertos and other forms, but even if he had had time I doubt if he would have chosen otherwise. The symphony was his *Wunderhorn* of plenty, and he fertilized it from the great Austro-German tradition of song. It was his chosen vessel for self-expression, as music-drama was Wagner's and the mazurka Chopin's. It is ironically amusing to consider Vaughan Williams's famous backhanded compliment to Mahler – 'intimate acquaintance with the executive side of music . . . made even Mahler into a very tolerable imitation of a composer'[1] – when one considers how fully Mahler fulfils Vaughan Williams's creative ideal: 'Have we not all about us forms of musical expression which we can purify and raise to the level of great art? . . . We must cultivate a sense of musical citizenship.'[2] This applies as much to the Mahler of the Third Symphony as it does to the composer of *A London Symphony*. Among English composers Elgar may be psychologically nearest to Mahler, but Vaughan Williams's symphonies are Mahlerian in ethos, if in nothing else. Mahler and Vaughan Williams erected imposing and inspiring structures often on unpromising material.

[1] R. Vaughan Williams, *Musical Autobiography*, which first appeared in Hubert Foss, *Ralph Vaughan Williams* (London, 1950).
[2] R. Vaughan Williams, *Who Wants the English Composer?* (London, 1912).

They stretched the symphony to wider terms of reference – not to mention the bond of folksong, so despised by Elgar.

Admirers of Mahler's music give three principal reasons for their enthusiasm: his melodic gift, his mastery of form, and his originality of sound (in other words, his brilliance as an orchestrator). The second has had to be defended strongly. The size of Mahler's symphonies makes them for some people synonymous with sprawl. But he needed a vast canvas on which to work out the intricate relationship of his themes, for it cannot be denied that his symphonies are complex. Their length is in proportion to their material. The allegation that he was a natural song-writer who mistakenly attempted to write symphonies shows a lack of understanding comparable with Bernard Shaw's strictures on Schubert for lack of 'head-work'.

The unmistakable 'Mahler sound' principally derives from his superb orchestral mastery – I say principally, because there is a certain shape, a tone of voice, in the very outline of a Mahler melody that proclaims its origin even on the pianoforte. Here again one discovers when one listens attentively to Mahler how mistaken was the old assertion that his music was an overblown, decadent swan song of Wagnerian Romanticism. Mahler's textures are often bare and stark, in spite of the very large orchestra he used. Partly his need for such large forces was determined by the dynamic contrasts necessary in the huge dimensions of his symphonic movements. Partly too it was dictated by his unceasing search for clarity above all else: the chief characteristic, also, of his conducting. Mahler's music is in reaction to the full orchestral textures of Wagnerian sound. His scores contain comparatively few *tutti* – though when he wants a *fortissimo* he can create a tremendous one – and are full of solos: for horn, flute, oboe, E flat clarinet, trumpet – all instruments with a very clear-cut sound. His enlargement of the woodwind department promoted it symphonically to the status of strings and brass. His writing for strings rarely has the comfortable, luxuriant 'richness' of Wagner and Bruckner: again, it is the insistence on exposed, clear part-writing. The result is that Mahler's orchestra can aptly be compared to a vast chamber orchestra, most memorably in *Das Lied von der Erde*, but in the earliest works too. In this connection it is instructive to quote his words to Natalie Bauer-Lechner in 1896: 'When I want passionate expression, I never use the middle strings, which do not sound effective. They are much better suited to softly veiled, mysterious passages.' He was above all the pioneer of a *concertante* style of writing for the modern symphony orchestra which has been carried to extreme lengths by composers working fifty years after his death. He pioneered, too, the range of colour to be obtained from the percussion.

Paramount concern with clarity led Mahler to highly detailed markings of dynamics in his scores and to sometimes lengthy printed adjurations to his interpreters. As a conductor he well knew orchestras' deficiencies and the difficulties of his own scores. Yet an intelligent English critic, Mr Desmond Shawe-Taylor, has written[3] that 'Mahler was hysterical, in fact neurotic to a high degree, as could be deduced without hearing a note of the music merely from the frenzied anxiety of his markings and instructions to the conductor'. Poor Mahler, the supreme professional: in some English eyes he cannot win. But the strange thing is that his intimate and profound practical knowledge of the orchestra did not give him absolute certainty of achieving his intentions. He was an inveterate reviser, the Fourth, Fifth, Sixth and Seventh Symphonies being subjected to constant alterations, not all of which are yet incorporated into published scores. The process of creation was for him never 'finished', in either sense of the word. During rehearsals of the Eighth Symphony at Munich in 1910 he turned to some of the musicians in the audience and said: 'If, after my death, something doesn't sound right, then change it. You have not only the right but the duty to do so.'[4] Egon Wellesz attended the final rehearsal of the Second Symphony in Vienna in 1907 when, for one passage in the finale, Mahler departed from the printed score and said aloud: 'Hail to the conductor who in the future will change my scores according to the acoustics of the concert hall'.[5]

The fundamental principle in Mahler's technique of composition was two-part counterpoint. This was a natural means for his expression of what lies at the root of all his work: conflict. Conflict is not satisfactorily conveyed by melody cushioned by changing harmonies. For Mahler the essence of his style seems to have been associated with the use of bare intervals, fourths and fifths, and pedal-points. As he developed, and as his scoring became ever more

[3] *Sunday Times*, 17th September 1972.
[4] P. Heyworth (ed.), *Conversations with Klemperer* (London, 1973), p. 34.
[5] E. Wellesz, 'Reminiscences of Mahler' (*The Score*, 28th January 1961), pp. 54–6.

Ex. 1

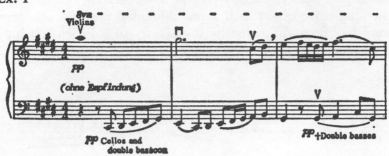

sinewy, he abandoned pedal-points so that his two-part contrapuntal form became detached from the conventional sense of
tonality, with each part independent of the other and liable to
separate development, as in the Ninth Symphony (Ex. 1)

To the ordinary listener and concert-goer the outstanding features
of Mahler's achievement are his convincing incorporation into his
immense structures of the everyday sounds which had so potent an
emotional effect upon him. It is here that he is a truly revolutionary
composer who took an established form, symphony, and gave it new
and fruitful life. For example, there is the folksong element, as found
in the tune from the *Lieder eines fahrenden Gesellen* which is used
again in Symphony No. 1:

Ex. 2

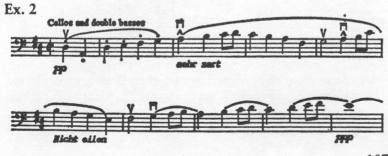

Mahler

Then there is Mahler's ability to give a deliberately vulgar tune a frightening twist, rather as if some childhood memory of a fairground had been shadowed by the cruelty of a Punch-and-Judy episode (also from the First Symphony):

Ex. 3

Like Bach and Bruckner — and, later, Berg and others — Mahler knew the power of a hymn-like tune (chorale) at crucial moments, as in the Symphony No. 2:

Ex. 4

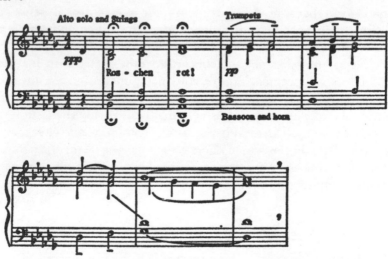

Then, antedating Skriabin, Messiaen and even Delius, he exploited in the most poetic manner imitations of the calls of birds — his cuckoo in Symphony No. 1 calls in the interval of a fourth — lending a mystical sense of loneliness to the music. This device reached its highest artistic point in *Das Lied von der Erde*. He produces similar emotional and dramatic effect from the continual use of march tunes and rhythms, as in this example from Symphony No. 3:

Ex. 5

Other pervasive fingerprints are the use of *Ländler* dance-tunes and the impressive atmosphere created by such simple yet imaginative touches as horns calling to each other across a valley (Symphony No. 5) and the cow-bells episode in Symphony No. 6.

Some discussion of Mahler's musical ancestry is inevitable, although the hunting down of 'influences' on such a personal composer is even less helpful than usual. Allied to this there is the problem, if such it be, of his eclecticism. Most composers are eclectic: they borrow from each other, they imitate the same models. It matters little as long as they can impart their own personality to what they borrow. Again one may call Vaughan Williams to Mahler's defence: 'Why should music be original? ... The duty of the composer is to find the *mot juste*. It does not matter if this word has been said a thousand times before as long as it is the right thing to say at that moment.' Mahler's genius as a conductor must have contributed towards his eclecticism: it was impossible for a man who sank himself so deeply into the works of others not to absorb subconsciously their spirit and sometimes their letter.

Mahler belongs to the symphonic lineage of Haydn, Schubert, Beethoven and Bruckner. He often has a Haydnesque pastoral flavour; like Schubert he imparted the breadth of strophic song to symphonic thinking; he emulated Beethoven in awareness of humanity and humanity's aspirations; like Bruckner, he worked best over a huge span, with room to move and time to breathe. But to none of these did he owe as much in substance as he did to Berlioz, whose masterly and unconventional way of handling a symphony, as in the *Fantastique* with its waltz, march, pastoral scene and witches' round dance, was obviously etched into Mahler's mind as ineradicably as his clear and colourful orchestration. Much as he admired Wagner for his thematic development, there is little of Wagner in Mahler, who saw clearly that Wagner represented an impasse. Though he is often linked with Bruckner, they inhabit different spiritual atmospheres. Superficial resemblances exist, but to experience the dissimilarity of Bruckner and Mahler one has only to listen to an *adagio* by each. A Bruckner *adagio* cannot progress beyond a few bars before we feel we are being lifted into another world; a Mahler *adagio* is inescapably of this world. Even when Mahler raises his eyes to heaven seeking redemption, even when he is 'lost to the world', he is shackled to it by his sense of mortality. Sometimes, as in the Fourth Symphony, there is peace of a sort, a spiritual armistice, but the tension of the counterpoint remains. It has been well said that Mahler was always looking for God, but Bruckner had found Him. Strauss never began the search. Mahler said in 1899: 'Music must always contain a yearning, a yearning for what is beyond the things of this world. Even in my childhood, music, for me, was something mysterious that lifted me above the world.'

Mahler's wife and several of his friends, notably Schoenberg, described him as a saint. They did not mean, we may be sure, any effete, stained-glass saint. Saints are toughened by suffering; they are men of steel, stoics, lashed by the world and their own sense of sin. Of this company was Mahler; and in exploring his work this steeliness of purpose and strength of fibre should not be overlooked.

10
Songs and Symphony No. 1

Mahler's earliest works need not detain us for more than a few lines. Some have already been mentioned. Mahler told Natalie Bauer-Lechner:

> At the Conservatoire I never finished a single score. I usually stopped after the first or second movement, occasionally after the third . . . not because I was impatient to start another but because, before even finishing my work, I was no longer satisfied with it. I had already moved beyond it.

Some of the earliest compositions which he allowed to be published are in the three books of *Lieder und Gesänge aus der Jugendzeit* (*Songs from the Days of Youth*). The first of the three books, all published in 1892, comprises five songs written between 1880 and 1883. The remaining books contain nine settings from *Des Knaben Wunderhorn*, which will be considered in that context. Of Book 1, the third song, *Hans und Grethe*, to a text by Mahler, was composed on 5th March 1880 as one of a proposed set of five songs dedicated to Josephine Poisl, daughter of the postmaster at Iglau, of which three survived. It was originally called *Maitanz im Grünen*. It is a delightful song and is important because it is Mahler's first use of the *Ländler* dance-rhythm and also because it became the main theme of the *scherzo* of the First Symphony, the first example of Mahler's thematic linking of song and symphony. *Erinnerung* is even more prophetic, the first highly organized example of the type of melancholy song in which Mahler excelled. *Frühlingsmorgen*, wistful and animated, belongs to the *Lied* as understood by Schumann. Two settings of text from Tirso de Molina's *Don Juan*, the *Serenade* and *Phantasie*, are pleasant folkish songs, noteworthy because they provide a clue to Mahler's natural inclination to think of his accompaniments in orchestral terms. He recommends a harp as the accompaniment to *Phantasie*, and the *Serenade* is subtitled 'with accompaniment by wind instruments', although no score has come to light.

Roughly contemporary with the first five *Lieder und Gesänge* – the chronology of Mahler's early works is still far from having been established definitively – is the large-scale cantata *Das klagende Lied* (*The Song of Sorrow*). Mahler followed Wagner's practice by writing the libretto before composing the music. He completed the text on 18th March 1878 and the music of the original three-part version on 1st November 1880. Mahler adapted the text from a story in an anthology of folk-tales published in 1856 by Ludwig Bechstein.[1] He introduced certain variations taken from a Grimm tale *Der singende Knochen* (*The Singing Bone*) which appeared in 1870. In Mahler's poem – written in the *Wunderhorn* style – a queen offers herself in marriage to the man who shall find a certain red flower. Two brothers search for it. The younger finds it, puts it in his hat and lies down to sleep. The elder brother discovers him, kills him, takes the flower and buries him beneath a willow tree. He claims his bride. In Part II the minstrel (*Der Spielmann*) finds a bone under the willow tree. He makes it into a flute. When he plays it, the 'flute' tells of his murder by his brother. In Part III the minstrel arrives at the castle on the queen's wedding day. He plays the flute, which again repeats the story of murder. The king seizes the flute and puts it to his lips, the 'singing bone' then accuses him: 'Oh brother, it was you who murdered me.' The queen collapses, the guests run away and the castle begins to fall to the ground. It is worth noting that in the Bechstein tale a brother and sister are involved. Mahler substituted two brothers, and this has been linked by some writers, not implausibly, with his feelings of guilt that he had been spared while his beloved younger brother Ernst had died in 1874.

The musical history of *Das klagende Lied* is complicated. Some writers have said it was originally planned as an opera, but this seems to be unlikely because there is no documentary – and not much musical – evidence for the theory. The three parts of the first version were entitled *Waldmärchen* (Forest Legend), *Der Spielmann* and *Hochzeitstück* (Wedding Piece). This version was not performed in Mahler's lifetime. Having failed to win the Beethoven Prize with it in 1881, he left it untouched until September 1893 in Hamburg when

---

[1] *Neues deutsches Märchenbuch* (Leipzig and Pesth). No. 3 is *Das klagende Lied*.

Gustav Mahler in Hamburg in 1896

Left A silhouette drawn in Vienna, 190:
Right Cartoon of Mahler the conducto

Mahler relaxing on board ship

Alma Mahler with her daughters Maria and Anna, 1906

Rodin's bust of Mahler, 1909

Mahler in 1907 in the Vienna Opera House

Mahler and his wife Alma, in Rome in 1910

Mahler and Bruno Walter, Munich, September 1910

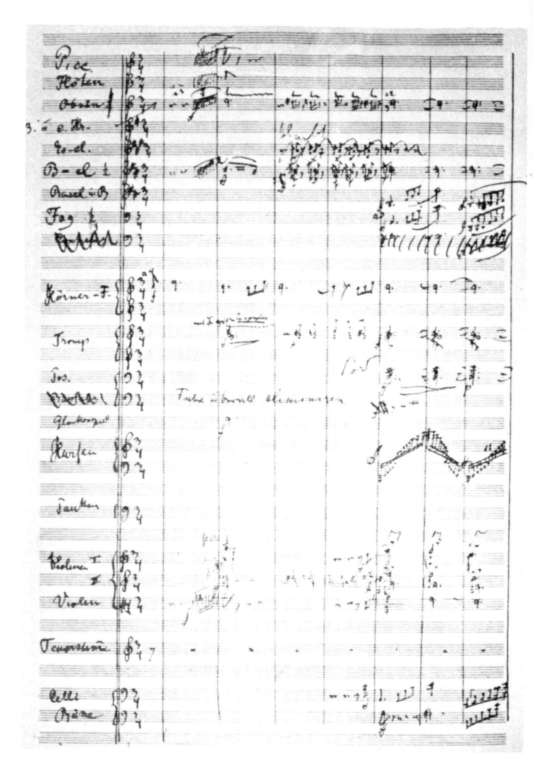

A page from the manuscript of *Das Lied von der Erde*

he excised Part I. The revised version, therefore, comprises only *Der Spielmann* and *Hochzeitstück*. It was published in 1902 and first performed on 17th February 1901 in Vienna, conducted by Mahler. The score of *Waldmärchen* was kept by Mahler's sister Justine, who bequeathed it to her son, Alfred Rosé. He conducted it on Radio Brno in 1934 and again, with the revised versions of Parts 2 and 3, on Vienna Radio in 1935. Rosé sold the full original 1880 score to an American collector in 1969 and the cantata in this form (never heard by Mahler) was first performed at a Hallé concert in Manchester on 7 October 1997.

The original version has been recorded by Pierre Boulez and Simon Rattle, convinced champions of this cantata. It remains a puzzle why Mahler should have discarded *Waldmärchen*. It cannot have been because of length: he was soon to write longer compositions. Musically and dramatically this first section is essential to the shape and atmosphere of the work. Its orchestral opening is magnificent, the key of A minor imbued with that mystery and tension which always surrounded it in Mahler. The horn-calls tell us that this young composer knows his early Wagner: but the oboe and other woodwind tell us that his name is Mahler. *Das klagende Lied* largely retains interest today—it is no masterpiece, and to insist that it is merely devalues his later achievements—because of its flashes of the real Mahler. Already there is the clarity, though rarely the pungency, of the mature scoring; there is the gift for broad-spanned melody, such as the serene passage describing the young man's death, 'Der Junge lächelt wie im Traum' (the youth smiles as if in a dream); there is the mastery in handling a large design. Most significant from this point of view are the use and recurrence of orchestral interludes which develop the material and carry the drama a stage further, just as they do in *Das Lied von der Erde*. Indeed it becomes tedious to point out the foreshadowings of later works in the early works, the predilection for a falling fourth, the major-minor modulations: they will be obvious to attuned listeners. Suffice it to say that certain musical shapes (images) were intuitive to Mahler and give his music an organic unity carrying over from one work to the next. He was a very consistent composer. The one really operatic section of the cantata is Part III, the wedding scene, where the opening set-piece for orchestra and chorus seems to belong to the theatre, as does the strikingly effective use of an off-stage wind band—Mahler's first use of a deliberately vulgar thematic contrast. The Hoffmannesque world of the romantic novel is the milieu of *Das klagende Lied*. Its weakness lies in its too obvious derivation from Weber and Wagner and in the comparatively staid writing for the chorus and the soloists. Only the soprano has a really exciting part, containing some extravagant vocal leaps. But the reason that the cantata fails to grip the listener as much as it might is, I think, that it is too objective. The tragedy happens to someone else, not to Mahler himself, and neither he nor we feel sufficiently involved.

What Mahler learned from practical experience in the four years between the completion of *Das klagende Lied* and the composition in 1884 of the song-cycle *Lieder eines fahrenden Gesellen* is obvious from the first orchestral sounds of the latter, even allowing for the revisions which he made in his prime. Although the songs were composed with pianoforte accompaniment (and are still performed in that version), it was always Mahler's intention that the accompaniment should be orchestral. Written as a memorial to the affair with Johanna Richter, the 'Wayfarer' cycle is in the tradition of Schubert's *Winterreise*, the same tradition that led in English music to Vaughan Williams's *Songs of Travel*. In the first song Mahler's wanderer, on his sweetheart's wedding day, contrasts the loveliness of nature with his own grief. As he walks through the fields, in the second song, the birds and flowers greet him, but his heart cannot respond. In the third song the girl's blue eyes haunt him so that he wishes he were dead. These eyes drive him, in the last song, into the world lonely and sad – a funeral march in E minor, a semitone higher than the ending of the previous song. But under a lime tree he sleeps and forgets his grief – a passage moving from F major into the minor and similar to the Young Knight's death under the willow in *Das klagende Lied*. But this time we know the wanderer is Mahler himself. The *Gesellen* songs constitute a masterpiece because they still sound original, fresh and evolutionary – only Berlioz's *Les Nuits d'Été* can compare with them in this respect. Mahler perfectly reconciles the simple folk-like lilt of his vocal tunes with the sophisticated tone-painting of the accompaniment. The use of tonality is startlingly unorthodox, as it was always to be. Keys are roughly and illogically contrasted. The cycle begins in D minor, and ends in F minor after experiencing F sharp minor, B major and E minor. The music, for all its attractive tunefulness, has a sharp edge, verging on bitter irony, which is far more characteristic of Mahler than sentimentality. The orchestration (1892–3) of the songs is an impressive early example of the chamber-music clarity that Mahler was always able to achieve. The harmonies are far from being exotic, and the changing moods of the songs are pervaded by repeated fifths in the bass and the use of the interval of a fourth. The first song begins with a curt figure for clarinets and harps which, lengthened, becomes the singer's opening phrase: the descending fourth is prominent. The sombre hues of F sharp shroud the closing lines of the second song. It is the anguished D minor of the later symphonies that we hear in the introduction to the third song, with its grating muted trumpets – later the cries of 'O weh!' melt into C major. Throughout the cycle, the scoring for woodwind is especially pungent and it ends with the funeral-march rhythm on the flutes while the harp tolls like a bell, not too far from the sound-world of *Das Lied von der Erde*.

The song-cycle is intimately connected, thematically and emotionally, with the Symphony No. I in D, the two together making a remarkable autobiographical commentary on Mahler's youth. Since there are cross-references also in the symphony to *Das klagende Lied*, the songs and another work, it will be seen that these works must be taken together, with the symphony as the summing-up. This was no doubt why Mahler first described the symphony as a symphonic poem: he could have called it 'The Wayfarer', because it follows the plan of the song-cycle. The blithe second song, *Ging heut' Morgen übers Feld* becomes the principal theme of the first movement, and the gentle epilogue of the fourth song reappears in the slow movement. Not only that, but the opening of the rustic *scherzo* derives from the song *Hans und Grethe*, a cross-reference to the affair with Josephine Poisl. Another of the songs dedicated to her, *Im Lenz*, is used in *Das klagende Lied*:

Ex. 6

The symphony, then, is a love story; but Mahler, in a letter to Max Marschalk dated 26th March 1896, explains not only that but his attitude to the then burning question of programme music (and, incidentally, why he disapproved of analytical notes):

> I should like to see it emphasized that the symphony begins at a point beyond the *love-affair*; it forms the basis, i.e. it dates from earlier in the composer's emotional life. But the real life experience was the *reason* for the work, not its content . . . The need to express myself musically – in symphonic terms – begins only on the plane of *obscure* feelings, at the gate that opens into the 'other world', the world in which things no longer fall apart in time and space. Just as I find it banal to compose programme-music, I regard it as unsatisfactory and unfruitful to try to make programme notes for a piece of music. This remains so despite the fact that the *reason* why a composition comes into being at all is bound to be something the composer has experienced, something real . . .

In 1967 the original five-movement score of the First Symphony came to light, including the short second movement which Mahler eliminated before publication in 1899. This was a delicately scored *Andante* entitled *Blumine*, and it was a remnant of the incidental music Mahler wrote for *Der Trompeter von Säkkingen*, where it did duty as a 'moonlight serenade on the trumpet blown across the Rhine'. Mahler not only incorporated it into the symphony but made it an integral part of the work by quoting it in the finale. His abandonment of it, for whatever reason, again seems to me to be a mistake both for itself – it is beautiful – and for its place in the structure. Without *Blumine* the second subject of the finale seems to have no function in that movement: it is just a luscious tune. But when *Blumine* has been included the whole point of recalling the theme in this form becomes apparent (Ex. 7). However, the fact remains that Mahler deleted the movement, and his revisions are not subject to the reservations one has about Bruckner's. In any case, any conductor who reinstates *Blumine* must also reinstate the 1893 orchestration of the symphony. The principal differences from the final version were the use in the first-movement introduction of four muted horns in place of clarinets for the distant fanfares and, when they were repeated, the use of two trumpets and two horns, playing in pairs and also muted, instead of three trumpets (two off-stage). At the start of the *scherzo* the figures in the double basses were doubled by timpani, and the horn-call leading to the trio is divided between horn and clarinet. The muted solo double bass which so strikingly begins the third movement was originally doubled by a muted solo

Ex. 7

cello. There was no repeat of the first-movement exposition, nor of the *scherzo*.

One can understand why the symphony was so unpopular in Mahler's lifetime only when one remembers how bizarre its orchestration must have sounded. Audiences were uncomfortable with the touches of *grotesquerie* in the otherwise benignly lyrical slow movement, the Callot-inspired funeral procession of the

117

huntsman accompanied to his grave by forest animals, all to a parody of the popular round *Bruder Martin* (or *Frère Jacques*). But this picturesque Romantic work belongs to the world of Dvořák and Tchaikovsky. Its beautiful opening, depicting a spring dawn, with birdsong and cuckoo-calls, is a vivid and imaginative piece of nature-painting; the *Ländler-scherzo* is a Mahlerian version of the Austrian peasant dance-forms hallowed by Bruckner and Haydn – it is the latter's spirit which predominates. Perhaps the triumphant climax of the finale (with horn-players ordered to stand) is too blatantly stage-managed after the recall of the first movement dawn-music, but it will be actively disliked only by those who cringe at Elgar's revised ending of the *Enigma Variations*. Today this revolutionary masterpiece is a popular work; yet its first Vienna performance on 19th November 1900 ended in pandemonium. What hurt Mahler most was that the Philharmonic Orchestra, 'which is able to understand my work better than anyone else, deserted me at the end of the concert. The musicians positively rejoiced at the fiasco and averted their faces to hide the malice in their eyes'. Thus Vienna once again maltreated genius.

Somewhere, perhaps, are the scores of apprentice works which would show Mahler's journey towards the maturity shown in this symphony, especially his mastery of by far the largest orchestra used in a symphony up to that date. The organic unity of the work, achieved by thematic cross-reference (and therefore strengthened by the inclusion of *Blumine*) and the employment of a progressive scheme of tonality, indicate the distance travelled by Mahler in eight years. It marked the end of the beginning.

Not the least of Mahler's achievements in these years was his reconstruction of Weber's comic opera *Die drei Pintos*, of which sketches for only seven numbers existed at the time of Weber's death in 1826, together with bare indications for instrumentation on only a very few bars. By using these sketches, composing new sections based on the themes they contained, and skilfully incorporating other music by Weber, Mahler extended the opera to twenty-one numbers and restored a delightful work to the stage. In the orchestral entr'acte and in other anachronistic touches of scoring, the Mahler of the First Symphony can easily be detected, but the remarkable feature of this posthumous collaboration is its fidelity to the spirit of Weber.

11

Wunderhorn Symphonies

The Second, Third and Fourth Symphonies are usually classified as the *Wunderhorn* symphonies because of their links with Mahler's settings of poems from *Des Knaben Wunderhorn*. This could apply equally to the First Symphony, for the words of *Das klagende Lied* and the *Gesellen* cycle are Mahler's pastiche of the *Wunderhorn* poems, proving how deeply embedded in his mind were the style and spirit of the anthology.

Mahler's first settings of *Wunderhorn* poems were for voice and pianoforte, although obviously conceived for orchestral accompaniment, and were written in the late 1880s. Twelve more, originally entitled *Humoresken*, date from 1892 to 1901. They alternate between a charming fairy-tale delicacy and a grimly ironic, nightmarish realization and interpenetration of the moods of military bluster and nocturnal mystery. They are outstanding for the quivering sensitivity of the composer's response to the text of each poem and, once again, for the beauty and aptness of sound with which this response is matched. The cornerstones of Mahler's style were cross-reference, variation and development, and even in such small-scale works as the songs the constant change enacted gives them a scope beyond the ordinary. Even in such an overtly simple and 'innocent' (though seductive) song as *Rheinlegendchen*, the range of tonality beyond the nominal home key of A major is remarkable. In *Das irdische Leben* the development by means of major-minor contrasts gives the song its psychological depth. Mahler's exploitation of contrast, his genius for savage juxtapositions, can be heard at their starkest in the 'duologue' *Wunderhorn* songs such as *Der Schildwache Nachtlied*.

The finest and most significant of the songs are what may be called the 'military nocturnes', where trumpet-calls, march rhythms and hollow drums are transformed into symphonic microcosms, such songs as the masterpieces *Nicht Wiedersehen*, *Revelge*, *Der Tamboursg'sell* and, greatest of all, *Wo die schönen Trompeten blasen*. These are at the extreme in mood from the no less masterly expression of pastoral freshness in *Ich ging mit Lust durch einen grünen Wald*. Hearing the macabre relentlessness of *Der Tamboursg'sell*, in which the drummer-boy awaits execution, one ponders on the marvellous setting Mahler might have made of Kipling's poem 'Danny Deever'. Incidentally, the *Wunderhorn* songs are most effective when a selection of four or five is performed. They were not composed as an entity and to perform them together exposes too clearly the superiority to the remainder of three or four of them.

In each of the next three symphonies Mahler used a *Wunderhorn* song as an emotional climacteric. And in each he took an enormous step forward: he grew as man and artist from symphony to symphony, almost from song to song. Although in some ways the First Symphony is a better organized work than the Second, containing more 'advanced' music in the finale, the sheer audacity of the scale of the Second shows how Mahler's powers were growing. The *Wunderhorn* symphonies are a religious triptych, representing Mahler's search for a firm belief and for an answer to his questions about the mystery of existence.

The human voice is used in the Second, Third and Fourth Symphonies and Mahler provided a 'programme' for each of them, although he snatched it away again because he was hypersensitive about being dubbed a 'programmatic' instead of an 'absolute' composer, regarding himself as the antithesis of Richard Strauss. In 1897, when Symphony No. 2 was published, he wrote to Arthur Seidl:[1]

> You are right in saying my 'music generates a programme as a final imaginative elucidation, whereas with Strauss the programme is a set task'. . . . Whenever I plan a large musical structure, I always come to a point where I have to resort to 'the word' as a vehicle for my musical idea – it must have been pretty much the same for Beethoven in his Ninth, except that the right materials were not yet available in his day.

The programme of the Second Symphony is self-evident, even without Mahler's 'crutch', as is the use of Beethoven's Ninth Symphony as a musical model. The first movement is the funeral rite of the 'Titan' of the First Symphony; it asks: 'What did you live for?

[1] Alma Mahler, *Gustav Mahler Briefe, 1879–1911* (Berlin, 1924).

Why did you suffer? Is it all only a vast, terrifying joke?' Although when he began the work in 1888, Mahler headed it 'Symphony in C minor', he crossed this out, substituting 'Totenfeier' (Funeral Rite) and offered it in this form three years later for publication as a symphonic-poem. The second and third movements are nostalgia, happy and bitter; for the fourth movement a voice leads the soul to God and in the colossal finale there are the Day of Judgment, resurrection and love. Death and transfiguration, in other words.

Mahler's genius for creating a world of sound in which to convey the full force of his ideas, musical and moral, is at high pressure in the first movement.[2] That marvellous stormy opening (Ex.8) – whether it

Ex. 8

derives from Berlioz or Wagner is irrelevant – is fissionary material for a host of derivative themes, all centred on C minor, all funeral-march-like in character. The contrast comes with a harmonic change to E major and a simple, aspiring and beautiful melody that could

[2] Letter to M. Marschalk, 26th March 1896.

only have been written by Mahler (and not only because of the *appoggiature*). This theme, first heard with a version of Ex. 8 as a counterpoint, is scored and used at each of its appearances with almost tentative restraint. If Mahler had been the composer his detractors believe that he was, one could imagine the lush treatment this tune would have received. It is, of course, the first hint of the 'Resurrection' theme of the finale:

Ex. 9

Mahler's scheme in this movement allows for an enlarged exposition and compressed development, each shedding different light on the material. Although he writes for a vast orchestra in this symphony (with six horns and six trumpets, increased to ten of each for the finale) his economy in its use is very marked. Mahler is, in fact, an economical composer except where inventiveness is concerned. What could be lovelier than the G minor introduction to the return of the slow theme in C major, when two oboes are accompanied by trumpets? Or more shattering than the famous dissonant chords containing every note of the C minor scale? The movement is one of Mahler's finest and best organized. His problem was how to follow it, knowing that he had planned the finale as the true climax of the symphony. He rejected, as he had in the First Symphony, the traditional symphonic *Adagio* and substituted – after specifying a five-minute pause – two short movements in complete contrast. His thoughts about this, expressed in a letter dated 25th March 1903 to Julius Buths (who was to conduct the symphony at the Lower Rhine Festival), are important and surprising:

Well then, this would mean that the main interval in the concert would come between the fourth and fifth movements. I marvel at the sensitive intuition with which you (in contrast with my own arrangement) have recognised the natural break in the work. I have long tended to this view, and all performances I have hitherto conducted have reinforced the same impression.

(It seems extraordinary that Mahler should have sanctioned a long pause between the *Urlicht* movement and the finale, the practice of playing them almost without a break now being standard.)

> Still, there really ought *also* to be a lengthy pause for reflection after the first movement, because the second movement does *not* have the effect of a *contrast*, but simply of a discrepancy after the first. This is my fault, not inadequate appreciation on the listener's part . . . The andante was composed as a kind of *intermezzo* (as the echo of *long* past days in the life of the man borne to his grave in the first movement 'when the sun still smiled on him'). While the first, third, fourth and fifth movements are related in theme and mood, the second stands alone, in a certain sense interrupting the strict, austere sequences of events.

He was right. The *Andante moderato* is too great a contrast, enchanting though it is as a piece of music. A little too artfully contrived, though, in its sophisticated bucolicism, too consciously an orchestral showpiece in its elegant, relaxed delicacy, a nineteenth-century reflection of Haydn's Paris symphonies with a Tchaikovskyan *pizzicato* for good measure. Yet entrancing. The third movement, too, presents similar problems. This is an orchestral version of the *Wunderhorn* song about St Anthony preaching to the fishes, who, like mankind also, listen but do not mend their ways. The song and the text are ironic and satirical, but can music express satire and irony in purely instrumental sound? Well, if anyone can provide an affirmative answer it is Mahler, with his burlesque dance tunes and bizarre solos for E flat clarinet. The movement succeeds as a brilliantly original *scherzo* with very potent suggestions of terror and disillusionment.

It is by the masterly cumulative tension of the coda of this *scherzo* that Mahler re-establishes his grip on his design. The two final movements can be regarded as one, the fourth being an integral prelude in D flat to the fifth. The contralto sings the *Wunderhorn* song *Urlicht* (composed in 1892), her voice unforgettably breaking the silence after the end of the preceding movement. A chorale for brass and woodwind emphasizes the solemnity of the mood, an example of Mahler in spellbinding vein. It seems and sounds so simple, so motionless, so timeless, yet there are twenty-one changes of time-signature in the first thirty-five bars and such inventive subtleties of orchestration as the use of two piccolos for a counterpoint to the vocal line, a delightfully ethereal effect.

The huge finale shows the young Mahler handling the most ambitious set-piece he had yet written with unerring confidence. The orchestral upheaval at the start, pointing the parallel with Beethoven's Ninth, gives way to a magnificent passage of scene-setting, unhurried, theatrical and portentous. Eclectic too, as there is little point in denying; not only are there reminiscences of Beethoven but of the Wagner of *Lohengrin* and, even more fruitfully and significantly, of Verdi. As usual Mahler weaves his fabric from a skein of thematic cross-references, anticipations and cross-fertilizations. Off-stage horn-calls and what can only be called fanfare-fantasias prepare for the violent percussive outburst which precedes a wild popular march. This passage has aroused scorn, even from avowed Mahlerians, but one of the features for which we cherish him is this ability to take basic elements of popular, even vulgar music, whether folk-pastoral or from the barracks tavern, and metamorphose them into symphonic material, as Beethoven did in the finale of the Ninth Symphony, as Puccini did in Act II of *La Bohème* and Vaughan Williams was to do in *A London Symphony*. Mahler saw this passage as a 'procession of rich and poor . . . a march of the dead to the Judgement'. It is like a Resurrection scene painted by Breughel (or, nearer to our day, by Stanley Spencer).

The last section of the finale, prefaced by a strange orchestral stillness, punctuated by distant fanfares and mysterious bird-calls – a forerunner of the similar passage in the *Abschied* of *Das Lied von der Erde* – culminates in the magical soft entry of the chorus singing Klopstock's hymn *Auferstehung* (Resurrection). Yet, to clinch his point, Mahler adds a verse of his own, given first to the contralto soloist: 'O glaube, mein Herz, O glaube' – 'O believe, my heart . . . thou wert not born in vain, hast not suffered in vain.' He is at his best setting his own words: one senses the joint inspiration. The tremendous peroration is an uplifting experience; hearing it, one receives a vicarious impression of what it must have been like to hear a great operatic finale controlled by Mahler from the conductor's desk. The end is in E flat major, the key of the Eighth Symphony, with which this 'Resurrection' symphony is linked. The work rarely fails in performance: it is more than a religious experience, it is both spiritual and humanitarian.

A Viennese critic after the first performance there of the Third Symphony in D minor wrote that its composer deserved a few years in gaol. Since then, by less hostile pens, it has been described as a formal disaster. I disagree. Not only do I think it shows an advance in musical power on the Second, but I think it is a better balanced artistic design, in spite of its six movements; and especially that the difficulties of the first movement have been much exaggerated (its duration too: 'nearly forty-five minutes', says one writer, who must have heard some odd performances. Thirty-five suffice).

Mahler, as stated earlier, had contemplated calling the symphony *Pan*, or even *The Joyful Science*, after Nietzsche's book *Die fröhliche Wissenschaft*. He planned seven movements, the last being a *Wunderhorn* setting, *Wir geniessen die himmlischen Freuden*, which later found its proper place as the finale of the Fourth Symphony. In its final version No. 3 has six movements: 1. Summer marches in. 2. What the flowers of the meadow tell me. 3. What the animals of the forest tell me. 4. What night tells me. 5. What the morning bells tell me. 6. What love tells me. These titles are pointers, no more: the symphony is an exultant celebration of life, physical and spiritual, sensuous and animal. While he was finishing it he described it to Anna von Mildenburg as 'a major work, liberally reflecting the whole world – one is oneself only, as it were, an instrument played by the whole universe . . . In it Nature herself acquires a voice and tells secrets so profound that they are perhaps glimpsed only in dreams! I assure you there are passages where I myself get an eerie feeling; it seems as though it were not I who composed them!' Schoenberg, as we have seen, heard the symphony as a battle between good and evil.

The gigantic first movement is better appreciated if the listener eschews analysis and concentrates instead on absorbing its atmosphere, its astonishing creation of a mood of protean energy unleashed. Its impressive and portentous opening theme for eight horns:

Ex. 10

symbolizes the force of nature but gives way at once to a long mysterious prelude, another example of potent Mahlerian scene-setting, with eerie brass *glissandi*, declamatory trumpet solos, exhortatory trombones – all the fingerprints which the kleptomaniac Mahler impresses on his score, pressing their emotional connotations into his service and rendering them Mahlerian. Twice, like some aural flashbacks to a vivid image retained from childhood or youth, come extraordinary episodes of plebeian brass music. A great conductor of this symphony, as Barbirolli was, can convey the hallucinatory quality of these outbursts and set them within the context of the surrounding music, so that the movement sounds vast but also concise, its stormy coda the inevitable conclusion to an immense drama.

It is Mahler's triumph in this symphony that the succeeding shorter inner movements 'fit' the scheme more comfortably than in the 'Resurrection'. The second movement, another in the *Blumine* mould, is again highly sophisticated, even prettified, far from elemental. But the kaleidoscopic effect of the orchestration is sufficient in itself for most ears; Mahler can scarcely be blamed if his turns of phrase have become clichés for a later generation because of the uses to which they were put by the émigré musicians who, knowing their Mahler better than most at the time, drew so heavily on him for Hollywood film scores in the 1930s and 1940s. The rustic start to the third movement, though it derives from the early *Wunderhorn* song *Ablösung im Sommer*, has an unmistakable affinity with the ballet music of *Aida*. The level of inspiration drops, despite much ingenuity, until the trio, where the mood-painter's magic takes over for a wonderful evocative posthorn solo, the memory of . . . of what? A bugle in childhood, a horn sounding in the Salzkammergut? Youth's Magic Horn itself? It hardly matters. Its spacious, distant quality is as haunting as the natural trumpet solo in a similar atavistic passage in Vaughan Williams's *Pastoral Symphony*.

Although another riotous popular outburst occurs in the *scherzo* repeat, it is the posthorn that stays in the mind and prepares us for the Nietzsche setting in the fourth movement: 'O Mensch! Gib acht' – 'O Man, take heed, what saith the midnight?', the same midnight song of Zarathustra which also inspired some of Delius's finest music in *A Mass of Life*. Mahler sets it for contralto, with one of his most profound and 'yearning' melodies as a counterpoint. It is one of

126

Mahler's 'lost-to-the-world' movements, the words 'Gib acht' set to the descending F sharp–E which opens the first theme of the first movement of the Ninth Symphony, both passages being in D major, and similar to the 'Ewig' phrase in the *Abschied* of *Das Lied von der Erde*. There is a wealth of musical and psychological interest to be derived from the cross-references, intentional or subconscious, between Mahler works – a game any listener can play; in this symphony there are several important cross-references between movements, notably the return of the climax of the first-movement exposition as the climax of the finale.

From the darkness of this sublime movement Mahler jerks us into the joyous light of another circle of the *Wunderhorn* paradise, where 'the quiring of the young-ey'd cherubins' (or, to be musically more accurate, of the *Otello ragazzi*) is heard – 'Bimm bamm' – and the bells chime for noonday joy, not midnight melancholy. (Britten, I suspect, was influenced by these sounds when he wrote *Noye's Fludde* and parts of the *War Requiem*.) The women's chorus sing 'Es sungen drei Engel' (Three angels sang a sweet song, the sound to heaven rises). The contralto sings the refrain which will recur in the finale of the Fourth Symphony in another context. Here it is the melody for St Peter's 'I have broken Thy commandments'; there for the angels who bake the bread, but, more significantly, for St Peter in heaven.

In the Second Symphony Mahler's grand design was to work to a climacteric in the finale. A finale on that scale in No. 3 would have been ridiculously out of mood, but a substantial clinching movement was needed. He gives us his first full-scale symphonic *Adagio*, the nearest he was to go to a Brucknerian fullness of harmony and spiritual calm (was it, perhaps, designed as a tribute to his old friend and encourager?). To Anna von Mildenburg he confided:

> You would like to know 'what love tells me'? Dearest Annerl, love tells me very beautiful things! And when love speaks to me now, it always talks about you! But the love in my symphony is one different from what you suppose. The motto of this movement is 'Father, see these wounds of mine. Let not be lost one creature of thine'. . . . I could equally well call the movement something like 'What God tells me!' And this in the sense that God can, after all, only be comprehended as 'love'. And so my work is a musical poem that goes through all the stages of evolution, step by step. It begins with inanimate Nature and progresses to God's love! People will need time to crack the nuts I am shaking down from this tree for them . . .

The *adagios* of Beethoven and of Elgar come to mind as one listens to this movement, in which the two melodies on which it is based are subjected, with infinite resource, to Mahler's doctrine of continuous development and variation – real 'unending melody'. Yet there is a crisis – Mahler cannot leave the world behind, however hard he may try; the dissonance in the central section is a forceful reminder to listeners today that Mahler was little more than a decade away from the Ninth and Tenth Symphonies. In the coda D major is reached in an apotheosis which is perhaps too rhetorically overblown, too extended, to carry conviction. Yet when one has said that, the overwhelming impression is of a masterpiece – one that seems to grow shorter and simpler the more one hears it. For all its size and scale, it is an intimate work.

The Fourth Symphony in G major of 1899–1900 can be regarded as an epilogue to the first three symphonies. It is Mahler's most intimate, small-scale symphony, with a reduced orchestra and hardly any grandiose effects. One cannot speak of naïveté in connection with such a subtle and disciplined composition, but its mood is certainly childlike in the most felicitous way. No wonder it is Mahler's most popular and approachable symphony, and it is the first in which he kept to the four movements of the classical pattern. He thought of subtitling it *Humoreske* – a clue (if any were needed) to its links with the *Wunderhorn* songs and especially with *Wir geniessen die himmlischen Freuden*, composed in March 1892. An early 'blueprint' for the symphony shows that its conception preceded the Second and Third – still further proof that Mahler's symphonies are a continuous interlinked chain, or, to use a literary parallel, a vast autobiographical novel, of which each symphony is a chapter. Paul Bekker's theory, disparaged by Neville Cardus, that the whole symphony was germinated by this song seems to me to be convincing. Each movement is thematically interconnected, in Mahler's usual allusively subtle way. Writing in February 1911 to Georg Göhler, who had sent him from Leipzig his 'entrancing analysis' of the Fourth, Mahler said: 'Did you overlook the thematic relationships that are so extremely important both in themselves and in relation to the idea of the whole work? . . . Each of the first three movements is thematically most closely and most significantly related to the last.' In any case, here are Mahler's words to Natalie Bauer-Lechner in 1901: 'I only wanted to write a symphonic humoresque and out of it came a symphony of the normal dimensions – whereas, earlier, what I imagined would be a symphony turned out, in my Second and Third, to be three times the normal length!'

The first movement is melodically profuse, its texture and structure an advance on anything Mahler had hitherto composed, the counterpoint never more inventive, the lucidity and freshness of the material often recalling Haydn rather than Schubert. Mahler's mood here is relaxed, the world's slings and arrows ignored if not forgotten. Not only is the delightful *insouciance* of the jingling opening unforgettable – he called it 'a divinely gay and deeply melancholical tune' and added: 'It begins as if it couldn't count to three, but then launches out into the full multiplication table' – but there is the piercing beauty of this flute vision of paradise:

Ex. 11

which is to play so important a part.

Of such a well-known and well-loved work it is hardly necessary to do more than to give a reminder of its beauties: the exquisite coda of the first movement, for example – *sancta simplicitas* if ever one heard it; and the mildly spooky *scherzo*, so marvellously likened by Cardus to the shadows cast by candlelight on a nursery wall. In this fantasy-*Ländler* Mahler makes much use of a solo violin with a *scordatura* tuning of the strings, so that it plays a whole tone higher than the rest, to sound like 'ein Fiedel', a medieval forerunner of the violin and the origin of the word 'fiddle'. In an early sketch Mahler wrote of this passage 'Freund Hain spielt auf'. The friend Hain who plays was a ghostly fiddler leading the way to eternity or perdition. Mahler's devils and demons are off duty in this symphony and friend Hain is picturesque rather than macabre. However, one must recall Mahler's description of composing this symphony:[3]

[3] Natalie Bauer-Lechner, *Recollections of Gustav Mahler*, op. cit., p. 150.

Compelled by the irresistible logic of a passage that I had to alter, everything that followed transferred itself so completely that suddenly, to my astonishment, I became aware that I was in a completely different world: as if you had imagined yourself to be wandering in flowery Elysian fields, but suddenly find yourself transported into the midst of the nocturnal terrors of Tartarus, with your blood running cold in your veins. In my works there are many traces and emanations of such worlds, which excite even in me a sense of horror and mystery. This time, too, it's the forest, with its marvels and terrors, that dominates me and steals into my world of sound. I see it more and more: one does not compose, one *is* composed!

Hence the chill that often grips this sunny work, even in the *Adagio*.

The end of the *scherzo*, after a subtle thematic allusion to the theme of the finale,

Ex. 12

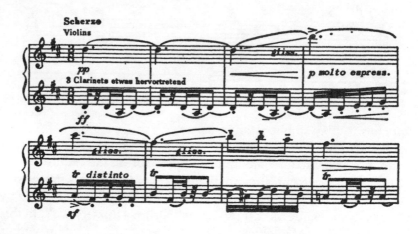

Ex. 13

has a touch of astringency which vanishes in the *Adagio*, Mahler's most untroubled movement, although its serene flow is interrupted first by dancing and later by a passionate 'disintegrating', as powerful as anything in the Fifth and Sixth Symphonies and obviously the 'terrors of Tartarus' mentioned above. In a superb passage near the end Ex. 11 bursts upon the listener like a religious fresco of Paradise. Mahler used variation form in this movement, and was thus able with uncanny skill to sustain moods of childlike bliss and adult devotion side by side and interlinked. It is the perfect prelude to the song-finale, in which the soprano, who must sound unaffectedly simple with no trace of archness, sings of the child's vision of heaven, 'cloudless blue sky' with Martha baking the bread and angelic voices hymning St Cecilia. The scoring is delicate, the key is a radiant consoling E major.

The G major symphony was published in 1902 but Mahler revised it several times. It is hard to believe that so enchanting a work should have had so cool an initial reception – even Alma disliked it at first – and that Mahler described it as a 'persecuted stepchild'. His final revision, for his two New York performances, was on 11th October 1910, but Erwin Stein in the 1920s discovered a set of proofs with still further extensive revisions aimed, as usual, at extra clarity.[4] These include changes of dynamics and expression marks and such alterations in the scoring as the reinforcement of the oboe melody at four bars after fig. 7 in the slow movement by muted trumpet, cor anglais and horn, and a thinning out of the accompaniment in the finale. Various *tempo* directions are also changed. It is as if, every time he conducted his own works, he recomposed them.

[4] See 'The Unknown Last Version of Mahler's Fourth Symphony' in *Orpheus in New Guises* (London, 1953), pp. 31–3.

12

Rückert Symphonies

When discussing the three central instrumental symphonies, Nos. 5, 6 and 7, several writers seem to have been so dazzled by their complexity and ingenuity that it is difficult, when listening to the music, to equate it with the verbal contortions and metaphors employed. There is perhaps a parallel with the late quartets of Beethoven, which for years were regarded as on such a high plane of musical philosophy that hardly a coherent paragraph could be written about them. Bernard Shaw was not merely an iconoclast but a heretic when he wrote in 1894 of the late quartets as 'beautiful, simple, straightforward, unpretentious, perfectly intelligible'. Mahler's three middle symphonies are not simple and straightforward, but they are beautiful and intelligible. Few composers have benefited more from the invention of the long-playing record and tape-recording. Only in the second half of the twentieth century has it been possible fully to absorb these works, not through the score and the memories of isolated performances but by constant study of their sound in a series of superb interpretations. Far from breeding contempt, familiarity increases admiration for their mastery. They are complex, but Mahler's grand designs are logical and purposive, becoming clearer and simpler with each repetition.

Mahler was sensitive to the taunt of 'programme music', and there is perhaps an element of determination to be 'absolute' about these instrumental works. But they mark an intensification of his processes of musical thought, and, for all their size and elaborate orchestration, a further refinement of the means of expression. Together they form one vast symphony and, as always, there are thematic allusions and cross-references. The *Wunderhorn* is still an influence, but the germinating songs for these three symphonies are the settings of poems by Friedrich Rückert (1788–1866) which Mahler began at Maiernigg in 1901. These songs were conceived with an orchestral accompaniment of refined, subtle and almost sparse texture, an extension of the clarity everywhere found in the Fourth Symphony and which he outlined in 1899 to Natalie Bauer-Lechner:[1]

> In earlier years, I used to like to do unusual things in my compositions. Even in outward form, I departed from the beaten track, in the way that a young man likes to dress strikingly, whereas later on one is glad enough to conform outwardly and not to excite notice. One's inner difference from other people is great enough without that! So, at present, I'm quite happy if I can somehow only pour my content into the usual formal mould, and I avoid all innovations unless they're absolutely *necessary*.

Not to be taken wholly at face value, of course, but certainly a confession of a change of tactics. At this time he was making a detailed study of polyphony and regularly received and pored over the volumes of the *Bachgesellschaft* as they were published. 'Bach teaches me something every day', he told Natalie, 'for my method of composing is innately "Bachic"!'

Mahler composed four Rückert songs in 1901 and began the Fifth Symphony. He set the first three of what was to become the cycle *Kindertotenlieder* (*Songs about the death of children*). At the time he was unmarried and had not met Alma: what moved him in these poems was that one of the two children whom Rückert had lost was named Ernst, the name of Mahler's beloved younger brother who had died in 1874. This boy's death was the most searing experience of Mahler's childhood and one can easily perceive that he would wish, as a mature artist, to commemorate him. One might imagine such a thing had never been done before when one reads such accusations as 'self-tormenting exhibitionism' (Redlich) made against Mahler, many of them no doubt deriving from Alma's superstitions about the songs' application to their own children — superstitions which I suspect did not occur to her until she wrote her book some years after Mahler's death. He completed the cycle with two more songs composed in 1904. It is his greatest song-cycle. Though sombre in mood as befits the subject, there is no trace of sentimentality nor of morbid introspection. If this was a conscious attempt to exorcize a ghost, it must have proved successful because tragedy is transcended and the music attains a mood of serene acceptance. Moreover, there is surely a deliberate symbolism in the

[1] *Recollections of Gustav Mahler*, op. cit., p. 131.

poems Mahler chose (five out of a total of 428): in the first the rising sun, 'the light that gladdens all the world'; in the second, brightness returning 'to the source of all light'; the vision in the fourth song of sunlight on the hills; and, finally, God's hand protecting the children from the storm. A compassionate, affirmatory approach, matched by music of tenderness and insight, scored with infallible mastery. The first, *Nun will die Sonn' so hell aufgeh'n*, is perhaps the most wonderful but the second, *Nun seh' ich wohl*, anticipates the lyrical line of *Das Lied von der Erde*. The cor anglais and *pizzicato* in the third song suggest Bach, and the last two songs make a perfect contrast, the fourth being visionary and the fifth dramatic, with its representation of the storm (so economically yet graphically depicted) and ending with the consoling lullaby – note the horn solo –which gives another 'child's view of heaven' and is an outstanding example of Mahler's ability to convey poignancy as effectively in the major mode as in the minor. The greatness of the music lies in the fusion of the sinuous melodic vocal line with an orchestral support in which every instrumental inflection is a counterpoint. Tonality is not progressive, as in the *Gesellen* cycle, but concentrates within a fairly narrow range. A detail of scoring that should be noted is the subtle use of the glockenspiel in the first, funeral song – a child's bell, reminiscent of the sleigh bells of the Fourth Symphony and its child's view of heaven. Mahler does not use it again until the last song, when it recurs towards the end of the storm and, in a dramatic intervention, leads into the serene D major of the final verse. Although there are no thematic links between the songs, the impression of organic unity is strong, so powerfully unifying is the mood of the cycle.

The five other Rückert settings, all composed in 1901–2, are beautiful individually but have no binding emotional theme. They too are notable for subtle refinement of scoring, a pointer to Mahler's progress towards the marvels of the introduction to Part II of the Eighth Symphony and to the almost vocal eloquence of the instrumental writing in *Das Lied von der Erde*. The delicacy of *Ich atmet' einen linden Duft* and of *Blicke mir nicht* are no distance from the Chinese porcelain of the inner movements of *Das Lied*. The airy summer magic of *Ich atmet* is achieved with single woodwind and no cellos and basses. The lower strings are absent, too, from *Blicke mir nicht*. The best known of Mahler's songs, *Ich bin der Welt abhanden gekommen*, has become an epitome of his spiritual withdrawal – though in fact no man was more engaged with life at all levels, an active not a passive artist – but it illustrates the deep satisfaction he found in his annual retreat from the hurly-burly of opera to the inner hurly-burly of composing. He said of it: 'It is my very self'. Such a beautiful melody it is, expressive of the escapist in us all. The countryside, love, poetry, music – would we not abandon ourselves to them if only . . . This idealistic personal yearning Mahler embodied in this great song, but its wider universal significance was to be expressed in the *Abschied* of *Das Lied von der Erde* in similar but even more subtle melodic curves. The most remarkable song of the five is *Um Mitternacht* (At Midnight), scored for woodwind and brass, with timpani, pianoforte and harp. In the friendless midnight the poet gives his power into the hands of God. Mahler's precise delineation of tone-colour calls here for an oboe d'amore to convey the lonely melancholy of Rückert's mood:

Ex. 14

The song has the solemnity of a chorale, but the note of passionate individual entreaty is strong. Whereas *Ich bin der Welt* represents Mahler the spiritual hedonist, *Um Mitternacht* shows us the religious ascetic. The last song to be composed, the simple and delicate *Liebst du um Schönheit*, was an offering to Alma on their first summer holiday after their marriage. It was not orchestrated by Mahler but by Max Puttmann, a writer on music who was employed for editorial work by the Leipzig publisher C. F. Kahnt. The first edition of the orchestral score in 1905 acknowledges Puttmann's work.

Symphonies 5, 6 and 7 may be designated the most 'Viennese' of Mahler's works, with Symphonies 2, 3 and 4 the most 'Austrian' and Nos. 9 and 10 the most cosmopolitan. The Fifth is Mahler's 'Eroica', progressing from tragedy to triumph. Although it is designated as in C sharp minor, the symphony 'feels' to be in D major. It begins in C sharp minor and moves through A minor, D major and F major to end in D – these tonal centres combine to give a major seventh with D in root position. This chord provides the symphony with overall tension. The symphony's form is also misleading. Although there are five movements, the symphony is in three parts. Part I comprises the opening funeral march and its thematically related stormy sequel; Part II is the *Scherzo*; and Part III consists of two linked movements, the *Adagietto* and Rondo-Finale.

The opening trumpet-call, derived from the first movement of the Fourth Symphony, is followed by a funeral march, obviously related to the 1901 *Wunderhorn* song *Der Tamboursg'sell*. Being a symphonic march, it is given two trios, the first a wild and intensely contrapuntal section in B flat minor, which is followed by a recapitulation of the march ending with a direct quotation from the first of the *Kindertotenlieder*, its last line 'Heil sei dem Freudenlicht der Welt!' (I bless the light that gladdens all the world). This is a signal for the second trio (A minor), quieter in mood and given to the strings. It is thematically related to a brass motif in the first trio but utterly transformed (see Ex. 15).

Binding each section together is the trumpet-call, sometimes strident, sometimes bodeful and, at the end, muted and echoed by a flute. The second movement is marked 'with the utmost vehemence' and develops the B flat minor section of the march as a Tchaikovskyan battleground on which Mahler can fight his demons. It is savage, exhilarating music, a classic passage of Mahlerian ability to extract the maximum emotional and contrapuntal effect from fairly commonplace material. At one point there is a deliberately vulgar perversion of one of the first movement's most poignant motifs (a rising minor ninth falling to the octave). But it is not all storm. Cellos and clarinets are given a consoling theme, later heard with poetic effect on the horns. The climax is a chorale in D major, majestically intoned, but it is not allowed at this stage to emerge triumphantly, and the movement ends with a mysterious coda, all half-lights and fantasies.

The central *Scherzo* is on a large scale, which has deluded some commentators into an excessively ponderous view of it. Mahler, after its first performance, wrote of 'dancing stars' in connection with this movement, which is mainly cheerful and gay – and rather Lehárish. The gently lilting second section for strings is the stuff of operetta, but the movement is dominated by the *concertante* part for solo horn. Some of this is boisterous, but Mahler's understanding of the instrument's romantic capability is at its most acute in the Trio

Ex. 15

section where the colours and moods of twilight descend over the orchestra and the horn calls poignantly while the strings suggest an Austrian lake across which the echoes come. The whole passage, with its marvellous use of *pizzicato*, is intensely atmospheric, as if it evoked some legend or folk-memory in Mahler's subconscious mind. It lasts too long for the good of the proportions of the movement, but the return to the hectic world of the *scherzo* is managed in a manner worthy of Schubert:

Ex. 16

The joyous recapitulation of the waltz cannot banish the poetic
memory, and before the coda the horn's evocation of faery lands
forlorn is heard again – and again during the coda.

Part III begins with the famous *Adagietto* for harp and strings
which used to be wrenched from its context and played separately.
(This was fair enough when it was the only way of introducing
Mahler's name into an orchestra's repertory, but the practice must
now be abhorred.) Its relationship to the Rückert song *Ich bin der
Welt* is obvious, though it is always an instrumental symphonic
movement, never a symphonic song, its middle section expressing an
unfulfilled yearning of special poignancy. The movement, as might
be surmised, had a personal origin in Mahler's love for Alma
Schindler. In his conducting score of the symphony, Willem
Mengelberg wrote: 'This *Adagietto* was Gustav Mahler's declaration of love to Alma! Instead of a letter, he confided it in this
movement without a word of explanation. She understood and
replied: *He should come!!!* (I have this from both of them!)' We are
roused from its lulling reverie by a gentle horn-call; the bassoon
quotes a phrase from the *Wunderhorn* song, *Lob des hohen
Verstandes*, about the song-contest between the cuckoo and the
nightingale judged by the donkey. Thus Mahler serves notice that he
is about to give a display of academic prowess, fugue and all. It is a
brilliant display combining rondo and sonata, the main theme

assembled from the fragments hinted at the start, each theme emerging effortlessly from its predecessor, the *Adagietto* theme made joyous in a quick tempo.

There is nothing neurotic in this exuberant exhibition of Mahler's mastery. Only towards the end does he falter while 'filling in' rather repetitively before his final climax – the return of the chorale from the second movement. This is perhaps rather contrived and is certainly too long signalled, but it is a hard heart which cannot rejoice in the life-giving zest of this astonishing movement, in itself proof that Mahler had a sense of fun.

With Symphony No. 6 in A minor Mahler took another protean step in his development as a musician. It is a tragic work, but it is tragedy on a high plane, classical in conception and execution. To describe this music in the jargon of the psychoanalyst's couch, in terms of neuroses and complexes, is to traduce its finely tempered steely spirit. For while it is of the utmost sensitivity and responsiveness, it is also the music of a valiant and noble-hearted man, grappling with fears, doubts and the fates but remaining resolute, even in defeat. Serious though it is, it is not unrelievedly gloomy. Mahler knew the need for constant contrast: '*Variety* and *contrast*! That is, as it always was, the secret of effectiveness.'[2] In all his works he lays immense responsibilities and burdens on the conductor but never more than in the last five symphonies. Not only must the 'architecture' of each work be comprehensively grasped, but there must be acute appreciation of the need for continuously fluctuating variations of tempo.

Mahler himself found No. 6 difficult to conduct and correctly prophesied that its day would dawn only when conductors, orchestras and audiences were familiar with all his work. For years it was rarely performed – the United States did not hear it until Mitropoulos conducted it in New York in 1947 – but this unhappy state of affairs no longer obtains and now it is regarded by many as Mahler's greatest symphony. He revised it several times. He planned the work with the *Scherzo* second and the *Andante* third, but at the first performance he reversed the order. However, the score, which was published almost at once, had the *Scherzo* second, but with a printed slip indicating the revised order. When the International Mahler Society published a new score in 1963 based on Mahler's revisions of the orchestration, the editor, Erwin Ratz, reverted to

[2] Letter to Marschalk, 12th April 1896.

139

placing the *Scherzo* second, saying that Mahler had changed his mind again towards the end of his life. No documentary evidence was adduced to support this flagrant assertion, nor has any been discovered since. Most conductors choose to follow this score, but there are exceptions. There is also the question of the three hammer-blows of fate in the finale. Mahler, as we have seen, was powerfully affected by this symphony and later, from superstition, deleted the third blow. But many conductors now restore it, and there seems to be no good reason why this should not be common practice.

Notwithstanding the length (eighty-one minutes) of this work and the very large orchestra used, the symphonic argument is comparatively taut and unified. Once again Mahler's favourite interval of a fourth is exploited to its full capacity, but the principal organic feature of the thematic material is the tragedy motif, the major-minor chord, heard in the first instance as a loud common chord fading away while the major third is turned into the minor:

Ex. 17

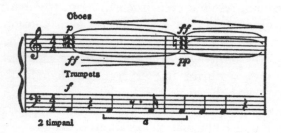

The rhythm in the accompaniment, marked *a*, pervades the symphony.

Much depends on the interpretation of the very first bars. Not summer this time, but 'modern music' marches in with this sinister, tramping start. It is marked *Allegro energico, ma non troppo*, and this is reinforced by a further instruction in German: *Heftig, aber markig* (vehement, but plenty of vigour). If, as often (alas) happens, only the *energico* and *heftig* are observed, without their qualifying speed limit, disaster inevitably follows and the movement, instead of being tragic, becomes merely strident and aggressive. True, vehemence and fury are there, but if they are allowed to become unbridled ferocity the point of the work is lost. Those who regard Mahler as an undisciplined composer might profitably study the design of this first movement – not excessively long at just over twenty minutes – and note especially the restraint with which he treats his F major second subject (said by Alma to depict her) – a consoling but by no means over-romanticized contrast with the opening march, although it has already been foreshadowed in the first-subject group:

Ex. 18

The interested listener may detect a *Heldenleben*-like sound in the richness of some of the scoring. Ironically, for Mahler referred to himself as an 'old-fashioned' composer, it was the 'boldness of harmony' in this symphony which Schoenberg admired. Alban Berg was equally impressed, describing it to Webern as 'the *only* Sixth, despite the *Pastoral*' – a meaningless but well-meant tribute. Perhaps he was thinking of three remarkably imaginative episodes in this movement: one in which the sleigh bells of the Fourth Symphony seem to be purposely distorted; the second in which Mahler evokes the sound of cow-bells heard from afar when one is high in the Alps, a passage of unforgettable poetry, unearthly, the cow-bells strangely like some electronic pastoral ghost-noise; and the third an equally strange evocation, this time with the celesta making its symphonic début, suggesting eighteenth-century echoes amid the twentieth-century *Sturm und Drang*. The cow-bells, Mahler explained, 'are the last earthly sounds heard from the valley far below by the departing spirit on the mountain top'. Clearly, too, their sound vividly recalled his youth. When he was nineteen he described to his friend Steiner how 'the pallid shapes that people my life pass by me like shadows of long-lost happiness'. He recalled that 'the tinkling of cow-bells has lulled me into dreams' and 'the chime of the eventide bells is wafted to me on a kindly breeze'.

The *Scherzo* also opens with a strong tramping rhythm, but it is a fatal interpretative mistake to fail to differentiate between the *tempi* of the first movement and this *Scherzo*. It is a remarkable and elusive movement. In fifteen lines about it that fine scholar Hans Redlich,[3] after describing it as a 'sinister Hoffmannesque puppet-show'

---

[3] H. F. Redlich, *Bruckner and Mahler* (London, 1963), p. 207.

(because of the xylophone), uses the adjectives 'spookish', 'ghostly', 'diabolical', 'exotic', 'catastrophic', 'grim', 'fiery', 'lurid' and 'demoniacal'. Mahler, it seems to me, accomplished his purpose with more subtlety. Might it not be that the personal experiences of Hans Redlich and his like, their enforced exile from Germany or Austria through the scourge of Nazism, distorted their responses to certain aspects of Mahler's music, lending it a specific personal association which — understandably enough — overlaid its substance with an almost hysterical intensity? Each listener, of course, may interpret the music to his own fancy. There are underlying sardonic humour, brief hints of the horn passage from the *Scherzo* of No. 5, and some delicate pastiche Haydn of uncloying charm which prepares the way for the *altväterisch* (in the style of a bygone age) trio, with its elegant oboe. The movement ends with an enigmatic passage — beating drum, flutes, violin solo — thoroughly in keeping with the tragic mood of the symphony.

For the main theme of the *Andante moderato* in E flat major Mahler refers to one of the *Kindertotenlieder*, but the movement is mellow, relaxed and even idyllic, in the form of a slow rondo. The cow-bells are heard again, the horn calls romantically. Restraint is once more the keynote, but the beauty of the music may easily cause us to overlook (as, indeed it should) the technical skill, notably the novel and subtle merging, or overlapping, of themes (as in the minuet of Symphony No. 3 and in the first movement of No. 4, where the development section and recapitulation are so intricately and effectively interlinked). Placed third, this *Andante* undoubtedly makes a poignant prelude to the crushing power of the immense finale. Mahler here seems to challenge his superb mastery of large-scale structures and wins triumphantly. All that has gone before is but the preface to this clinching essay in tragedy, opening in C minor with a tense and mysterious introduction containing the principal material — swirling harp *glissandi*, a soaring violin theme (note the rhythm *a* from Ex. 17):

Ex. 19

the tragedy-motif, a baying tuba whose theme is also flavoured by the pervasive rhythm *a* and is based on the ascending octave of Ex. 19. Among further themes is a sombre woodwind chorale. The trumpets for this movement are increased from four to six, there is a bass trombone and a remarkable array of percussion.

A march tune, still in C minor, leads into the A minor *Allegro energico*, invigorating and strident. Twice the cow-bells return, enclosing a savage march. Three times the *Allegro energico* is interrupted by the return of the introduction. After the first interruption it resumes with two development sections. At the height of each, a hammer-blow is heard followed by the tragedy-motif roared by trombones, with unison trumpets as background. After the second return of the introduction, the *Allegro* reaches an exultant climax but the tragedy-motif halts it. This is where the third hammer-blow occurs. Those who expect a melodramatic metallic crash for these blows, as Richard Strauss did, are disappointed; Mahler specified a non-metallic thud, 'like an axe-stroke', of the bass drum. The excitement of the movement is cumulative and intensified by moments of lyrical expansiveness. Despite its thirty-two minutes, it is so packed with incident that it seems almost compressed. In the coda there is a lofty Brucknerian chorale for the horns, as though the malignancy of Fate had been quelled. But, like Thomas Hardy, Mahler the fatalist – for such he was, rather than a pessimist – believed that someone was waiting round the corner to club him down, and this mighty work ends in its original key with the tragedy-motif as a *fortissimo* minor triad, subsiding into the sullen silence of defeat, a soft *pizzicato* A over a stroke on the bass drum.

In the Sixth Symphony, and especially in its finale, Mahler's individual use of symphonic form reached its highest peak so far. The sonorities are still new-sounding and fascinating, the counterpoint supreme; his constant variation of his themes is masterly – the 'Alma' theme, for example, always slightly different, always elusive; but the sonorities and the substance seem to have been simultaneously created, so inseparable are they. Much may therefore be expected from Symphony No. 7 for we have seen how Mahler developed with each successive work – shed a skin, in Cardus's graphic phrase. Yet even though Mahler's symphonies are now as much appreciated as they were formerly derided, the Seventh has remained the least understood and accepted of the ten; even long-serving champions in his cause have called it a failure, or 'cranky', or repetitive (because its design is so similar to that of No. 5). Few conductors can bring this work off as effectively as they can No. 5, or even No. 9. Does this mean that the fault lies in the music itself? I do not think so. It is a complex, extravagant, highly sophisticated, mercurial symphony beside which No. 6 is comparatively straightforward. It needs exceptionally close understanding and co-operation between conductor and orchestra if it is to make its proper effect, not to mention thorough rehearsal. In none of Mahler's symphonies is it more essential for a modern orchestra's string sections to be taught the correct and subtle use of *portamento*. Much is made of Mahler's admission that the second and fourth movements were composed in 1904 and the three others added a year later, a lack of unity being adduced. This criticism must be respected; one can refute it only by saying that 'unity' in a symphony is partly sensed as an emotional inevitability. (Binding movements together thematically is not an infallible passport to unity.) I sense this unity in the Seventh, and am convinced that Mahler's grand design succeeds.

After the taut, almost classical, four-movement Sixth, the Seventh appears loose-limbed and sprawling, a reversion to the form of the Second and Third Symphonies, where huge outer movements enclose three shorter *intermezzos*. But there is a difference. The second and fourth movements complement and balance each other, both being given the title *Nachtmusik*. Between them comes a substantial *Scherzo*, only it is no joke but a nightmare in the midst of the Night Music. The Seventh is, in fact, the other side of the coin of the Sixth, with certain rhythms and thematic shapes common to both. Although much of the Sixth is optimistic, cheerful music and its slow movement is less anguished than that of the Fourth, even, it suddenly takes a wrong road in the finale and a tragic outcome is therefore inevitable. In that respect it is like a Hardy novel – one twist of fate, or destiny, and the skies fall. The Seventh is optimistic, amorous and, at the end, jovial. It contains grotesque and disruptive episodes and the *Scherzo* is spooky and sinister, but for most of its length it is music in which human resilience, charm and humour are celebrated. It is a masterpiece on several levels, besides being one of Mahler's most outgoing, straightforward and accessible works.

Its subtitle could be 'the Romantic' or 'Nocturnes', for this is music 'about' night and dreams and, eventually, the return of day. It is Mahler's most glamorous symphony and it is a vast canvas, nearly eighty-seven minutes in length, the first movement lasting over twenty-three minutes. It is scored for a large orchestra (2 piccolos, 4 flutes, 3 oboes, cor anglais, E-flat clarinet, 3 clarinets in A, bass clarinet, 3 bassoons, contra-bassoon, tenor horn in B flat, 4 horns, 3 trumpets, 3 trombones, tuba, 2 harps, mandoline, guitar, much percussion, and strings). Yet the texture is translucent. Clarity, always clarity, every detail telling. In orchestration alone, this work is spellbinding. 'With me,' he boasted, 'all the instruments sing, even the brass and the kettle-drums.' There are prophetic features in the harmony, such as the superimposed fourths in the first movement, and the work appealed strongly on its first appearance to the new generation – to Hermann Scherchen, for instance, who was a viola-player before he became a conductor and was eighteen when No. 7 was first performed. He described it as 'my first whiff of a new artistic feeling, one that marked the transition to expressionism'. Schoenberg was impressed by its massive flexibility and poise. Writing to Mahler on 29th December 1909 he mentioned

> perfect repose based on artistic harmony; something that set me in motion without simply upsetting my centre of gravity and leaving me to my fate; that drew me calmly and pleasingly into its orbit ... in a manner so measured and preordained that there are never any sudden jolts. ... I felt so many subtleties of form.

He had penetrated to the secret of this astonishing symphony: that Mahler's grip on the Haydn-Beethoven-Mozart sonata-form tradition was so strong and his own individuality so potent that an extraordinary impression of novelty and experiment is given within a classical structure on which a copious imagination has been given full play. The key structure of the symphony is B minor, followed by an E minor *Allegro con fuoco* which ends in E major; C minor for the second movement, D minor for the third, F major for the fourth and C major for the fifth.

The slow introduction to the first movement is dramatic and deliberate, the magnificent and pregnant first theme being allotted to the tenor horn. ('Here Nature roars', said Mahler.) As in the first movement of No. 4, the mosaic effect of the treatment of the material shows the cunningly experienced hand of an ultra-sophisticated musician. The intensely Romantic and 'Mahlerian' second subject, in C major, is a strong clue to the pervading mood of the work; it is juxtaposed with a typical march-like rhythm (similar to a comparable passage in No. 6). Part of the expressionism which attracted Scherchen is to be found in the trumpet-calls, the hushed strings, the anticipation of Bartók's night-music. With what mastery the movement is built to an ecstatic climax – a blaze of light in the darkness which returns, even more doom-laden and mysterious, before the aggressive coda.

The first of the two 'night-music' movements seems to recapture, in twentieth-century terms, the moonlit Romanticism of Mozart's *Don Giovanni* and *Marriage of Figaro* – perhaps the Spanish rhythm has a relevance to Seville. The echoing horns and woodwind, the *pizzicato* strings and the marvellous assortment of sounds –particularly the A flat theme for the cellos – seem to constitute a determined re-creation of the elegance of eighteenth-century manners, yet with a sinister twist. Cow-bells are used, but how differently from No. 6. There they drifted to the ear impressionistically, the very sound of solitude; here they are near and mundane.

Mahler's direction for the central *Scherzo* is 'Fluently, but not brisk (shadowy)'. For some commentators this haunting movement has a 'whiff of death'; others find it horrific and bitter, expressing cynicism and sarcasm. I am sceptical of the ability of instrumental music to be sarcastic, and while in no way wishing to deny the mysterious atmosphere of this movement, I align myself with Erwin Stein's poetic description: 'It is a child's fear of the dark that Mahler so compassionately describes.' That can be horrific enough, of course, and this *Scherzo* marvellously depicts flickering firelight and grotesque shadows, with the gentle trio a calming lullaby. Waltz, *Ländler* and march are parodied during this satirical essay, which ends like a frenzied *danse macabre*.

But night is for love too, and just as the Fifth had its *Adagietto* at this point, the Seventh has its *Andante amoroso* – a tender and romantic serenade, with swooning harmonies, the sound of the mandoline for wooing and a lyrical cello theme (the trio) for sensuous fulfilment. The movement is rather too long (sixteen and a half minutes) for its material, but by the time the poetic coda has been heard, all is forgiven. The C major Rondo-Finale, in a Mahlerian version of variation-form, is the music of broad daylight, drums and trumpets suggesting a *Meistersinger*-like pageantry (perhaps a parody of the Masters' theme is intentional, just as the later suggestion of the *Merry Widow* waltz is too witty not to be meant – a highly topical joke too in 1905, the year the *Widow* started her career). Such parodies – including one of the *Adagietto* of No. 5 – have suggested to some that Mahler ran out of ideas in this finale and simply makes music, or not so simply. It is a point of view. Yet a great interpretation of this symphony will crown it with this Rondo, its gaiety so open-hearted, its sudden retreat to the simplicity of the *Wunderhorn* so touchingly effective, and its final peroration not entirely free from doubt despite the overt triumph (rather like the coda of Elgar's First Symphony). Once again the symphony has embraced everything.

These three symphonies stand like a mighty arch at the gateway to twentieth-century music. The Fifth and Seventh are the two sturdy supports to the roof – the pinnacle – the Sixth. Why is No. 6 the greatest? Because it is his most perfect reconciliation of form and matter. He set out to compose a true Tragic Symphony, even giving it that title for a time. Mahler the intellectual and student of literary classics knew that real tragedy must have both universality and objectivity. Yet he was the most subjective of composers, and Alma has called the Sixth his most personal work. She is right; but Mahler here disciplined and controlled his emotions without diminishing them. No references to bugle-calls or bird-calls, no *Ländler* or popular songs in this symphony, only one brief allusion to *Kindertotenlieder*. He does not carry themes from one movement to another: thematic unity is achieved by two chords and a rhythmic phrase. Three of the four movements are in A minor, the movements are classical in design (repeated exposition in the first movement). All this is sufficient refutation of the old gibe that Mahler was an undisciplined sentimentalist. The severe classical training of his youth and his genius as a conductor of Beethoven and Mozart are the keystones of the Sixth Symphony. It is also a demonstration that his conducting was an integral part of his composing.

Yet there is an extra poignancy when we contemplate these masterpieces. They were composed when Mahler's music was not merely misunderstood by the critics but attacked with such vehemence that even he was thrown off balance and lost faith in his work. His anxieties when he conducted the first performances were more than first-night nerves. He made himself ill with revisions of the orchestral parts, constantly worrying over them. Schoenberg's words, published in an essay on Mahler in *Der Merker*, should be recalled:

147

How will they seek to answer for this: that Mahler had to say 'It seems I have been in error'? How will they seek to justify themselves when they are accused of having brought one of the greatest composers of all time to the point where he was deprived of the sole, the highest recompense for a creative mind, the recompense found when the artist's faith in himself allows him to say: 'I have *not* been in error'?

13

The Eighth Symphony

The Eighth Symphony is a throwback to the Mahler of Symphonies 2, 3 and 4 and a return to words as the carriers of his ideas. It is as if, after the secular, worldly confessions of Nos. 5, 6 and 7, he had returned to the search for redemption which had obsessed him in the 1890s. Alma is reported to have said, in a moment of exasperation, that 'Gustav is always on the telephone to God'. In No. 8 he was on the hot line. I have already quoted his description of how 'the *Spiritus Creator* took hold of me and shook me and drove me on' when he went to Maiernigg in 1906. He composed the symphony between 21st June and 18th August, and he told Schoenberg it was 'as if it had been dictated to me' – again the sense of 'being composed'. That it represents a profound spiritual experience cannot be gainsaid. Mahler even went so far as to say to Specht that he regarded it as 'a gift to the whole nation'.

The intellectual plan of the symphony is characteristic of Mahler: to affirm the Christian faith and belief in the power of the Spirit as expressed in the ancient hymn *Veni, Creator Spiritus*, and to link this with Goethe's symbolic vision, in the closing scene of *Faust*, Part II, of the redemption of mankind through love as represented by the Eternal-Feminine (*Das Ewig-Weibliche*). In this scene Faust's soul is borne aloft by angels and granted salvation by the Virgin Mary (Mater Gloriosa). Mahler allots only two lines to the Virgin, but they are the key to the affinity he found between Goethe and Hrabanus Maurus, the ninth-century Archbishop of Mainz who is supposed to have written the hymn:

> Komm! hebe dich zu höhern Sphären!
> Wenn er dich ahnet, folgt er nach.
>
> (Come then! rise to higher spheres!
> Divining you, he will follow.)

And from the hymn:

> Accende lumen sensibus,
> Infunde amorem cordibus.
>
> (Illuminate our senses,
> Pour love into our hearts.)

There was a further association in Mahler's mind with what, in a letter to Alma written in June 1910 while he was rehearsing the symphony in Munich, he called 'the misunderstood "Platonic love" '. He continued:

> The essence of it is really Goethe's idea that all love is generative, creative, and that there is a physical and spiritual generation which is the emanation of this 'Eros'. You have it in the last scene of *Faust*, presented symbolically . . . The wonderful discussion between Diotima and Socrates . . . gives the core of Plato's thought, his whole outlook on the world . . . The comparison between [Socrates] and Christ is obvious and has arisen spontaneously in all ages . . . In each case Eros as Creator of the world.

It may be helpful here to recall some of Diotima's discourse on love in Plato's *Symposium*, as translated by Shelley:

> 'Love then, O Socrates, is not as you imagine the love of the beautiful.' – 'What, then?' – 'Of generation and production in the beautiful.' – 'Why then of generation?' – 'Generation is something eternal and immortal in immortality. It necessarily, from what has been confessed, follows that we must desire immortality together with what is good, since Love is the desire that good be for ever present to us. Of necessity Love must also be the desire of immortality.'

Now Mahler again, writing to Alma in June 1909 about the Goethe scene:

> That which draws us by its mystic force, what every created thing, perhaps even the very stones, feels with absolute certainty as the centre of its being, what Goethe here – again employing an image – calls the eternal feminine – that is to say, the resting-place, the goal, in opposition to the striving and struggling towards the goal (the eternal masculine) – you are quite right in calling the force of love. Goethe . . .

expresses it with a growing clearness and certainty right on to the Mater Gloriosa – the personification of the eternal feminine!

Could there be more eloquent testimony to the extraordinary breadth of Mahler's human sympathy and to the power of the mysticism which impelled his creative activity, a mysticism with roots far deeper than the Catholicism superficially implicit in some of Goethe's text and deeper too than any atavistic Judaism? Indeed Mahler is an exemplar of Bryan Magee's assertion, in his splendid *Aspects of Wagner* (London, 1968), that 'it is only Jews who have escaped from their religious and intellectual tradition who have achieved greatness'.

So much for the impulse behind the Eighth Symphony. What of the music? It was the first completely choral symphony to be written – Vaughan Williams's *Sea Symphony* was not finished until 1908–9 – and it justifies the title of symphony first by being indubitably symphonic in conception and secondly by its adaptation of sonata form in Part I. Some eminent commentators descry slow movement, scherzo and finale in Part II, but I think this involves 'bending' the music to fit the theory. Because of the vast forces involved, the work has become known as the 'Symphony of a Thousand', a description to be deplored because it encourages the view of No. 8 as a 'Barnum and Bailey' show, whereas Mahler's use of an exceptionally large orchestra was obviously not for grandiose effect but to ensure that balance between chorus and orchestra was as near perfect as possible. The scoring is for piccolo, 4 flutes, 4 oboes, cor anglais, 3 clarinets, E flat clarinet, bass clarinet, 4 bassoons, contra-bassoon, 8 horns, 4 trumpets, 4 trombones, bass tuba, 3 timpani, bass drum, cymbals, gong, triangle, bells, glockenspiel, celesta, pianoforte, harmonium, organ, 2 harps, mandoline, strings, double chorus, boys' choir and eight soloists (three sopranos, two contraltos, tenor, baritone and bass). This was lampooned in the German press in 1911, just as the scoring of the Sixth Symphony had occasioned a cartoon of Mahler in 1906 captioned: 'My God, I've forgotten the motorhorn. Now I shall have to write another symphony.' Yet the predominant impression of No. 8 is not of torrents of sound but of the contrasts of subtle tone-colours and the luminous quality of the scoring. Rarely had Mahler shown such mastery of the large forces he required, rarely scored with such certainty. Unusually for him, there were few revisions and the score was ready for publication in

1907, though not published until 1911. Repeated hearings, such as the gramophone affords, reveal the remarkable thematic unity of the two movements: the work seems to grow shorter. In fact it is far from being the longest of his symphonies. At roughly seventy-seven minutes, it is nearly ten minutes shorter than No. 7, for instance.

Part I, the setting of *Veni, Creator Spiritus*, opens on a chord of E flat for organ, woodwind and lower strings, followed by the choir's outburst of:

Ex. 20

marked *allegro impetuoso*. Three important themes are at once introduced in this opening passage, which is of elemental strength. Mahler's polyphonic supremacy is demonstrated throughout in a way which entitles him to rank, in terms of technical ability alone, with the Venetian masters of three centuries earlier. Donald Mitchell believes, and I agree with him, that this movement was inspired by Bach's motets, particularly *Singet dem Herrn* (which Mahler included in the programme in 1905 when he conducted the first Vienna performance of the Fifth). Yet from the first entry of the soloists, after the majestic cries of 'Veni', the unmistakable presence of twentieth-century Mahler is felt as he broods over the words: 'Fill with divine grace the hearts of thy creatures.' A modulation from D minor to E major brings the triumphant 'Accende' theme and, eventually, a double fugue in the tempo of a march and an ecstatic *Gloria*. In spite of the introspective central episode, this movement has an irresistible vitality, rushing headlong to its apotheosis.

Part II is nearer to the Mahler world: we seem to have passed into a totally different atmosphere. Now the orchestra comes into its own, setting the Faustian scene – a rocky mountain gorge, with lions prowling – in bleak and remote writing for woodwind over a plodding bass. The connection with the 'Accende' motif is soon established – its three rising notes occur time and again. As the

Anchorites softly echo each other, the music becomes richer and the baritone (Pater ecstaticus) invokes 'eternal rapture'; the bass (Pater profundus) has a more dramatic song, vividly accompanied by 'nature music' for the stormy sea and thunderbolts whereby the imagery of love is depicted. A relic of the proposed *Wunderhorn* 'Christmas Games' *scherzo* is the entry of 'angels, blessed boys, younger angels, and more perfect angels'. We are back in the world of the Fourth Symphony until Dr Marianus's (tenor) rapturous plea to the Virgin to unveil herself to the world. An E major chord for harps and harmonium sustains this elevated theme, marked *adagissimo*:

Ex. 21

which begins the final section. The three women, Magna peccatrix (soprano), Mulier Samaritana annd Maria Aegyptiaca (contraltos) describe Christ's agony and death and plead for Faust's soul, reinforced by the Penitent (formerly Gretchen), whose soprano solo is of limpid beauty. The Virgin speaks, and the work reaches its emotional climax with Marianus's prayer to the 'Virgin, Mother, Queen and Goddess' followed by the final Mystic Chorus, beginning in hushed awe and ending in a blaze of E flat sound and an orchestral coda in which the *Veni, Creator* theme returns, its interval of the seventh changed into a major ninth for trumpets and trombones 'as if', Redlich wrote, 'trying to reach the stars'.

Well, did Mahler reach the stars in this ambitious symphony? There is no doubt that in a superb performance (such as Klaus Tennstedt has recorded) it can be an overwhelming emotional experience, temporarily sweeping aside doubts and uncertainties. Even if the expense of performing it did not ensure its rarity, it is a work which ought to be reserved for special occasions. Repeated hearings expose its weaknesses, especially the fitful nature of Mahler's inspiration. Whereas the more one hears the other symphonies, the more one comes to admire and understand them – I can speak only for myself – the Eighth does not constantly surprise and amaze the listener, as No. 6 and No. 7 do however familiar they become. The thematic simplicity and diatonic harmony are not supported by the sustained inventiveness which alone could have assured Mahler a total realization of his immense conception. As a declaration of religious faith I find the Second Symphony more convincing and moving; as an expression of pantheistic mysticism I find the Third more impressive. Both those works are more original than No. 8, and are more truly and organically symphonic, whereas No. 8, especially in Part II, is markedly episodic and is perhaps best regarded as a series of tableaux or frescoes. Part I, a magnificent display of Mahler's unrivalled contrapuntal skill, cannot be wholly absolved of the suggestion that he is saying: 'Just listen to this, all those of you who say I'm an unbridled Romantic megalomaniac.'

The great moments in the work are great indeed: the opening pages, for instance, where one still recaptures the feeling of Mahler's burst of sudden inspiration; the Beethovenian effect (as cruel to the singers too) of the massive double fugue; the spare and sparse scoring of the prelude to Part II (too long, though); and the ecstatic solo arias for Marianus and Gretchen. Where Mahler may be thought to have failed – not surprisingly, really – is in achieving the musical personification of his vision of the Goethean Eternal-Feminine-Alma synthesized with the Platonic Eros. For this he resorts (but wonderfully) to the soaring strings and glittering harps of Ex. 21, a beautiful and sensuous passage but perilously near to the idiom of Mascagni and Puccini.[1] It is not, we may be forgiven for thinking, the Mater Gloriosa who 'swims into view', but Santuzza. The artistic judgment which in the other symphonies, particularly No. 4, kept sentimentality at bay by the tartness of the orchestration here temporarily deserted Mahler. Later, after Marianus's final prayer and the chorus's inspired 'Blicket auf', the way to the Mystic Chorus is prepared by a strange orchestral interlude the texture of which is dominated by the sound of harmonium, pianoforte, celesta, organ, harps and woodwind. It suggests irresistibly a parallel with the spangled interior decoration of certain Austrian Catholic churches. The final chorus, 'Alles Vergängliche', achieves exaltation of a rare kind, although its similarity to the end of the Second Symphony must blunt its impact on experienced Mahlerians.

[1] It is perhaps not without significance that Mahler admired the music of Mascagni and adored Liszt's *Legend of Saint Elizabeth*.

14

Das Lied von der Erde

When Theobald Pollak gave Hans Bethge's *The Chinese Flute* to Mahler, he set in motion a masterpiece in which the words acquired an extra dimension and became inseparable from the marvellous music to which they were set.

The genesis of *Das Lied von der Erde* has been described in Chapter 8. In Mahler's depressed state in 1907 and 1908, when he was suddenly conscious of his physical limitations and therefore exceptionally aware of his mortality, the eighty-three poems which Bethge paraphrased from English, German and French translations of the Chinese originals aroused profound thoughts and distant echoes. Bethge's sources were Hans Heilmann's *Chinesische Lyrik*, Judith Gautier's *Le Livre de Jade* and the Marquis d'Hervey-Saint-Denys's *Poésies de l'épilogue des Thang*. Gautier's translations provided the models for both Heilmann, in 1905, and Bethge. But her translations were very free and she was careless, or uncaring, about her attributions. Certain of the poems Bethge adapted from her book are not by the Chinese poets she names; and in *Von der Jugend* (which is not by Li-Tai-Po) the way clothes were worn at that period in Chinese history meant that what she described in the fourth stanza – 'their silken sleeves slip backwards, their silken caps perch gaily on the back of their necks' – could not have occurred.[1]

Mahler made certain significant alterations to the text. For example (in *Der Abschied*), Bethge's original has these two lines:

> Die arbeitsamen Menschen
> Geh'n heimwärts, voller Sehnsucht nach dem Schlaf.
> (Labouring men wend homewards,
> Filled with longing for sleep.)

[1] For a comprehensive analysis of *Das Lied von der Erde* in a detail impossible within the scope of this book, the interested reader is referred to Donald Mitchell's magnificent Volume III of his *Gustav Mahler* (London, 1985).

Mahler inserted a phrase from a poem, *Die Nacht blickt mild*, he had written to Johanna Richter in December 1884 so that his version reads:

> Die müden Menschen
> Geh'n heimwärts,
> Um im Schlaf vergess'ness Glück
> Und Jugend neu zu lernen!

> (Tired men wend homewards
> to recapture in sleep forgotten happiness and youth.)

It was an alteration symbolic of the mood of nostalgia which the music so perfectly conveys. Further significant alterations will be mentioned in context.

Mahler's description of *Das Lied von der Erde* is 'A Symphony for tenor, alto (or baritone) and orchestra'. It is said, by Alma and others, that he was superstitious of a ninth symphony because Beethoven, Schubert, Bruckner and Dvořák had died after completing nine, and that by calling this elaborate symphonic song-cycle a symphony his ninth would be his tenth. One accepts this theory with some reluctance and scepticism because Mahler, great musician that he was, is likely to have realized that although *Das Lied von der Erde* is symphonic, it stands apart from the rest of the series.

Because a work achieves the greatest popularity with the public does not mean that it is its creator's best work. In the case of *Das Lied von der Erde*, however, the public have chosen wisely. It has everything: it is filled with indefinable sadness and longing yet ultimately it is not depressing; it is simple in design; it is fantastically beautifully scored; and it provides the soloists with wonderful opportunities.

So familiar is it today, and so widely admired, that it is easy to overlook its originality and the supreme skill with which it was composed. One of the hallmarks of a masterpiece is that it should appear inevitable, spontaneous. *Das Lied von der Erde* seems continuously new, constantly renewing itself. Yet it represents the culmination of the technique which Mahler had been developing since the First Symphony: perpetual variation, no exact repetitions, and a magical web of melodic counterpoint. The result sounds like a vast inspired improvisation combined with hypersensitive attention to details of tone-colour. He used again the basic ingredients which had supplied him with so much fine music in the past, but here their use was heightened by his response to the poems. He used the intervals of the perfect fourth, the ascending minor third (symbol of space and solitude), the falling second (yearning), and – sole concession to *chinoiserie* – a three-note pentatonic phrase which occurs throughout the work in many permutations, as here in the Finale:

Ex. 22

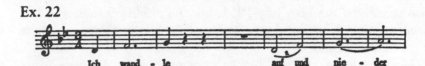

By masterly deployment of these fragments Mahler gives this work – as he gave other works – a binding unity which subconsciously is communicated to a listener unable to read a note of music and ought to convince those who can that he is a symphonist of the first magnitude. Donald Mitchell has drawn attention to two important influences on Mahler at the time he was composing *Das Lied von der Erde*. At Toblach, Mahler was visited by the banker Paul Hammerschlag, who gave him some cylinders of Chinese music, recorded in China, which he had bought in Vienna in a shop near St Stephen's Cathedral. Secondly, in 1908 Guido Adler published an article on heterophony, which he described as 'rudimentary irregular polyphony'. This term is usually applied to exotic, or ethnic, music and is the use of two parts simultaneously performed in different versions, one more elaborate than the other. Scholars have identified Mahler's use of heterophony in the *Rückert* and *Kindertotenlieder* and in the Eighth Symphony. The work is scored for a large, but not mammoth, orchestra, triple woodwind except for five clarinets, and a much enlarged (but most economically used) percussion section to include the exoticism of mandoline, glockenspiel, triangle, cymbals and tambourine. Part of the marvel of the scoring of *Das Lied von der Erde* is that Mahler projects the duality at the heart of the work – the contrast of spring and autumn, dream and reality, life and death – through the use not of one big orchestra but of several independent orchestras with varying constituents, i.e. wind and percussion for the pentatonic melodies and mainly string textures for other passages.

The first performance of *Das Lied von der Erde* was conducted by

Bruno Walter in Munich on 20th November 1911, six months after Mahler's death. Writing to Berg before they set out to be there, Webern wrote: 'Once you have read the end of the poem of *Das Lied von der Erde* in the enclosed cutting [from the *Berliner Tageblatt* of 29th October 1911], would you not expect to hear the most wonderful music that there is? Something of such magnificence as has never yet existed? . . . For heaven's sake, what kind of music must that be? I feel I must already be able to imagine it before having heard it'. The first performance had been offered to Mengelberg and was scheduled for 16th July 1911, but the publisher intervened to point out that Walter had been assigned the first performance of the posthumous works.

Mahler selected seven of Bethge's poems to make six movements —his first use of this form since the crucial Third Symphony, which has many affinities with *Das Lied von der Erde*, the most obvious being that they both have a long *adagio* as finale preceded by short *intermezzi*. The first movement (*Allegro pesante*) is *Das Trinklied vom Jammer der Erde* (Drinking song of Earth's sorrow), one of Mahler's best constructed and most powerful first movements. The Chinese poem by Li-Tai-Po advocates wine as the best means of coming to terms with the fact that man has less than a hundred years of life in which to delight 'in all the decaying trifles of this earth' (not a theory, incidentally, that Mahler put into practice, because he was abstemious in matters of food and drink). The music begins with a fanfare on the horns, suggesting the defiant desperation of the poem, followed by a burst of manic laughter before the tenor launches into the first of the three stanzas – he needs to be a *Heldentenor* for this notoriously difficult passage, which all too often exposes the weaknesses of the singer's high register in *fortissimo* (the late Fritz Wunderlich pre-eminently showed that it was not a Mahlerian miscalculation). Each stanza ends with the haunting and haunted refrain 'Dunkel ist das Leben, ist der Tod' ('Dark is life, dark is death') which rises a semitone at each appearance (G minor, A flat minor, A minor).

It is soon clear that Mahler is to cover the whole range of emotion and to use every orchestral device (including the remarkable 'flutter-tonguing' by the wind) to heighten the tension. Never did he score more delicately, more imaginatively, more vividly. Never did he draw purer sound from the strings. Sometimes we almost seem to hear the stillness of the air. 'Not all the best of music is in the notes,' he said on one occasion, and in *Das Lied von der Erde* every pause is pregnant. When the tenor sings of the eternal blue sky and the earth blossoming in spring, we can feel Mahler's pulse quicken just as it must have quickened when he first read these words; we can sense how, while composing this music, his fear for his own weakness was conquered and he became extra-sensitively alive to the beauty of the world of nature which had inspired him for so long. 'I am thirstier for life!' It is the eternal wonder of music that it can convey emotion at several different levels simultaneously. Throughout *Das Lied von der Erde* we feel Mahler's hedonism, we feel his rapturous rapport with Nature, we feel his loneliness, his overpowering sense of poignancy at the brevity of man's existence, and we feel his joy in the beauty of the earth and the return of spring. There is nothing nihilistic or defeatist about *Das Lied von der Erde*: its final effect is to uplift the heart. But there are terrors to be faced boldly too: consequently we have the remarkable passage in this first song where the poet describes the ape howling on the graves in the moonlight – a passage that is the musical equivalent of some of the expressionist painting of the time and takes us momentarily into the world of *Pierrot Lunaire*.

The second movement is the second longest, *Der Einsame im Herbst* (The lonely one in autumn), after Tchang-Tsi, according to Bethge.[2] This is a slow movement in D minor; Mahler's marking is 'somewhat dragging and weary'. It is a *locus classicus* for the means by which to obtain a chamber-music effect from a symphony orchestra: figuration for muted strings, an oboe like a solitary bird-call, dialogue between horn and cellos, and the contralto voice sometimes expressionless and despairing (at the line 'Mein Herz ist müde', 'My heart is weary') and radiantly ecstatic at the invocation to the 'Sun of Love' to shine again and dry her tears. The movement ends in gloom with an orchestral coda of extraordinary beauty pointing the comparison between human tears and the autumn mists over the lake with which the movement began.

This is perhaps the place to mention the use of male or female voice in some of Mahler's works. The baritone is a bracketed alternative in *Das Lied*, suggesting that Mahler envisaged a contralto as the norm. It is, nevertheless, fascinating to hear a baritone in the part, for

[2] No Chinese source of Gautier's poem, which Bethge adapted, has been identified, but it has been suggested that it could have been a poem by a Tang poet, Qian Qi.

although the range tests even Fischer-Dieskau's upper register, there is no doubt that the use of the male voice intensifies the personal emotional content of the music – it is as if Mahler himself were singing to us. For this reason, and also for the subtle changes in tone-colour, some may always prefer the alternative version, but they will remain a minority because this is one of the supreme challenges to a contralto or a mezzo-soprano; while singers like Kerstin Thorborg, Kathleen Ferrier, Christa Ludwig and Janet Baker bring such interpretative insight to the sheer vocal beauty of this work, the public will continue to prefer the contrast which the contralto and tenor provide. In the case of *Lieder eines fahrenden Gesellen* and *Kindertotenlieder* the choice is less equivocal. It has become the custom – because of the popularity and high standard of contraltos in recent years – for women to sing these works. But both really belong to men, notably the *Kindertotenlieder* in which Mahler himself always preferred a male voice, even engaging a tenor in New York, Ludwig Wüllner (who, incidentally, had sung Elgar's Gerontius in Düsseldorf and London in 1901, 1902 and 1903).

The third, fourth and fifth movements of *Das Lied von der Erde* are short, simply designed miniatures. *Von der Jugend* (Of youth) is in B flat major. Despite the woodwinds' initial pentatonic scale and the fact that 'The Porcelain Pavilion' depicts a Chinese scene which everyone knows – willow-pattern, in effect – the flavour of the music is sophisticatedly Viennese. It is all very artificial and mannered, as formal as the mirror-image of the pavilion and the bridge reflected in the pool. Every note, every solo, is polished and precise. The effect is of detached emotion. The fourth movement, *Von der Schönheit* (Of beauty), in G major, is a Li-Tai-Po poem dealing with another characteristic Chinese scene – girls pick flowers on the river bank; young men on horseback gallop past; and one of them inspires a passionate and longing glance from a girl. For this Mahler provided some of his most graceful and poised music, with an almost fragile orchestral texture except in the riotous outburst of the riders where more than a hint of savagery rises to the surface. The strings make explicit every implication of the girl's glance, and the exquisite piece ends with a kind of berceuse. The mood is broken by the *scherzo*-like fifth movement, in A major, *Der Trunkene im Frühling* (The drunken man in spring). Again Li-Tai-Po commends the merits of drinking, this time to excess. The opening *Allegro* is brittle and strident, essentially light-hearted, but the mood changes poetically when a bird awakens the drunken man and tells him spring has come in the night – a brilliant theme for the piccolo (and how magically the word *Lenz* – spring – resonates through the whole work). The fifth verse, mellower and restrained, forms a short trio before the *scherzo* section returns.

At this point the work has lasted just over thirty minutes. The incomparable finale, *Der Abschied* (The Farewell), is itself to last

Ex. 23

another thirty. It opens with an unforgettable sound: a low C on cellos, basses, harp, contra-bassoon, horns and tam-tam, above which the oboe, like an *obbligato* in a Bach cantata, cries out in an anguished *gruppetto* which is to dominate the movement (see Ex. 23). The initiating strokes on the tam-tam strike a chill terror into the listener's heart, but in the first sketch were scored for double bassoon and harp, with no tam-tam. It seems extraordinary that something so inseparable from the sound of that passage should have been an afterthought! Similarly, when the tam-tam is used at the start of the great orchestral funeral march later in the movement, in the first sketch Mahler did not bring it in until three bars later. He scribbled in the margin '*Grabgeläute*' ('death-knell'). The celesta, which gives such a distinctive quality to the final bars of the work, was added at a late stage.

The impression of funereal chill given by this orchestral introduction cannot easily be described, so stark and 'hollow' is the harmony. When the contralto enters above a low C held by the cellos the effect is of a lost soul, an impression intensified by the transference of the oboe's lament to the flute. The poem, by Mong-Kao-Jen, describes sunset and twilight, with the moon 'like a silver bark on the blue lake of heaven' – an aspiring passage in which for the first time warmth floods into the orchestral tone.

The second section is freer, the tonality ambiguous, the voice accompanied by thirds for clarinets and harp. Its principal feature is the long and beautiful introductory oboe solo:

Ex. 24

which incorporates elements of all the principal motifs of the movement. It becomes an accompaniment to the soloist as she describes the brook singing in the darkness and Nature and the world going to sleep, the birds roosting on the branches, while the poet awaits his friend 'to take the last farewell'. The orchestra thins out to nothing but the harp, vibrating in fourths. For the third section the mandoline joins the harp and Mahler introduces the melody for strings which is to dominate the last part of the movement. It is a variant of *Ich bin der Welt*, the idea of longing and the beauty of the earth producing a comparable musical image. The central climax of the first part of the finale is ablaze with ecstasy as the poet longs for his friend to join him. It is no exaggeration to claim that there is no comparable expression in music of the peculiar intensity of longing conveyed in these pages of the score. 'O beauty! O eternal love-and-life-intoxicated world.' Yet here are two more remarkable glimpses into the mysteries of artistic creation. Those words – in German, 'O Schönheit, O ewigen Liebens, Lebens, trunk'ne Welt' – were Mahler's own, a substitution for Bethge's prosaic original 'O kämst du, kämst du ungetreuer Freund' ('O com'st thou, com'st thou, unfaithful friend'). Yet, and this is what is so amazing, Mahler did not substitute his own words until he was working on an orchestral draft score, but the ecstatic, rapturous music *had already been written* as a setting for Bethge's line. Again, the wonderfully calm music for Mahler's words 'Still ist mein Herz und harret seiner Stunde!' ('My heart is still and awaits its hour!') was conceived for Bethge's line 'Müd ist mein Fuss, und Müd ist meine Seele' ('My foot is weary and so is my soul'). Time and again the *music* was there first, and Mahler had to find the right words for it.

For the fourth section Mahler wrote his finest and noblest funeral march as a long interlude between the two poems which constitute the finale. It is constructed from motifs already heard, with the *gruppetto* phrase and the baleful tam-tam as chilly reminders of extinction. As this superbly scored episode sinks into the depth of gloom, the voice re-enters with the first lines of Wang-Wei's poem as recitative. The march rhythm continues, ominous and insistent, while the contralto describes the arrival of the poet's friend and his farewell. At the words 'Du, mein Freund' the compassionate music modulates into the major. In the subsequent passage, a subtle alteration in the printed score has been convincingly propounded by Donald Mitchell after a study of all Mahler's sketches and drafts.

The printed full score shows the words 'Ich werde' in 'Ich werde niemals in die Ferne schweifen' ('I shall never again go seeking the far distance') set to three repeated As. This is how it appears in Mahler's fair copy of the manuscript (now in the Pierpont Morgan Library, New York). But in at least three other Mahler manuscripts the syllable 'wer' is set to a G, giving A-G-A, as in the very first sketch. The fair copy seems to be a slip of Mahler's pen as he anticipated the three As to which he set 'Still ist mein Herz' in the next line, where he specifically wanted an effect of calm and tranquillity. The correctness of the A-G-A version of 'Ich werde' is supported by the heterophonic character of the first violins' counter-melody, the 'unfocused unison' in which identical parts 'differ slightly from one another in rhythm', as Theodor Adorno put it. It may seem a trivial matter but if one hears the phrase sung in the corrected (and incontrovertibly correct) manner, there is a world of difference.[3] The coda, in C major, begins with the return of the 'Longing' theme, and the soloist sings the words that Mahler himself added:

The dear earth everywhere
Blossoms in spring and grows green again!
Everywhere and eternally the distance shines bright and blue!
Eternally . . . eternally.

This famous passage never loses its miraculous power to grip the listener. As the contralto sings her last words, 'Ewig . . . ewig', the music fades imperceptibly from our hearing as the orchestration is thinned down to *pianissimo* held chords on the strings, with arpeggios from harp and celesta and the uncanny impersonality of the mandoline. The pentatonic scale which has lent its flavour to the whole work is omnipresent. It is almost always impossible to determine the exact moment when the music ceases, so remote and unearthly are the last bars.

---

[3] The first performance of the work with this note corrected to a G was in the Royal Festival Hall, London, on 19 April 1985, when Simon Rattle conducted the Philharmonia Orchestra. The contralto was Florence Quivar. Two hitherto undetected misprints in the score of this work, one in *Der Trunkene im Frühling,* the other in *Der Abschied,* were the subject of an article by the conductor Theodore Bloomfield in *The Musical Times* of May 1989, pp. 266–7.

This great *Abschied*, inspired as it is, is very skilfully planned – a cool, calculating brain has controlled music which springs direct from the heart. Mahler's artistic judgment was never surer than in his placing of the orchestral interlude between the poems and in his uncloying use of his fine *Sehnsucht* (longing) theme. If, as has been suggested, the finale of *Die Walküre* was his model, he rose to comparable heights.

Das Lied von der Erde is Mahler's supreme masterpiece because he, who was essentially a programmatic composer however much he may have wished to deny this, found in it the ideal programme for the projection of his musical character and capability. It is music filled with his love of life, a love sharpened to the limits of poignancy by awareness of man's mortality and the transitory nature of existence. I do not find it morbid with death-obsession. As in the Sixth Symphony, he brought to its composition an element of artistic objectivity and detachment while at the same time being gripped by intense emotion. When he said of the *Abschied* to Bruno Walter, 'Is it at all bearable? Will it drive people to do away with themselves?' he knew that he had achieved his aim of expressing a passionate longing for life, not for death. If, through some unimaginable folly, it were to be decreed that only one work by each composer should survive, there could be no hesitation about preserving *Das Lied von der Erde*. It is the best of Mahler, his speaking likeness; and admirers of the work have only to hear a fragment of it to be transported at once into its unique atmosphere. It becomes part of one's metabolism.

15

Symphonies 9 and 10

Mahler's last two symphonies and *Das Lied von der Erde* are already barnacled with romantic mythology. Because they were performed for the first time after his death, because he died comparatively young, leaving a beautiful young widow (and, better still, an unfinished symphony), because he regarded them as excessively difficult to conduct, and because he had been under medical sentence of death, they have invited every kind of subjective interpretation, to some extent justified by their elegiac nature. While I would not suggest that the subject of death was not present in his mind from 1907, I doubt if it obsessed him to the pitch of morbid superstition which has led to statements that he dreaded the idea of performances of *Das Lied von der Erde* and the Ninth Symphony. I do not believe there is any portentous significance in the fact that Mahler did nothing to promote performances of these two works. Here are the practicalities:

Because of the circumstances of his life and the customary difficulties involved in performing new works, especially elaborate and expensive ones for huge orchestras, Mahler was accustomed to long intervals between completion, and sometimes publication, of his works and their first performances, nor does he seem to have been unduly worried about this. The act of creation was the important part for him – once a symphony was finished, all his energies were devoted to sketching the next one and to scoring and re-scoring the completed work. Also, there is every indication that during his decade in Vienna he was determined to avoid any accusation that he used his position to have his symphonies performed. So No. 3, completed 1896, published 1898, waited until 1902; No. 4, completed 1900, was quicker – 1901; No. 5, competed 1902, was first played late in 1904; No. 6, scored in 1905, performed 1906; No. 7, finished 1905, first performance 1908; No. 8, composed 1906–7, performed 1910.

From 1908 Mahler divided his time between New York and

Europe. He could no longer call on the services of the Vienna Philharmonic to play through his works. But by now he was hearing his symphonies magnificently played by Mengelberg's Concertgebouw Orchestra, and this led him to revise several of them thoroughly. Symphonies 3, 5, 6 and 7 were revised between 1907 and 1909. Symphony No. 2 was revised in 1910, so was No. 4. He revised No. 5 again in 1910–11. He wrote to the Leipzig conductor and writer Georg Göhler from New York on 8th February 1911: 'I have finished my Fifth – it had to be almost completely re-orchestrated. I simply can't understand why I still had to make such mistakes, like the merest beginner. (It is clear that all the experience I had gained in writing the first four symphonies completely let me down in this one – for a completely new style demanded a new technique)'. All this took time. He did not finish scoring *Das Lied von der Erde* until 1909 and the Ninth Symphony until the spring of 1910, whereupon he immediately began to compose No. 10 and to devote four months to rehearsals for No. 8, which meant so much to him. In addition to this, he had the responsibility of re-forming and training the New York Philharmonic, choosing its programmes, rehearsing them, and studying the works by other composers which he was conducting for the first time. It must have disappointed him that he judged the American orchestra incapable of doing justice to his later, more complex works, and the audience incapable of appreciating them. 'I have made up my mind not to start in New York with a performance of the Seventh,' he wrote to Alma in 1909. 'The Seventh is too complicated for a public which knows nothing of me.' It is unlikely, then, that he would have considered a New York first performance for a work of his last period. None of this suggests the outlook of a neurotic. It suggests the sensible attitude of a busy man and of a conscientious musician who had even contemplated cancelling the first performance of No. 8 because, as he wrote to his wife, 'I am absolutely determined *not* to put up with artistic sloppiness'. If he had been obsessed merely with hearing it before he died, he would have put up with anything.

Nor can the argument be sustained that Mahler's inspiration failed him in his last two years. The long first movement of the Ninth Symphony (twenty-six minutes) is his most advanced and original instrumental movement. Here is the epitome of Mahler's duality, essential Romanticism combining with amazing anticipations of the developments of the next and later generations. This great

167

movement is sufficient testimony to why the evolutionary Mahler has had a greater influence than the revolutionary Schoenberg. In it we hear the sparse, fragmentary textures of Webern, the epigrammatic style of Berg, the 'total thematicism' of Schoenberg. The music has linear complexity and rich polyphony, and its shape is peculiar to Mahler: a combination of sonata-form and rondo with elements of the 'perpetual variation' technique. The principal theme of the movement, a nostalgic D major melody based on two falling seconds and marked *andante comodo* (a leisurely walking-pace), returns several times, as a rondo theme does. It is a significant theme, because it is related intentionally to the 'farewell' *leitmotif* of Beethoven's 'Les Adieux' sonata Op. 81a – the work which had been his 'passport' to the Vienna Conservatory – and at one point is varied to become a pathetic transformation of a Johann Strauss waltz, 'Enjoy life' (*Freut euch des Lebens*, Op. 340).

This idea of farewell was obviously carried over from *Das Lied von der Erde*, for the symphony opens with the tolling of the harp which had dominated *Der Abschied* (an even more direct allusion occurs in the finale) and with a faltering rhythmic phrase for cellos which Leonard Bernstein has suggested may represent Mahler's erratic pulse-beat. This is plausible because the conviction grows that this movement recollects, in intermittent tranquillity, Mahler's emotional crisis at Toblach in 1908 when he had to adapt himself to a new pace of life. No wonder 'Enjoy life' is quoted so wistfully.

The movement is marvellously full of contrast: Romantic nostalgia, as when the principal subject first returns (a passage above which Mahler scribbled in the short score 'O vanished days of youth! O scattered love'), tragic (heroic) defiance, uncanny quiet, a desperate climax, muted trumpet fanfares, and a prophetic and remarkable coda when the orchestra is reduced to a small group of solo instruments toying with fragments of themes and a solo horn takes us back to a simpler musical world while the 'farewell' theme slowly disintegrates. So profoundly had Mahler been stirred by the Bethge poems that clearly he felt that the symphonic song-cycle had not exhausted their musical possibilities: the Ninth Symphony is therefore an extension of *Das Lied*, almost a symphonic commentary upon it. How strongly this is conveyed is evident from Alban Berg's reaction, expressed in a letter to his wife in the summer of 1910. Mahler had lent him the score. 'The first movement is the most heavenly thing Mahler ever wrote,' Berg said. 'It is the expression of an exceptional fondness for this earth, the longing to live in peace on it, to enjoy nature to its depths – before death comes. For he comes irresistibly. The whole movement is permeated by premonitions of death.'

Deryck Cooke has suggested that Mahler took Tchaikovsky's *Pathétique* Symphony as a model for the Ninth, in spite of the fact that Mahler described this work to Adler as 'shallow, superficial, distressingly homophonic – no better than salon music'. Where the Russian followed his impassioned first movement with a waltz, Mahler returned to the pastoral *Ländler* which had served him well for light relief. For this movement is certainly light relief, even if presented with a heavy touch (it is marked 'rather clumsy and rough'). Those who perceive death in every bar of this symphony easily find a nightmarish quality in the humour – condemned man eating a hearty breakfast, I suppose. But if we regard it solely from its place in the symphonic scheme, we may see that Mahler had still not quite, but almost wholly, exhausted the musical possibilities of satirical *Ländlers*. The dance-themes are decked out in orchestration that is sometimes witty, sometimes grotesque, sometimes bizarre. There are two trios, in different *tempi*, the first a quick waltz, the second gentle and lilting, its theme based on the falling seconds of the first movement. The coda is Mahler at his spookiest, with the hollow sound of the horn as a spectral intruder.

For his third movement Tchaikovsky wrote his most brilliant march. Mahler too introduces a march tune into his novel Rondo-Burleske. This is in A minor like the first movement of *Das Lied*, which its resembles. Mahler dedicated this movement privately 'to my brothers in Apollo', implying a sarcastic parody of those who accused him of lack of contrapuntal skill. Its marking is 'very defiantly' and that is how it sounds – harsh, disjointed music built on short thematic cells, the first of which echoes figures from the second and third movements of the Fifth Symphony. When the trio section returns, it contains a parody of the march from the first movement of the Third – thus does Mahler continue to bind his works into one vast unity (see Ex. 25).

The prevailing high pitch of the movement is relaxed by a return to D major when first the trumpet, then the strings, transform one of the jagged rondo themes into a consoling diatonic theme characterized by its octave fall on B. But this is gradually ousted by the fiercer music, which erupts into a final outburst of savagery.

Ex. 25

(a) 9th Symphony

4 Horns

(b) 3rd Symphony

Woodwind *ppp*

After this comes the *Adagio* last movement. The key is D flat major (a semitone lower than the first movement) and after a short introductory flourish like a cry of despair, the strings play the solemn threnody which contains elements of several previous themes, including the Beethoven quotation and the first trio of the *Ländler scherzo*. As it progresses, this movement prophesies some of the writing by Mahler's heir-apparent, Berg, in its simultaneous use of strings in their highest register and basses at their lowest, and of wisps of theme drifting about in a sparse orchestral texture. But the emotional passion of the strings' main theme is never long absent, alternating in the style of a rondo with the woodwind's concertante episodes. There are references to the *Abschied* of *Das Lied von der Erde* and to the consolatory vision from the Rondo-Burleske, but the most significant cross-reference occurs just before the lingering fade-out when the strings quote, from the fourth of the *Kindertotenlieder*, the phrase associated with the children's imagined dwelling-place 'in the sunshine . . . on those heights':

Ex. 26

(a) 9th Symphony

ppp   ersterbend   zögernd   *ppp*

(b) Kindertotenlieder (original key E flat)

[Sonnen-]scheinl __ Der   Tag __ ist   schön __ auf je • nen Höh'nl

Is it right, therefore, to regard this movement as Mahler's obituary of himself, the egocentric wringing out the last drop of self-pity? That is the usual, Alma-inspired, view. Might it not be his requiem for his daughter, dead only two years when he began to compose it, and for his long-dead brothers and sisters, an elegy as touching as Berg's for Alma's daughter Manon Gropius in his Violin Concerto? Indeed, are we right to hang the label 'egocentric' round Mahler's neck at every opportunity? Allowing that every creator must give substance to his inner visions through the medium of personal experience, was not Mahler's principal preoccupation not so much his own destiny as that of mankind? He was a compassionate artist. His search for God or redemption is mankind's search. The 'hero' of his First and Second Symphonies is Mankind-Mahler, not merely Gustav Mahler. And are we not guilty of the naïveté of which Mahler is so boringly accused when we cry 'megalomaniac' because he said to Anna von Mildenburg: 'My Third Symphony reflects the whole world,' and told Bruno Walter not to bother to look at the mountains of the Salzkammergut because 'I've already composed it all'? Is this not the dedicated composer's joy in creation? Here is the essential Mahler in words he wrote to Alma while he was sketching the Ninth Symphony at Toblach in June 1909:

> The 'works' of this person or that . . . are the ephemeral and mortal part of him; but what a man makes of himself – what he becomes through the untiring effort to live and to be – is permanent . . . What we leave behind us is only the husk, the shell. The *Meistersinger*, the Ninth, *Faust* – all of them are only the discarded husk! No more, properly speaking, than our bodies are. I don't mean that artistic creation is superfluous. It is a necessity of men for growth and *joy*, which again is a question of health and creative energy. But what actual need is there of notes?

A great Mahler conductor told me that, notwithstanding the Third and Seventh, he regarded the Ninth as the most difficult of the symphonies, technically and interpretatively. He was perhaps acknowledging that, for all its masterly and close-knit organization, it has a fundamental structural weakness which only the most compelling performance will conceal. There is something top-heavy about it. Nothing, not even the lovely *Adagio*, is on the inspired level of the first movement; and although Mahler must have intended the Rondo-Burleske to be the balancing weight, there is something artificial and contrived about that movement so that it fails to carry full conviction.

The history of the Tenth Symphony is fascinating. For thirteen years after Mahler's death Alma kept the sketches locked away. In 1924, on advice from Richard Specht, she published them in a 116-page photographic facsimile,[1] though it has since transpired that she did not publish them all. Her twenty-four-year-old son-in-law (husband of Anna Mahler) Ernst Křenek, with some help from Berg and Franz Schalk, prepared a performing version of the first and third movements which was played in Vienna in the autumn of 1924. These movements were published in 1951 (with unacknowledged instrumental retouchings by Zemlinsky and Schalk) by Associated Music Publishers of New York under the editorship of a Berg pupil, Otto Jokl. Specht, incidentally, had suggested that a performing version should be prepared 'by some musician of high standing who is devoted to Mahler and intimate with his style and who, by comparing the sketches and completed scores of his earlier works, would surely find the right way to the goal'. Specht died in 1932 and it was not until 1942 that the Mahler scholar Jack Diether took up his suggestion and approached Shostakovich, who refused. Similarly, in 1949, Schoenberg declared himself unable to attempt such a task. It is unlikely, in any case, that a composer, with an individual style, would have been able to obscure his own musical *persona* sufficiently.

In 1960, to mark the centenary of Mahler's birth, the British Broadcasting Corporation performed the nine symphonies and published a booklet about them by Deryck Cooke. He found himself unable to discuss the Tenth on the basis of the two published movements and proceeded to copy the manuscript himself as a means of thorough study. He then proposed a broadcast talk with orchestral illustrations. As he worked on the sketches, he discovered that they were far more than the disconnected assortment of jottings which others had dismissed as making no sense. In his own words, he had deciphered 'not a "might-have-been", but an "almost-is": five full-length movements in various stages of textural completion, but all sufficiently coherent to add up to a magnificent Symphony in F sharp, a symphony in two parts'.[2] Working with the conductor

[1] Published by the Paul Zsolnay Verlag (Berlin, Vienna, Leipzig).
[2] D. Cooke: 'Mahler's Unfinished Symphony', *The Listener*, 15th December 1960.

Berthold Goldschmidt, he was able for the broadcast on 19th December 1960 to offer the first, third and fifth movements complete and substantial fragments of the second and fourth.

The broadcast had several results. Cooke learned that other performing versions existed, though none had yet been heard; he was urged to complete his task, though Alma forbade re-broadcasts of the programme and any further performances. Three years later, after earnest representations on Cooke's behalf, she lifted the ban, although certain distinguished Mahlerians, among them Bruno Walter and Erwin Ratz, continued to maintain that the symphony should not be performed. However, Cooke was able to complete his performing version when a further forty-three pages of manuscript, including practically all the short score of the second movement, were made available to him. So the work was performed in London in August 1964, and introduced to America by Eugene Ormandy at Philadelphia on 5th November 1965. After that Cooke made further revisions based on later research.

It is important to know what Cooke had to work from. Mahler follows his usual practice of building a full-length sketch in four-stave 'open' score, with some indications of intended orchestration. He left five folders of these sketches, each representing a movement continuous from start to finish. Next he would elaborate this four-stave score into a full-score sketch. Half-way through this process he died and so did not begin the final stage of writing a definitive full score. But he left no doubt of the order of the movements, marking them from I to V in blue pencil on the folders. All that Cooke claimed[3] for his 'performing version' was that it represented 'the stage that the Tenth Symphony had reached when Mahler died'. It

---

[3] Readers interested in detailed accounts of the reconstruction are referred to three important articles by Cooke from which I quote in this chapter: in *The Listener*, op. cit.; 'Mahler's Tenth Symphony: sonority, texture and substance', *Composer*, No. 16, July 1965, pp. 2–8; and programme-note for Royal Liverpool Philharmonic Society concert, 23rd April 1968. Even more important are his introduction and explanatory notes included in the published full score of the symphony (A.M.P./Faber, 1976).

Extensive discussion *pro* and *con* Cooke's performing version may be read in these articles: William Malloch: 'Deryck Cooke's Mahler Tenth: an Interim Report', *Music Review*, Vol. XXIII (1962), pp. 292–304; D. Cooke's letter in reply, *Music Review*, Vol. XXIV (1963), pp. 95–6; and Charles Reid: 'Mahler's Tenth', *Music Review*, Vol. XXVI (1965), pp. 318–325.

cannot in any way be thought of as an intended completion of the symphony . . . If Mahler had lived to complete the work, he would have elaborated the music considerably, refined and perfected it in a thousand details, expanded or contracted or transposed a passage here or there, and of course clothed it in orchestral sound of a subtlety and vividness beyond all our conjectures.

On this last point, Cooke emphasized that 'approached purely as a Mahler sound-texture [the symphony] scarcely exists after bar 28 of the second movement (and not fully, in every detail, anywhere)'. Yet he believed he divined Mahler's essential orchestration to within eighty per cent: 'Mahler conceived his music orchestrally, and his short scores are blueprints of instrumentation; if studied and auralized persistently enough, they score themselves – in essentials.' Was Cooke's, then, a presumptuous undertaking, unjustified on moral and æsthetic grounds, as some still think? No. He believed, and I do, that the music, even in its unrevised state, has

such strength and beauty that it dwarfs into insignificance the few momentary uncertainties about notes and the subsidiary additions, and even survives being presented in conjectural orchestration. After all, the leading thematic line throughout, and something like ninety per cent of the counterpoint and harmony, are pure Mahler, and vintage Mahler at that.

Shortly before he died in 1976, Cooke wrote to me: 'The cards are on the table now, and people will be able to make up their own minds. I am sure it will be accepted because the whole *substance* of it is *Mahler*, after all. Even the orchestration of the last three movements *sounds* Mahlerian in essence – which is simply because I retained his harmonic spacing without adding any middle-register filling.' Cooke would not have objected to a continuous process of revisions and amendments to his version by sympathetic conductors, for example Simon Rattle who, in his 1980 recording added (with Berthold Goldschmidt's approval) percussion to the central climax of the finale, omitted the xylophone and substituted bass clarinet for bassoon at one point in the first movement. Rattle is convinced that 'the guillotine blow before the finale should link the two movements'. Others who have worked on performing versions of the symphony are Joe Wheeler in Britain, Clinton Carpenter in the United States and Hans Wollschläger in Germany. Carpenter's version, completed in 1966, was performed in England for the first time on 15th April 1987 at Poole, Dorset, by the Bournemouth Symphony Orchestra conducted by Harold Farbermann. Carpenter was less inhibited than Cooke, in several places inventing counterpoint and often preferring horns to Cooke's woodwind. There are inspired touches. At the opening of the finale, the slow ascending theme is given to double basses instead of bass tuba, a gain in smoothness though a loss in starkness. A reprise of the main theme of this movement is given to strings *fortissimo* instead of horns. The drum strokes are muffled. More controversially, in the first movement Carpenter has inserted an aggressive timpani part and a cymbal clash to end the climactic discord.

The world of music owes an incalculable debt to Deryck Cooke for three reasons: he enabled us to hear what must at the lowest estimate be called a remarkable approximation to Mahler's intentions; and he thereby completely altered the emotional interpretation of Mahler's last year. It is apparent from this symphony that it is wrong to regard Mahler as having died in a mood of valediction, defeated or resigned to the inevitable – assuming, which I do not, that the *Adagio-Finale* of No. 9 is a heartbroken egocentric leave-taking. No. 10 is a symphony which transcends thoughts of death and ends with a gloriously affirmatory and positive assertion of a man's spiritual victory. Thirdly, it establishes beyond doubt that Mahler was entering a new phase, in some ways simpler than the complex Ninth Symphony, yet even more prophetic of the collapse of tonality and, paradoxically, even more insistent upon the Classical-Romantic procedures which had always nurtured him.

There is the subsidiary matter of the imprecations to Alma written on the score which are painful to read because of their anguish and have misled some writers into a belief that the symphony was the work of a near-madman. These messages are connected with the Gropius affair of 1910. Perhaps this symphony reflects that experience, at least in part, but whatever passions swept him, they had no effect on his cool brain. There are many examples of the 'schizophrenia' of creative geniuses, of composers writing comic operas, for instance, while their personal world fell about their ears. Ordinary mortals habitually underestimate the ability of such men to concentrate on their work to the exclusion of all else.

Thanks to Cooke, it can be asserted that the Tenth Symphony is (or was to be) greater than the Ninth: it is better balanced and more thoroughly composed. The design is symmetrical: outer movements of about twenty minutes, *scherzos* (second and fourth) of about eleven minutes and a central movement of just under five minutes. Like the Fifth Symphony, it is in two parts, Part I an *Adagio* followed by *Scherzo I*, Part II an *Allegretto moderato* from which *Scherzo II* and the Finale derive their principal material. The opening *Adagio* is a marvellous elegy, more moving than the Finale of No. 9, its main theme (violas) of Brucknerian breadth and richness of harmony, borne aloft on a pulsing *pizzicato*. But it is not long before the strings are in their upper register, almost at the screaming-pitch that occasions Mahler to be labelled neurotic, although it is his obsessive concern for clarity and avoidance of muddy textures that is the musical reason for this stylistic feature (derived from Beethoven). All the European music of the 1920s seems to be stirring in the womb of this movement – *Wozzeck*, *Lulu* and others crying to be born. We are in a different sound-world from the Ninth Symphony. Its tensions and complexities boil up into an astonishing nine-note dissonance for the full orchestra pierced by a high A on the trumpet. A kind of serenity returns in the beautiful coda but one senses that nothing can be quite the same again.

Scherzo I in F sharp minor is more successful than its counterpart in the Ninth, its opening dance delightfully rhythmical and Haydn-like, its two trios respectively graceful and nostalgic before the jagged strings bring it to an exuberant end. No ghosts to lay there, but what of the enigmatic little movement that opens Part II and is known as *Purgatorio*? Mahler wrote the words 'Purgatorio or Inferno' on the score of this *Allegretto moderato* in B flat minor, then deleted the last two words. Was this a reference to his state of mind during the matrimonial crisis, was it because in 1910 he was re-reading the poems of his friend Lipiner, one of which has this title, or has it some bearing on the music, which is like a ghostly *danse macabre* and uses the *ostinato* accompaniment from his *Wunderhorn* song *Das irdische Leben* (about the child who dies from starvation)? There are sudden irruptions of warmth and a final impassioned question. Mahler wrote what can be taken as an almost perfect description of this movement fourteen years earlier in a letter to Marschalk about the Second Symphony's third movement:[4]

This surge of life, ceaselessly in motion, never resting, never

---

[4] 26th March, 1896, from Hamburg.

comprehensible, suddenly seems *eerie*, like the billowing of dancing figures in a brightly lit ballroom that you gaze into from outside in the dark – and from a *distance* so great that you can *no longer* hear the *music*! Life then becomes meaningless, an eerie phantom state out of which you may start up with a cry of disgust.

Some have called *Purgatorio* trivial, but its triviality is of the same kind as the short movements of Beethoven's late quartets. It is, whatever its emotional connotation, a vital factor in the design of the symphony. It is followed by *Scherzo II, allegro pesante*, beginning in E minor and ending in D minor. Here Mahler achieved the diabolism which he failed to bring off totally in the Rondo-Burleske. On the score he wrote: 'The devil dances it with me, madness takes hold of me, cursed one'; and there is a terrifying savagery in this music. But it is not overdone, and the thematic material is more distinctive. A theme from the *Purgatorio* becomes a slow waltz, there is a parody of the central orchestral interlude from the finale of *Das Lied von der Erde* and a direct quotation from that work's first movement where the drinker sings that 'joy and singing wither and die'. The movement ends with a Stravinskyan passage for percussion (timpani, bass drum and cymbals). Its last note is a single funereal crack on a muffled drum.

'Only you know what it means,' he wrote, to Alma, on the score. He was referring to an incident in New York during their first visit (December 1907–April 1908) when they stayed at the Hotel Majestic overlooking Central Park. The cortège of a fireman who had died heroically halted beneath their windows. Before it moved on there was a brief stroke on a muffled drum. Mahler, ever susceptible, watched with tears streaming down his cheeks. This incident occurred on Sunday afternoon, 16th February 1908. The funeral was of Charles W. Kruger, Deputy Chief of the City of New York Fire Department, commanding the 2nd Division, who died from injuries received while fighting a fire at 217 Canal Street at 1 a.m. on 14th February. He had been in the fire service for thirty-six years.

The drum-stroke opens the finale, which continues the key of D minor. Six times this sound of mortality is heard, while the bass tuba and horns intensify the solemn mood. The tuba's theme is a slow version of the *Purgatorio* dance. A long, sinuous melody for the solo flute, poignant with hope (and derived from the slow waltz of

Scherzo II), leads the music back to Brucknerian rapture, the strings' warmth suggesting the sun returning in spring. But this new life is cut short by the funeral drum and the tuba's theme. Mahler now introduces a central *Allegro* in which all the *Purgatorio* themes are developed and contrasted with a lyrical 'yearning' theme. The climax of this section is the dissonant chord from the *Adagio* and its trumpet note, followed by a progressively more lyrical and impassioned episode as the music returns to F sharp major and the violas' theme from the *Adagio* becomes a great song of life and love – the most fervently intense ending to any Mahler symphony and a triumphant vindication of his spiritual courage.

Mahler died on the full crest of his creative powers. What would his Eleventh Symphony have been like? Would he have moved further along the path which his followers were to take? Useless to speculate, of course, especially as one fears to think of the effect on such a sensitive man of the carnage of the First World War. But it remains uncanny to think that he would have celebrated his eightieth birthday in 1940, would have heard the great works of Berg, Bartók and Stravinsky and the twelve-note revolution of Schoenberg. He would have seen the rape of his native Czechoslovakia and Austria; and his conversion to Catholicism would not have saved him from permanent exile with so many other Jews. And we should not forget that his niece Alma Rosé, daughter of his sister Justine and her husband Arnold Rosé, perished in Auschwitz, where she had conducted the famous 'women's orchestra'.

Wherein lies Mahler's immense appeal? He is not so easy to listen to as Tchaikovsky; he wrote no concerto with which brilliant executants can display their skill; his brand of nostalgia is not the sensuous heartbreak so marvellously expressed by Delius in *Sea-Drift*, but a spiritual longing for loneliness; he offers us no certainty as a result of his constant search for an answer to the questions which bewildered him: he is often contradictory, and Bruno Walter called his attitude 'desultory'.

But although the emotional and autobiographical elements of Mahler's music should never be left out of account, he must be judged primarily as a musician – and not exclusively as a musician whose anticipation of the future is so remarkable. He must be assessed on what he did, not on what others took and developed from him. After all, even his most advanced passages are basically within the context of the nineteenth century. Taking a hint from

Berlioz, he created the orchestral song-cycle, realizing that the complex emotions of Romantic poetry required the resources of an orchestra to do them justice. With *Das Lied von der Erde* he created a new form from which have sprung Britten's *Spring Symphony* and *Nocturne* and Shostakovich's Fourteenth Symphony, to name but three. He showed that the symphony was still a valid and fruitful form, and he did this by expansion, as it were, while his contemporary, Sibelius, also put new life into the symphony by compression. He created an entirely individual sound, unmistakable, inimitable – a Mahler world.

It is true that there is an element of the actor in Mahler, that he strikes attitudes not from conviction but as a spiritual experiment. But the result is never insincere. To some temperaments he will always be anathema because it is felt that he did not subject his musical thought-processes to enough refining self-criticism, that he was too much the suffering human and not sufficiently the detached artist. There is something in this, though study of his scores reveals a musical headwork, as Shaw would have described it, of a peculiarly intricate nature.

'Thrice homeless . . . always an outsider,' he said. 'How alien and lonely I feel at times.' This lack of identification with any roots is surely the fundamental cause of the contrasts and conflicts in his music and therefore a source of artistic strength. Born in Bohemia, he developed very differently from his contemporary, the Moravian Janáček. He turns a quizzical, detached musical eye on both the folksongs of his boyhood and the sophisticated Viennese music of his manhood. Yet this sense of alienation in no way detracts from the emotional impact of his music. Its compassion, its humanity, its wry humour, shine through its complexities, its self-questioning, its anguished doubting. Those who love Mahler's music may give a variety of reasons for their love. Common to them all, I believe, would be agreement with Schoenberg: 'I sensed a human being, a drama, *truth*, the most ruthless truth.' In a world of collapsing values Mahler's truth about music and about Mahler is something to cherish.

16

Afterthoughts

In the decade since I revised this book, research on Mahler has continued unabated. New books about him have been written, wonderful facsimile editions of some of his scores have been issued, and performances
and recordings of his music have multiplied. As the twenty-first century
arrives, there seems little likelihood of any diminution of interest in any
aspect of Mahler. Much of the latest research has been brought together
in one large and handsome volume, *The Mahler Companion* (Oxford,
1999), edited by Britain's leading and indefatigable Mahler scholar
Donald Mitchell and by Andrew Nicholson. It is to this book that I am
indebted for most of this chapter, a debt I acknowledge with gratitude.

The early cantata *Das klagende Lied* was heard in 1997 for the first
time in its original form and scoring and has since been recorded.
Mahler himself never heard this 1880 version, in which there were four
soloists, an off-stage band and a children's choir. This original version
is more radical than the two-movement version which Mahler eventually conducted in Vienna in February 1901 after a lengthy process of
revision, begun in Hamburg in 1893. That Mahler recognized how far
advanced his 'child of sorrow' was is shown in a letter to his sister
Justine on 17 December 1893: 'The nuts that my tree produced at that
time are perhaps the hardest to crack of all those I have offered to the
world'. His revisions were directed towards making the cantata easier
(and less expensive) to perform. He reduced the harps from six to two
and omitted D flat flutes and E flat cornets in favour of more common
orchestral instruments. The off-stage band was deleted from the second
and third movements (*Der Spielmann* and *Hochzeitsstück*) but was
restored to the third movement in the 1898 revision before publication.

Until 1997 the three-movement version had been performed since
1970 in a hybrid edition: the original unrevised score of the first movement, *Waldmärchen* (which had been bequeathed by Justine to her son
Alfred Rosé, who conducted it on Czech Radio in 1934) together with
Mahler's revised scores of *Der Spielmann* and *Hochzeitsstück*. Among
the differences from the revised version which may be heard in Kent
Nagano's 1997 recording are the use of more clarinets than oboes and

of more horns than trumpets and trombones. In *Der Spielmann*, an extra section of trumpets and timpani enters when the minstrel carves a flute from the bone of the murdered younger brother. The orchestral passage which follows harks back to an episode in *Waldmärchen* and anticipates the wedding music in *Hochzeitsstück*. Three-in-a-bar is played against four-in-a-bar, with C flat major in the main orchestra and C major in the off-stage band. Similar rhythmical and harmonic dissonances of an Ivesian character recur in *Hochzeitsstück*. The choral writing and the use of boys' voices in the original version are strikingly vivid. As Donald Mitchell has pointed out, Mahler's preoccupation with indicating *precisely* the sound effect he was after emerged, virtually fully fledged, at a time when he had had only the barest experience of conducting or working with an orchestra. The 1880 *Das klagende Lied* is an even more important and significant work than anyone had realized.

Further documentation of Symphony No. 5 comes from the score which was used by Willem Mengelberg when he was conductor of the Concertgebouw Orchestra of Amsterdam. Inscriptions on the flyleaf are followed by Mengelberg's heavily underlined declaration: 'These were Mahler's very own words'. This refers to the detailed programme of the symphony (in which Mengelberg classifies the first and second movements as a single movement):

First movement: deepest sorrow, melancholy, sadness—tears, tears!—a face distorted by constant weeping—worn out by violent outbreaks of despair, fury, frenzy close to madness (laughing!!! !!!) The end: half delirious with sorrow, gruesome, ghostly

Second movement: forced gaiety—wants to get over suffering—but it can't be yet; sounds forced, sad undertone—here and there a Dance of Death.

Third movement: *Love, love comes into his life!* return to nature, motif of nature d c♯ b a first motif. Then comes the fourth's entry d a, a b c♯ d—

Fourth movement: friendly—exuberant gaiety, starts with a mood of happiness and contentedness—more and more 'exuberant'. The end: mad with joy and happiness.

Mengelberg's description of the *Adagietto* as Mahler's declaration of love for Alma (see p. 138) has been sceptically received by the scholar Henry-Louis de La Grange, who is surprised that Alma never mentioned the episode in her diary and never boasted about it in later life, as one might have expected of her. Mitchell, on the other hand, is more convinced and finds in it clues to the chronology of composition of the symphony. Presumably Mahler gave Alma a sketch or a completed short score of the movement before their official engagement at the end of December 1901. In which case the *Adagietto* may have been sketched or composed very soon after the *Scherzo* (the first movement to be composed) and the first and second movements. This also means that it was composed very soon after the Rückert song *Ich bin der Welt abhanden gekommen* to which it is so often compared (although Mitchell thinks that there is more to be gained from a comparison with *Nun seh' ich wohl*, the second of the *Kindertotenlieder*).

Mahler's many revisions of the orchestration of this symphony have been extensively documented and can be studied at length in *The Mahler Companion* and also in the book wholly devoted to the symphony, *New Sounds, New Century* (Amsterdam 1997). His last revisions were made in the last year of his life. Together with his earlier revisions of both the orchestral parts and of the full score, these created what has been called by Paul Banks 'a tangled web of sources'. The 'new version' of the score, put together from these sources, was first performed in Leipzig on 9 January 1914, conducted by Georg Göhler. No published full score incorporated all Mahler's revisions until 1964 when the fifth volume of the Collected Works appeared. In this context, there is a particular interest in the recording by the Royal Concertgebouw Orchestra of Amsterdam, conducted by Riccardo Chailly (issued with *New Sounds, New Century*) of the 1904 orchestration of the second trio from the *Trauermarsch* (first movement). This had not previously been heard since Mahler conducted the Vienna Philharmonic in a play-through of the symphony in 1904. On the disc is the same passage as revised and published in the 1919 edition of the full score. The passage as printed in the 1904 study score is reproduced, showing additions and amendments, in *New Sounds, New Century*.

The character of the Fifth Symphony—its progress from the stormy and funereal beginning through love of nature and love of woman to the final joyous abandon—can now be seen to be related to the haemorrhage Mahler suffered in February 1901 from which it appears that he nearly died. Recovered, he composed in the summer of 1901 at Maiernigg eight songs with orchestra and three—perhaps four—movements of the Fifth Symphony. The shock of his brush with death is reflected in the gloomy character of some of the music he wrote: three of the *Kindertotenlieder*, *Der Tamboursg'sell* and *Um Mitternacht* and the first two movements of the symphony, while the Rückert settings *Ich bin der Welt* and *Ich atmet' einen Lindenduft* are almost other-worldly meditations. Only the *Scherzo* of the symphony expressed some happiness. Yet we have his words about this movement as quoted by Mengelberg: 'Forced gaiety . . . sad undertone . . . here and there a Dance of Death'. And there are certainly dark, frenetic moments in the movement. Richard Specht in his 1905 monograph on Mahler quotes Bruno Walter (who would in all probability have heard it from Mahler) as saying that the *Scherzo* grew from Goethe's poem *An Schwager Kronos* (To

Brother Time the Coachman)—set by Schubert (D 369). It can be paraphrased thus:

Hurry on, Time, at a rattling trot! On briskly, over stick and stone, stumbling headlong into life! High, wide and glorious the prospect of life rings us round. A shadowy doorway beckons you aside across the threshold of the girl's house, and her eyes promise refreshment. Take comfort! Down then, faster down! See, the sun sinks. Before it sets. Before the mist from the marshes envelops me in old age, snatch me, drunk with the sun's last ray, a sea of fire boiling up before my eyes, blind and reeling through the dark gate of hell. Blow your horn, brother, clatter on at a noisy trot. Let Orcus know we are coming, so that mine host will be at the door to welcome us.

Like Mahler's *Scherzo*, Schubert's song is marked *Nicht zu schnell* and ends, like the *Scherzo*, in D major.

The *Scherzo* is dominated—like Goethe's poem—by the sound of the horn(s), and Donald Mirchell has called it 'the horn concerto that Mahler never wrote'. Dr Mitchell was present at the first British public performance of the symphony in the Stoll Theatre, London, on 21 October 1945 when the conductor, Heinz Unger, for this movement placed the first horn at the front of the platform close to the leader. Unger evidently knew of Mengelberg's note in his score: 'The first horn should always stand out and be placed at the front next to the leader'. Undoubtedly he learned this from Mahler. The tradition is followed by Chailly in his 1997 recording.

Whether the *Adagietto* was or was not a 'love letter' to Alma, the Rückert song *Liebst du um Schönheit* certainly was. Her story that Mahler slipped it between the title-page and first page of her score of Wagner's *Die Walküre* is now shown by her autograph diary entry to be wrong: the score was that of *Siegfried*. (She also got the date wrong. It happened on 10 August 1902, not 1903.) Of more significance is Mahler's choice of poem. I am indebted to Donald Mitchell for the suggestion that Mahler guiltily set *Liebst du um Schönheit* because it had been set by Clara Schumann and he knew that Alma, whom he had ordered to give up her own song-writing, would also know that Clara's setting, from her Op. 12, had been published in 1841 together with Robert Schumann's seven *Lieder* and two duets as their joint Opus 37/12.

The vexed question of the order of the middle two movements, *Andante* and *Scherzo*, in the Sixth Symphony (discussed on pp. 139–40) is further dissected in *The Mahler Companion* by David Matthews. It has been established beyond doubt that on the three occasions when Mahler conducted No. 6, he placed the *Andante* second and the *Scherzo* third. This is how Mengelberg conducted it in the first Dutch performance in 1916 but, for a repeat performance in 1919, he asked Alma about the order and received the reply 'Erst Scherzo dann Andante'.

Matthews infers from this that Mahler had told her that he wished to revert to that order. But there is no proof. Matthews now believes this order is the more satisfactory. Paul Banks argues that because of Mahler's indecision, one has to think of two versions of the symphony. The advantage of compact discs is that the listener can decide in which order to hear these movements.

Less controversial is the case of 'the third hammer-blow of fate' which Mahler removed after the first performance because of superstition that it might be prophetic (in his case it was). He also thinned the orchestration and reduced the dynamics at this point. Both David Matthews and Norman Del Mar (in his *Mahler's Sixth Symphony*) argue for restoration of this blow and for reversion to the original scoring. Sir Simon Rattle's 1989 recording restores it. As Del Mar wrote (p. 152 of his book): 'Fate cannot still be felt to stand threateningly over the composer who has been dead and beyond her menace, real or imaginary, for over sixty [now nearly ninety] years. Superstition must play no further part in what is now primarily an artistic decision'.

Some recent research on the Seventh Symphony has concentrated on the true whereabouts of the first performance in Prague. The Swiss critic, William Ritter, describes rehearsals and the première in September 1908 as taking place 'in a hall which doubled as a banqueting hall. Here, while the Master and the orchestra were making strenuous efforts to rehearse on a very steep platform, the waiters would be laying the tables'. This hall has now been identified not as the Civic Hall (Obecní dům), built between 1905 and 1911, but as the Concert Pavilion (Koncertní síň), a timber hall seating 1,500, designed by Josef Zasche and built in the grounds of the Exhibition mounted by Prague Chamber of Commerce and Crafts to mark the sixtieth anniversary in 1908 of the accession of Emperor Franz Josef I. It has now been demolished. This means also that the photograph purporting to be of Mahler rehearsing the Seventh Symphony, reproduced on p. 41 of the 1995 facsimile edition of the Seventh Symphony and as No. 102 in Gilbert Kaplan's *The Mahler Album* (1995), is of him rehearsing a programme of Smetana, Wagner and Beethoven (Seventh Symphony) in the Merkur Society's hall in Prague in May 1908. The orchestra shown in the photograph consists of about 65 players and could not possibly have performed Mahler's Seventh.

Colin Matthews's fascinating chapter in *The Mahler Companion* on the Tenth Symphony points out that although 165 pages of manuscript sketches survived, many more are undoubtedly missing. Among these he specifies pages 6 and 7 of the opening *Adagio* short score and 1–3 of the composition sketch of the fourth movement. The first movement was initially much shorter and may have begun without the violas' introduction. Because the draft score of the movement can be played as it stands, it has been assumed that it was Mahler's final thoughts. This is not so; and David Matthews has suggested that Alma removed some of the pages because they contained inscriptions in Mahler's handwriting even more personal than those which have survived. This particularly relates to the lower half of the title-page of the third movement (*Purgatorio*) which has been cut away. Knud Martner has suggested that perhaps Mahler (who knew of Alma's adultery with Walter Gropius) wrote on this page a verse from his friend Siegfried Lipiner's sequence of 19 poems called 'Il Purgatorio'. Perhaps, he guesses, two verses ending: 'I cannot look you in the eye, as *you* are not ashamed, it is *I* who am: alas, I still love you'. Two of Mahler's inscriptions on the manuscript of *Purgatorio* refer to Wagner's *Parsifal*, and David Matthews is eloquent on the musical influence of *Parsifal* on the symphony. Mahler wrote *Erbarmen* ('Have mercy!') on his manuscript near a passage derived from the *Erbarmen* music of *Parsifal*. *Erbarmen* is the cry of Amfortas, whose wound will not heal; Mahler, wounded by Alma's betrayal, cried for his wound to be healed.

And when was *Das Lied von der Erde* composed? It is now known that Hans Bethge's *Die chinesische Flöte* was published on 5 October 1907 but was reviewed in a Leipzig publication on 8 July 1907 (according to de La Grange in his *Gustav Mahler. Vienna: Triumph and Disillusion* (1904–1907) (Oxford, 2000, p. 700, fn. 287)). Alma's statement that Mahler made some sketches for the music on walks in the woods around Schluderbach in the summer of 1907 is therefore probably accurate. Dated manuscripts show that the whole work was completed in the summer of 1908. Of special interest is the distribution of the solo voices in this work. Preliminary manuscripts show that Mahler was at first undecided. The short score and autograph keyboard version of the third song (*Von der Jugend*) indicate it as for tenor or soprano. The keyboard MS gives the first song to the tenor, the second simply to 'voice' and Nos. 4, 5 and 6 are unspecified. By the time of the autograph full score Nos. 1, 3 and 5 were allocated to tenor, Nos. 2, 4 and 6 for 'Alt-solo', 'Alt-Stimme' and 'Alt' respectively. Only in a printer's manuscript written by a copyist, at the first entrance of the Alt-Stimme in the second song, did Mahler write 'Could possibly be taken over by baritone'. He did not make this suggestion for Nos. 4 and 6. At no time did he give baritone as an alternative to contralto for the whole work. Bruno Walter substituted a baritone (Friedrich Weidemann) for the contralto at the first Vienna performance on 4 November 1912. 'Never again', he wrote to Wolfgang Stresemann in December 1957. 'From then on I have always used an alto voice . . . two male voices do the work no good. Mahler never heard *Das Lied von der Erde*—in my firm conviction, based on practical experience, he himself would have realized the error of giving the three songs to a baritone'.

Appendix A

Calendar

(Figures in brackets denote the age reached by the person mentioned during the year in question)

Year	Age	Life	Contemporary Musicians and Events
1860		Gustav Mahler born July 7 at Kališt, Bohemia, son of Bernhard Mahler (32) and Marie, née Hermann (23). Family move to Iglau (Jihlava) in December.	Wolf born, March 13; Albéniz born, May 29; Charpentier born, June 25; Paderewski born, Nov. 6; Berlioz 57; Bizet 22; Humperdinck 6; Marschner 65; Rossini 68; Smetana 36; J. Strauss (ii) 35; Wagner 47; Brahms (27) signs manifesto against 'the New Music'.
1866	6	Learns piano, goes to school.	Busoni born, April 1; Satie born, May 17; Debussy 4; Delius 4; Elgar 9; Weingartner 3; R. Strauss 2; Nielsen 1; Sibelius 1.
1869	9	Studies under piano-teacher Brosch and himself teaches younger boy.	Vienna Hofoper on Ringstrasse opens, May 25.
1870	10	Gives public recital in Iglau, Oct. 13.	Lehár born, April 30; Schmitt born, Sept. 28; Pfitzner 1; Franco-Prussian War; first Vienna *Meistersinger*, Feb. 27.
1871	11	Studying at Prague Gymnasium.	Mengelberg born, March 28; Auber (89) dies, May 12.

Year	Age	Life	Contemporary Musicians and Events
1874	14	His brother Ernst (13) dies.	Holst born, Sept. 21; Ives born, Oct. 20; Schoenberg born, Sept. 13; Skriabin 2; Vaughan Williams 2; Zemlinsky 2; Rakhmaninov 1; Reger 1.
1875	15	Enters Vienna Conservatory, Sept. 20. Begins opera *Herzog Ernst von Schwaben*.	Ravel born, March 7; Bizet (36) dies, June 3; Richter (32) becomes conductor, Vienna Hofoper.
1876	16	Wins prizes for piano and composition. Performs in his piano quintet in Vienna, July 10, and Iglau, Sept. 12, and in his violin sonata, Iglau, Sept. 12.	Falla born, Nov. 23; Bruno Walter born, Sept. 15; first cycle of *Ring*, Bayreuth, Aug. 13–17; Brahms's Symphony No. 1, first perfs.: Carlsruhe, Nov. 6, Vienna, Dec. 17.
1877	17	Wins another piano prize. Matriculates at Iglau. Asked by Bruckner (53) to make two-piano arrangement of his Symphony No. 3.	Dohnányi born, July 27; first Vienna *Walküre*, March 5; Brahms's Symphony No. 2, first perf., Vienna, Dec. 30.
1878	18	Leaves Conservatory, July 11. Gives piano lessons. Begins to write words of cantata *Das klagende Lied*. Attends Vienna University lectures on philosophy and history of painting.	First Vienna performances of *Rheingold*, Jan. 24, and of *Siegfried*, Nov. 9.
1879	19	Piano tutor in Hungary and Vienna.	Alma Schindler born, Aug. 31; Medtner born, Dec. 24. First Vienna *Götterdämmerung*, Feb. 14; *Ring*, May 26–30.

Mahler

Year	Age	Life	Contemporary Musicians and Events
1880	20	Three songs composed, Feb. and March. Conducts during summer at Hall spa. Completes *Das klagende Lied*, Nov. 1. Begins opera *Die Argonauten*.	Pizzetti born, Sept. 20.
1881	21	*Das klagende Lied* fails to win Beethoven Prize. Conducts at Laibach. Begins opera *Rübezahl*.	Bartók born, March 25; Mussorgsky (42) dies, March 28.
1882	22	Conducts at Iglau.	Kodály born, Dec. 16; Stravinsky born, June 17; first perf. of *Parsifal*, Bayreuth, July 25; Berlin Philharmonic Orch. founded.
1883	23	Conducts at Olmütz (Jan.). Visits Bayreuth, July. Appointed second conductor at Cassel court theatre.	Webern born, Dec. 3; Wagner (69) dies, Feb. 13. First perf. of Brahms's Symphony No. 3, Vienna, Dec. 2; first Vienna *Tristan*, Oct. 4.
1884	24	Composes incidental music for *Der Trompeter von Säkkingen*. Begins Symphony No. 1. Composes *Lieder eines fahrenden Gesellen*, Dec.	Smetana (60) dies, May 12; Bruckner's Symphony 7, first perf., Leipzig, Dec. 30.
1885	25	End of his love affair with Johanna Richter. Leaves Cassel post, July 1. Appointed second conductor, Deutsches Landestheater, Prague. Notable success as interpreter of Wagner and Mozart operas.	Berg born, Feb. 9; Wellesz born, Oct. 21; first perf. of Brahms's Symphony No. 4, Meiningen, Oct. 25.

Year	Age	Life	Contemporary Musicians and Events
1886	26	Three songs performed at Prague, April. Second conductor (under Nikisch) at Leipzig, Aug.	Liszt (74) dies, July 31. R. Strauss conductor at Meiningen.
1887	27	Conducts first *Siegfried* at Leipzig. Works on completing Weber's *Die drei Pintos*. Affair with Mathilde von Weber. Offered opera post in New York. Completing Symphony No. 1.	First perf. of Verdi's *Otello*, Milan, Feb. 5.
1888	28	First perf. *Die drei Pintos*, Leipzig, Jan. 20. Meets R. Strauss. Resigns Leipzig post, May. Returns to Prague in summer, but is dismissed after quarrel. Becomes musical director, Budapest opera. Begins Symphony No. 2.	Alkan (74) dies, March 29; N. Cardus born, April 3.
1889	29	Father dies, Feb. 18 and mother, Oct. 11. Symphony No. 1 first perf. Budapest, Nov. 20 (under title Symphonic Poem).	Boult born, April 8. First perf. of Strauss's *Don Juan*, Weimar, Nov. 11.
1890	30	Holiday in Italy with his sister Justine.	Franck (67) dies, Nov. 8.
1891	31	After quarrel with new Budapest Intendant, M. resigns, March 14. Begins as chief conductor, Hamburg, March 29. Plays part of Symphony No. 2 to Hans von Bülow. Holiday in Norway.	Prokofiev born, April 23.

Year	Age	Life	Contemporary Musicians and Events
1892	32	Visit to London as conductor, June and July. Vols. I, II and III of *Lieder und Gesänge* published. Songs with orchestra performed in Hamburg and Berlin.	First perf. of Bruckner's Symphony No. 8, Vienna, Dec. 18.
1893	33	Spends summer at Steinbach-am-Attersee where he works on Symphony No. 2. Symphony No. 1 performed in Hamburg, Oct. 27.	Tchaikovsky (53) dies, Nov. 6; first perf. of Verdi's *Falstaff*, Milan, Feb. 9.
1894	34	Symphony No. 1 (with sub-title *Titan*) performed Weimar Festival, June 29; Symphony No. 2 completed, Steinbach, July 25. Succeeds Bülow as conductor of Hamburg symphony concerts.	Bülow (63) dies, Feb. 12; first perf. of Bruckner's Symphony No. 5, Graz, April 8.
1895	35	His brother Otto shoots himself, Feb. M. conducts first three movements of Symphony No. 2, Berlin, March 4, and complete Symphony, Berlin, Dec. 13. Begins Symphony No. 3 at Steinbach in summer.	Hindemith born, Nov. 16; first perf. of Strauss's *Till Eulenspiegel*, Cologne, Nov. 5.
1896	36	First performance of *Lieder eines fahrenden Gesellen* and four-movement version of Symphony No. 1, Berlin, March 16. Completes Symphony No. 3, Steinbach, Aug. 6.	Bruckner (72) dies, Oct. 11; R. Strauss becomes chief conductor at Munich.

Year	Age	Life	Contemporary Musicians and Events
1897	37	Becomes Roman Catholic, Feb 23. Tour of Russia, March. Leaves Hamburg. Engaged as *Kapellmeister*, Vienna Hofoper, May 1; deputy director, July 13, director, Oct. 8. *Lieder eines fahrenden Gesellen* and Symphony No. 2 published.	Brahms (63) dies, April 3.
1898	38	Intensive work at Vienna Opera. Becomes conductor, Vienna Philharmonic, after Richter. Revises some of his works. Operation for haemorrhoids in June.	R. Strauss (34) becomes principal conductor, Berlin Opera, and composes *Ein Heldenleben*.
1899	39	Buys land for a house at Maiernigg (Wörthersee). Begins Symphony No. 4 in Aug. at Alt-Aussee (Styria) and composes songs.	Poulenc born, Jan. 7; Barbirolli born, Dec. 2; J. Strauss (ii) (73) dies, June 3; first perf. of Elgar's *Enigma Variations*, London, June 19; Richter settles in Manchester, Oct.
1900	40	Takes Vienna Philharmonic to Paris, June. Completes Symphony No. 4 at Maiernigg, Aug. 5.	Copland born, Nov. 14; Křenek born, Aug. 23; Weill born, March 2; first perfs. of Puccini's *Tosca*, Rome, Jan. 14, Charpentier's *Louise*, Paris, Feb. 2, and Elgar's *Dream of Gerontius*, Birmingham, Oct. 3.
1901	41	Conducts first performance *Das klagende Lied*, Vienna, Feb. 17. Resigns conductorship, Vienna Philharmonic, April. Begins Symphony No. 5	Verdi (87) dies, Jan. 27; first complete perf. of Debussy's *Nocturnes*, Paris, Oct. 27.

Year	Age	Life	Contemporary Musicians and Events
		at Maiernigg, summer, also composes Rückert settings including three of *Kindertotenlieder*. Meets Alma Schindler, Nov. 7. M. conducts first performance of Symphony No. 4 in Munich, Nov. 25.	
1902	42	Conducts first Vienna performances of Symphony No. 4 on Jan. 12 and 20. Marries Alma Schindler, March 9. Honeymoon while conducting in Russia. Conducts first performance Symphony No. 3, Crefeld, June 9. Meets Mengelberg. Symphony No. 5 completed, summer. Daughter Maria born, Nov. 3.	Walton born, March 29. First perfs. of Debussy's *Pelléas et Mélisande*, Paris, April 30, Schoenberg's *Verklärte Nacht*, Vienna, March 18, and Nielsen's Symphony No. 2, Copenhagen, Dec. 1.
1903	43	Increasing number of performances of Mahler's symphonies in Germany, many conducted by him. Association with stage designer Alfred Roller begins with *Tristan*, Vienna, Feb 21. Begins Symphony No. 6, Maiernigg. Conducts Symphony No. 3, Amsterdam, Oct. 22 and 23.	Wolf (42) dies, Feb. 22. Wood conducts first English perf. of a Mahler symphony (1), London, Oct. 21. First perf. of Bruckner's No. 9, Vienna, Feb. 11.

Year	Age	Life	Contemporary Musicians and Events
1904	44	Daughter Anna born, June 15. Completes Symphony No. 6 at Maiernigg, Sept. 9. Begins Symphony No. 7. Rückert settings completed. Conducts famous *Fidelio* production, Oct. 7, and first performance Symphony No. 5, Cologne, Oct 18.	Dvořák (62) dies, May 1; Hanslick (78) dies, Aug. 6. First perfs. of Bartók's *Kossuth*, Budapest, Jan. 13; Janáček's *Jenufa*, Brno, Jan. 21; Sibelius's violin concerto, Helsinki, Feb. 8; Puccini's *Madama Butterfly*, Milan, Feb. 17; R. Strauss's *Symphonia Domestica*, New York, March 21; Ravel's *Shéhérazade*, Paris, May 17. First American perf. of a Mahler symphony (4) conducted by W. Damrosch, New York, Nov. 6.
1905	45	First performance of *Kindertotenlieder*, Vienna, Jan. 29. Conducts his symphonies on several occasions. Completes Symphony No. 7 in summer. Notable Vienna revival of *Don Giovanni*, Dec. 21. Symphony No. 5, *Kindertotenlieder* and *Rückertlieder* published.	Tippett born, Jan. 2. First perfs. of Schoenberg's *Pelléas et Mélisande*, Vienna, Jan. 26; Debussy's *La Mer*, Paris, Oct. 15; Strauss's *Salome*, Dresden, Dec. 9; and Lehár's *Merry Widow*, Vienna, Dec. 30.
1906	46	Conducts Mozart revivals of *Seraglio*, Jan. 29, and *Figaro*, March 30. Conducts first performance of Symphony No. 6, Essen, May 27. Symphony No. 6 published. Composes Symphony No. 8, Maiernigg, June–Aug. Conducts at Salzburg in Aug.	Shostakovich born, Sept. 25. First perf. of Delius's *Sea-Drift*, Essen, May 24.

Year	Age	Life	Contemporary Musicians and Events
1907	47	Heart lesion diagnosed. Daughter Maria dies, July 5. Resigns from Vienna Hofoper, Aug.; accepts contract for Metropolitan, New York. Conducts last opera (*Fidelio*) in Vienna, Oct. 15; leaves for concerts in St Petersburg, Oct., and Helsinki, Nov., where he meets Sibelius. Conducts last concert in Vienna (his Symphony No. 2) Nov. 24. Sails for New York, Dec.	Grieg (64) dies, Sept. 4. First perf. of Schoenberg's String Quartet No. 1, Vienna, Feb. 15, and Sibelius's Symphony No. 3, Helsinki, Sept. 25.
1908	48	Début at Metropolitan, New York, in *Tristan*, Jan. 1. During summer at Toblach composes *Das Lied von der Erde*. Conducts first performance of Symphony No. 7, Prague, Sept. 19. Returns to New York Metropolitan and also conducts N.Y. Symphony Orchestra in his Symphony No. 2 on Dec. 8.	Messiaen born, Dec. 10; Rimsky-Korsakov (64) dies, June 21. First perfs. of Delius's *Brigg Fair*. Liverpool, Jan 18; Rakhmaninov's Symphony No. 2, Moscow, Nov. 8; Elgar's Symphony No. 1, Manchester, Dec. 3; and Schoenberg's String Quartet No. 2, Vienna, Dec. 21.
1909	49	Severs connection with Metropolitan. Accepts 3-year contract as conductor of reorganized New York Philharmonic. Returns to Europe for summer. Sits to Rodin in Paris. Begins Symphony No. 9 at Toblach and Göding. Returns to New York for first Philharmonic season (46 concerts). Conducts Symphony No. 1 on Dec. 16.	Albéniz (48) dies, May 18. First perfs. of Strauss's *Elektra*, Dresden, Jan 25, Bartók's Suite No. 2, Budapest, Nov. 22, and Rakhmaninov's Piano Concerto No. 3, New York (Damrosch), Nov. 28. Schoenberg completes *Drei Klavierstücke*, Op. 11, on Aug. 7.

Year	Age	Life	Contemporary Musicians and Events
1910	50	Takes N.Y. Philharmonic on tour. Completes Symphony No. 9. Conducts Symphony No. 2 in Paris, April; conducts in Rome in May; begins Symphony No. 10 at Toblach. Alma in sanatorium and precipitates marital crisis through friendship with Walter Gropius. M. consults Freud at Leyden in Aug. Conducts first two performances of Symphony No. 8 at Munich Sept. 12 and 13. Revises Symphonies Nos. 2 and 4. His second N.Y. Philharmonic season opens on Nov. 1.	Balakirev (73) dies, May 29. First perfs. of Debussy's *Rondes de Printemps*, Paris, March 2; Bartók's String Quartet No. 1, Budapest, March 19; Stravinsky's *Fire-Bird*, Paris, June 25; and Elgar's Violin Concerto, London, Nov. 10.
1911	50	Conducts Symphony No. 4 in New York, Jan. 17 and 20. After conducting on Feb. 21 he is seriously ill with severe streptococcal blood infection. Returns to Paris for serum treatment in April. Taken to sanatorium in Vienna, where he dies, May 18. Bruno Walter conducts first performance of *Das Lied von der Erde* at Munich on Nov. 20.	First perfs. of Strauss's *Der Rosenkavalier*, Dresden, Jan. 26; Skriabin's *Prometheus*, Moscow, March 15; Sibelius's Symphony No. 4, Helsinki, April 3; and Elgar's Symphony No. 2, May 24. Josef Stransky appointed conductor of New York Philharmonic, May 17.

Appendix B

Catalogue of Works

SONGS

1880 Three Songs for tenor and pianoforte (words by Mahler)
1. *Im Lenz* (19 Feb.)
2. *Winterlied* (27 Feb.)
3. *Maitanz im Grünen* (5 March) – see also *Hans und Grethe* below

All that survive of a projected Five Songs 'dedicated to Josephine'. First performance: Zdenek Knittl (tenor), Alfred Rosé (pianoforte), Brno Radio, 30 Sept. 1934.

1880–3 Five Songs for voice and pianoforte
1. *Frühlingsmorgen* (Leander)
2. *Erinnerung* (Leander)
3. *Hans und Grethe* (Mahler)
4. *Serenade aus 'Don Juan'* (Tirso de Molina)
5. *Phantasie aus 'Don Juan'* (Tirso de Molina)

No. 3 is same song as *Maitanz im Grünen*. First perf.: Prague, 20 April 1886, Betty Frank (soprano), accompanied by Mahler. These Five Songs were published as Book I of the *Lieder und Gesänge aus der Jugendzeit* by Schott, Mainz, in February 1892. Books II and III, all with words from *Des Knaben Wunderhorn*, were published at the same time, but were composed between 1888 and 1891:

II. 6. *Um schlimme Kinder artig zu machen*
7. *Ich ging mit Lust durch einen grünen Wald*
8. *Aus! Aus!*
9. *Starke Einbildungskraft*
III. 10. *Zu Strassburg auf der Schanz*
11. *Ablösung im Sommer*
12. *Scheiden und Meiden*
13. *Nicht Wiedersehen!*
14. *Selbstgefühl*

1884 *Lieder eines fahrenden Gesellen*, for voice and orchestra (or pianoforte). Words by Mahler, adapted from *Des Knaben Wunderhorn*. Composed in November and December of 1884. Orchestrated and revised 1892–3, further revised 1896, published 1897 (Vienna, Weinberger). Orchestral version published 1912.

196

1. *Wenn mein Schatz Hochzeit macht*
2. *Ging heut' Morgen übers Feld*
3. *Ich hab' ein glühend Messer*
4. *Die zwei blauen Augen*

First perf.: Berlin, 16 March 1896, Anton Sistermans (baritone), Berlin Philharmonic Orchestra (Mahler); first perf. in Britain: Queen's Hall, London, 3 Nov. 1927,[1] Maria Olczewska (contralto), Orchestra of Royal Philharmonic Society (Sir Henry Wood).

1888–99   *Lieder aus 'Des Knaben Wunderhorn'*, for voice and orchestra (or pianoforte). Originally named *Humoresken*. Published 1899 (Vienna, Weinberger). Dates of composition, where known, in brackets.

I.   1. *Der Schildwache Nachtlied* (1892)
      2. *Verlor'ne Müh'* (1892)
      3. *Trost im Unglück* (6 April 1892)
      4. *Wer hat dies Liedlein erdacht?* (1892)
      5. *Das irdische Leben* (1893)

II.   6. *Des Antonius von Padua Fischpredigt* (Steinbach, 1 Aug. 1893)
      7. *Rheinlegendchen* (originally *Tanzlegendchen*) (Steinbach, 10 Aug. 1893)
      8. *Lied des Verfolgten im Turm* (1895)
      9. *Wo die schönen Trompeten blasen* (1895)
      10. *Lob des hohen Verstandes* (21 June 1896)
      11. *Es sungen drei Engel* (Symphony No. 3) (1895)
      12. *Urlicht* (Symphony No. 2) (1892–4)

First perf. of Nos. 1 and 2 Berlin, 12 Dec. 1892, Amalie Joachim (mez.-sop.), Berlin Philharmonic cond. Raphael Maszkowski; of Nos. 3, 4, 7, Hamburg, 27 Oct. 1893, Clementine Schuch-Prosska (soprano) and Paul Bulss (baritone), with orchestra (Mahler); of Nos. 5 and 9, Vienna, 14 Jan. 1900, Selma Kurz (soprano), Vienna Philharmonic (Mahler); and of Nos. 6 and 8 Vienna, 29 Jan. 1905, Friedrich Weidemann (baritone) and orch. (Mahler). Other settings from *Des Knaben Wunderhorn*:

> *Wir geniessen die himmlischen Freuden* (Symphony No. 4). For soprano and orchestra (12 March 1892)
> *Revelge* (1899). Published 1905 (Leipzig, Kahnt)
> *Der Tamboursg'sell* (July 1901). Published 1905 (Leipzig, Kahnt)

1901–4   *Kindertotenlieder* (Rückert), for voice and orchestra (or pianoforte). Published 1905 (Leipzig, C. F. Kahnt Nachfolger).
1. *Nun will die Sonn' so hell aufgeh'n* (1901)
2. *Nun seh' ich wohl* (1901)

---

[1] This date is speculative. This cycle and *Kindertotenlieder* were scheduled for performance at a Promenade Concert on 17 October 1914, but it was cancelled.

Mahler

3. *Wenn dein Mütterlein* (1901)
4. *Oft denk' ich, sie sind nur ausgegangen* (1904)
5. *In diesem Wetter* (1904)

First perf.: Vienna, 29 Jan. 1905. Friedrich Weidemann (baritone) and orchestra (Mahler); first perf. in Britain: Bechstein Hall, London, 28 May 1913 (with pianoforte), Lula Mysz-Gmeiner (contralto), Richard Epstein (pianoforte); with orchestra, 27 May 1924, Elena Gerhardt (contralto), L.S.O. (Fritz Reiner); first U.S. perf.: New York, 26 January 1910, Ludwig Wüllner (tenor), N.Y.P.O. (Mahler).

Fünf Lieder nach Rückert (Five Rückert Songs) for voice and orchestra (or pianoforte). Published 1905 (Leipzig, C. F. Kahnt Nachf.).

1. *Blicke mir nicht in die Lieder* (1901)
2. *Ich atmet' einen linden Duft* (1901)
3. *Ich bin der Welt abhanden gekommen* (1901)
4. *Um Mitternacht* (1901)
5. *Liebst du um Schönheit* (1902) (orch. Puttmann)

First perf.: Vienna, 29 Jan. 1905 (excluding No. 2). F. Weidemann (baritone) and orch. (Mahler).

CANTATA

1878–80 *Das klagende Lied* (words by Mahler) for soprano, contralto, tenor, bass, chorus and orchestra. Original version in three parts completed 1 Nov. 1880: I *Waldmärchen*, II *Der Spielmann*, III *Hochzeitstück*.

Revised 1893 into two parts, *Waldmärchen* being deleted. Scoring further revised 1898–9, post-1900. Publication of revised version, 1902 (Vienna, Weinberger). First perf.: Vienna, 17 Feb. 1901, Vienna Philharmonic Orchestra and choir of Vienna *Singakademie* (Mahler) with Elise Elizza and Anna von Mildenburg sharing soprano role, Edyth Walker and Fritz Schrödter; first perf. in Britain: Royal Festival Hall, London, 13 May 1956, London Symphony Orchestra, Goldsmiths' Choral Union (Walter Goehr) with Joan Sutherland, Norma Procter, Peter Pears. (Adrian Boult conducted Parts II and III with piano accompaniment in the Judge's Lodgings, Oxford, on 26 July 1914.)

3-movement version: first perf. of *Waldmärchen* alone, Brno Radio, 28 Nov. 1934 (in Czech) conducted by Alfred Rosé; first perf. of complete hybrid version: Vienna Radio 8 April 1935 conducted by Alfred Rosé; in Britain, Royal Festival Hall, London, 21 April 1970, L.S.O. and Chorus (Pierre Boulez) with Elisabeth Söderström, Grace Hoffman, Ernst Häfliger; first U.S. perf.: New Haven, 13 Jan. 1970, New Haven S.O. (Frank Brieff), Veronica Tyler (soprano), Janet Baker (mez-soprano), Blake Stern (tenor), Richard McKee (bass); first perf. of original 1880 version, Bridgewater Hall, Manchester, 7 Oct. 1997, Hallé Orch. & Choir, Manchester Boys' Choir (Kent Nagano), Eva Urbanová, Jadwiga Rappé, Hans Peter Blochwitz, Håkan Hagegård.

[2] Two sopranos shared soprano role.

SONG-SYMPHONY

1907–9 *Das Lied von der Erde*, Symphony for alto (or baritone), tenor and orchestra (words by Hans Bethge, based on Chinese poems, with additions by Mahler). Published 1911 (Vienna, U.E.).

First perf.: Munich, 20 Nov. 1911, Sara Jane (Mme Charles) Cahier (contralto), William Miller (tenor), Orchestra of Munich Concert Society (Bruno Walter); first performance in Britain: Queen's Hall, London, 31 Jan. 1914, Doris Woodall, Gervase Elwes and Queen's Hall Orchestra (Wood); first U.S. perf.: Philadelphia, 14 Dec. 1916, Philadelphia Orchestra (Stokowski).

SYMPHONIES

1884–8 Symphony No. 1 in D major. Revised 1893, 1896 (reduced from five to four movements) and 1897–8. Published 1899 (Vienna, Weinberger).

First perf.: Budapest, 20 Nov. 1889 (Mahler); first perf. in Britain: Queen's Hall, London, 21 Oct. 1903, Queen's Hall Orchestra (Wood); first U.S. perf.: New York, 16 Dec. 1909, N.Y.P.O. (Mahler).
First 20th-century perf. of five-movement version: New Haven, 9 April 1968, New Haven S.O. (Frank Brieff); first perf. in Britain of *Blumine* movement: Aldeburgh, 18 June 1967, L.S.O. (Britten).

1888–94 Symphony No. 2 in C minor. For soprano, contralto, mixed chorus and orchestra. Revised 1910. Published 1897 (Leipzig, Hofmeister).

First perf.: first three movements only, Berlin, 4 March 1895, Berlin Philharmonic Orchestra (Mahler); complete, Berlin, 13 Dec. 1895, Berlin Philharmonic (Mahler), with Josephine von Artner (soprano), Hedwig Felden (contralto); first perf. in Britain: Queen's Hall, London, 16 April 1931, Queen's Hall Orchestra and Chorus (Bruno Walter), with Luise Helletsgruber (soprano), Enid Szanto (contralto); first U.S. perf.: New York, 8 Dec. 1908, N.Y. Symphony Orchestra (Mahler), with Laura L. Combs (soprano) and Gertrude Stein Bailey (contralto).

1895–6 Symphony No. 3 in D minor. For contralto, women's chorus, boys' chorus and orchestra. Published 1898 (Vienna, Weinberger).

First perf.: Crefeld, 9 June 1902 (Mahler) at festival of Allgemeine Deutsche Musikverein; first perf. in Britain: B.B.C. broadcast, 29 Nov. 1947, B.B.C. Symphony Orchestra, Chesham Ladies' Choir, boys of London Choir School (Sir Adrian Boult) with Kathleen Ferrier (contralto); (public) London, St Pancras Town Hall, 28 Feb. 1961, Polyphonia Symphony Orchestra, Wimbledon Girls' Choir, William Ellis School boys' choir (Bryan Fairfax), with Jean Evans (contralto); first U.S. perf.: New York, 8 Feb. 1922, New York Philharmonic (Mengelberg).

Mahler

1899–1900 Symphony No. 4 in G major. For soprano and orchestra, Revised 1910. Published 1902 (Vienna, Waldheim-Eberle).

First perf.: Munich, 25 Nov. 1901 (Mahler), with Margarete Michalek (soprano); first perf. in Britain: Queen's Hall, London, 25 Oct. 1905, Olga Urusova (Mrs Henry J. Wood) (soprano) and Queen's Hall Orchestra (Wood); first U.S. perf.: New York, 6 Nov. 1904, N.Y. Symphony Orchestra (Walter Damrosch), with Mme de Montjau (soprano).

1901–2 Symphony No. 5 in C sharp minor.[2] Revised 1904, 1905, 1907, 1909. Published 1905 (Leipzig, C. F. Peters).

First perf.: Cologne, 18 Oct. 1904 (Mahler); first perf. in Britain: Stoll Theatre, London, 21 Oct. 1945, London Philharmonic Orchestra (Heinz Unger); *Adagietto* only : Queen's Hall, London, 31 Aug. 1909, Queen's Hall Orchestra (Wood); first U.S. perf.: Cincinnati, 25 March 1905, Cincinnati S.O. (Frank van der Stucken).

1903–5 Symphony No. 6 in A minor. Revised 1908. Published 1906 (Leipzig, C. F. Kahnt Nachf.).

First perf.: Essen, 27 May 1906 (Mahler), festival of Allgemeine Deutsche Musikverein; first British broadcast (Hamburg perf.) 31 Dec. 1947; first British orch. broadcast: 28 Dec. 1950, B.B.C. Symphony Orchestra (Walter Goehr); first U.S. performance: New York, 11 Dec. 1947, N.Y.P.O. (Dmitri Mitropoulos).

1904–5 Symphony No. 7 in B minor. Revised 1909. Published 1908 (Berlin, Bote und Bock).

First perf.: Prague, 19 Sept. 1908 (Mahler); first perf. in Britain: Queen's Hall, London, 18 Jan. 1913, Queen's Hall Orchestra (Wood); first U.S. perf.: Chicago, 15 April 1921, Chicago S.O. (Frederick Stock).

1906–7 Symphony No. 8 in E flat major. For 8 soloists (3 sopranos, 2 contraltos, tenor, baritone and bass), mixed chorus, boys' chorus and orchestra.[3] Published 1911 (Vienna, U.E.).

First perf.: Munich, 12 Sept. 1910; soloists: Gertrud Förstel, Marta Winternitz-Dorda, Irma Koboth, Otillie Meyzger, Tilly Koenen, Felix Senius, Nicola Geisse-Winkel, Richard Mayr; Leipzig Riedelverein, Vienna Singverein, Munich Central School Children's Chorus, Festival Orchestra (Mahler); first perf. in Britain: Queen's Hall, London, 15 April 1930, B.B.C. Symphony Orchestra, B.B.C. National Chorus, boys of Southwark Cathedral and others (Wood), with Elsie Suddaby, May Blyth, Irene Mordern, Muriel Brunskill, Clara Serena, Walter Widdop, Harold

---

[2] The keys given for this symphony and Nos. 7–10 are merely those in which the works begin.

[3] The nickname 'Symphony of a Thousand' was true at Munich where over 1,000 performers were on the platform, comprising orchestra of over 150, the soloists, choruses of 500 voices and children's choir of 350.

Williams and Robert Easton; first U.S. perf.: Philadelphia, 2 March 1916 (Leopold Stokowski).

1909–10   Symphony No. 9 in D major. Published 1912 (Vienna U.E.).

First perf.: Vienna, 26 June 1912, Vienna Philharmonic (Bruno Walter); first perf. in Britain (also broadcast): Manchester, 27 Feb. 1930, The Hallé Orchestra (Sir Hamilton Harty); first London performance: Queen's Hall, 7 Feb. 1934, B.B.C.S.O. (Boult); first U.S. performance: Boston, 16 Oct. 1931, Boston S.O. (Koussevitzky).

1910   Symphony No. 10 in F sharp major. Left unfinished. Sketches published in facsimile 1924 (Berlin, Paul Zsolnay Verlag). Movements 1 and 3 published 1951 (New York, Assoc. Music Publishers).

First perf.: of *Adagio* and *Purgatorio*: Vienna, 14 Oct. 1924, Vienna Philharmonic (Franz Schalk); first perf. in Britain: *Adagio*, B.B.C. broadcast, 20 Nov. 1948, B.B.C.S.O. (Hermann Scherchen); *Adagio* and *Purgatorio*, Royal Festival Hall, London, 30 Nov. 1955, Royal Philharmonic Orchestra (Richard Austin); first U.S. perf.: Erie, 6 Dec. 1949, Erie S.O. (Fritz Mahler).

Deryck Cooke performing version: first perf. (both *Scherzos* incomplete), B.B.C. broadcast, 19 Dec. 1960, Philharmonia Orchestra (Berthold Goldschmidt); (complete) Royal Albert Hall, London, 13 Aug. 1964, London Symphony Orchestra (Goldschmidt); (revised) Royal Festival Hall, London, 15 Oct. 1972, New Philharmonia (Wyn Morris); first U.S. perf.: Philadelphia, 5 Nov. 1965, Philadelphia Orchestra (Ormandy). Published 1976 (Assoc. Music Publishers, N.Y. and Faber Music, London).

JUVENILIA AND FRAGMENTARY WORKS
(All unpublished)

PROJECTED BUT UNCOMPLETED OPERAS

1875   *Herzog Ernst von Schwaben* (libretto by J. Steiner, probably based on Uhland)

1879–80(?)   *Die Argonauten* (libretto by Mahler, probably based on Grillparzer)

1880–90   *Rübezahl* (libretto by Mahler)

ORCHESTRAL

1876–8   Symphony (rehearsed at Vienna Conservatory)
1876–8   Symphony in A minor (three movements in MS.)

Mahler

1876 *Sonata for violin and pianoforte.* Performed Iglau, 31 July 1876
(Mahler, pianist, Richard Schraml, violin).
1876 *Pianoforte Quintet in A minor* (first movement awarded prize at
Vienna Conservatory, 1 July 1876). First perf.: Iglau, 12 Sept. 1876
(Mahler, pianist).
1876 *Pianoforte Quartet in A minor* (one movement). First broadcast:
Station WBA1, New York, 1962; first public performance: London,
Purcell Room, 1 June 1968, Albert Landa (pianoforte) and Nemet
Ensemble; first U.S. public performance: Cultural Center, New York, 17
Feb. 1973, Thomas Muraco (pianoforte) and violinist, violist and cellist
of Concord Quartet.
1878 *Pianoforte Quintet (Scherzo).* Performed Vienna Conservatory, 11
July 1878 (Mahler, pianist).

INCIDENTAL MUSIC

For *Der Trompeter von Säkkingen* by Josef Viktor von Scheffel. For
orchestra. First performance: Hoftheater, Cassel, 23 June 1884
(Mahler).

ARRANGEMENTS AND EDITIONS

J. S. Bach: Suite for Orchestra in four movements
  1. Overture in B minor (from Suite No. 2)
  2. Rondeau and Badinerie in B minor (from Suite No. 2)
  3. Air in D (from Suite No. 3 in D major)
  4. Gavotte in D (from Suite No. 3 in D major)
First perf.: New York, 25 Nov. 1909, N.Y.P.O. (Mahler, who also played
continuo on pianoforte with action altered to resemble powerful
harpsichord). Published 1911 (New York, Schirmer).
Bruckner: Symphony No. 3, pianoforte arrangement for four hands
(Vienna, Rättig, 1878).
Mozart: *The Marriage of Figaro* (1906). Published 1908 (Leipzig, C. F.
Peters). Recitatives for judgement scene.
Schubert: String Quartet in D minor (*Der Tod und das Mädchen*) (D.810)
arranged for string orchestra. First perf.: *Andante con moto* only,
Hamburg, 19 Nov. 1894 (Mahler). First complete perf.: New York,
Carnegie Hall, 6 May 1984, American S.O. (Moshe Atzmon); first perf. in
Britain: London, Barbican Hall, 30 June 1985, English Chamber
Orchestra (Jeffrey Tate).
Weber: Completion of *Die drei Pintos* (libretto in collaboration with K. von

Weber). First perf.: Leipzig, 20 Jan. 1888 (Mahler). First perf. in England: London, 10 April 1962, cond. by David Lloyd-Jones. Published 1888 (Leipzig, C. F. Kahnt Nachf.).

Euryanthe (new libretto by Mahler), 1903–4.

Oberon (new libretto by Mahler), 1906. Published 1919 (Vienna, U.E.)

Rescorings by Mahler of the Schumann symphonies and of several Beethoven works have not been published. Mahler's annotated scores of his own works and of works by Beethoven, Schubert, Schumann and others were presented to Southampton University by the late Miss Anna Mahler in March 1973.

It is important to remember that Mahler said: 'I have made these retouchings for myself, not for anyone else. When I conduct, I can take responsibility for them.'

Appendix C
Personalia

Adler, Guido (1855–1941), Austrian musicologist who founded and was first director of the influential Institute for Music History at Vienna University, where he succeeded Hanslick as professor of musicology (1898–1927), Pupil of Bruckner and author of a study of Mahler published in a year book in 1914 and as a book in 1916. Knew Mahler from his student days onwards.

Barbirolli, Sir John (1899–1970), English conductor who in the last twenty years of his life regularly conducted Mahler symphonies throughout the world. Recorded Nos. 1, 5, 6 and 9; and off-the-air recordings of Nos. 3, 4 and 7 have been issued on CD.

Bauer-Lechner, Natalie (1858-1921), Austrian violinist who was a close friend of Mahler and his sisters up to the time of his marriage. Studied at Vienna Conservatory. Violinist in all-women Soldat-Röger Quartet. Her *Recollections of Gustav Mahler* (1923) is indispensable.

Berliner, Arnold (1862–1942), physicist who became a close friend of Mahler in Hamburg in 1891 and remained an intimate. He committed suicide on hearing that the Nazis intended to arrest him.

Bernstein, Leonard (1918–90), American conductor (especially of New York Philharmonic) who twice recorded all Mahler's symphonies and *Das Lied von der Erde* (with tenor and contralto and also with tenor and baritone).

Bodansky, Artur (1897–1939), violinist in Vienna Opera orchestra who became an assistant conductor during Mahler régime. He was devoted to Mahler and his music. Settled in 1915 in United States where, until his death, he was chief German conductor at the Metropolitan Opera.

Busoni, Ferruccio (1866–1924), composer, conductor, writer and virtuoso pianist who first met Mahler in Leipzig in 1887 and later was soloist with him in concerto performances in Hamburg, Vienna and New York. Mahler conducted several of Busoni's compositions.

Buths, Julius (1851–1920), German conductor of remarkably wide tastes whose pioneering work at the Lower Rhine Festival helped to win a hearing for Mahler, Strauss, Elgar and Delius.

Cardus, Sir Neville (1888–1975), English music critic and author whose championship of Mahler's cause never wavered. Published a volume of analysis of Mahler's first five symphonies, but his masterpiece is his essay on Mahler which first appeared in *Ten Composers* (1945).

Chantemesse, André (1851–1919), French physician and expert on bacteriological infections to whom Mahler went in Paris in April 1911. Associated with Pasteur Institute.

Chvostek, Franz (1864–1944), Viennese physician who treated Mahler in May 1911. Expert on blood diseases.

Conried, Heinrich (1848–1909), manager of the Metropolitan Opera, New York, 1903–8, who persuaded Mahler to work in the United States.

Cooke, Deryck (1919–76), English music critic, scholar and author specializing in Mahler, Wagner and Delius. His book *The Language of Music* is highly stimulating. Made an invaluable contribution to Mahlerian research through his performing version of the Tenth Symphony.

Damrosch, Walter (1862–1950), American conductor of German origin who, while conductor of New York Symphony Society 1885–1927, did remarkable work on behalf of contemporary composers. He first encountered Mahler at Hamburg in 1895 when he was impressed by a *Meistersinger* at the opera there. Conducted first American performance of a Mahler symphony (No. 4) in New York in 1904.

Dehmel, Richard (1863–1920), poet whose work was set to music by several of Mahler's contemporaries including Richard Strauss and Reger. His poem *Verklärte Nacht* inspired Schoenberg's string sextet of that name.

Foerster, Josef Bohuslav (1859–1951), Czech composer and organist. Born near Prague and succeeded Dvořák as organist of St Vojtech, Prague. Married in 1888 the soprano Berta Lauterer (1869–1936), who was engaged by Mahler for Hamburg Opera, 1893–1901, and in Vienna, 1901–13. Mahler described her as 'the best Seiglinde I have ever heard'. Foerster was music critic of the *Hamburger Nachrichten* and became a loyal and undemanding friend of Mahler's, about whom he wrote perceptively in his memoirs. Moved to Vienna, writing for *Die Zeit* and becoming professor of composition at the New Vienna Conservatory. Was director of Prague Conservatory, 1922–31. Composed symphonies, operas and chamber music.

Fremstad, Olive (1871–1951), American soprano of Swedish origin who was leading exponent of Wagnerian rôles at the Metropolitan, New York, until 1914.

Freund, Emil (1859–1928), Austrian lawyer who met Mahler in Vienna in 1873. Became Mahler's financial adviser, especially about contracts with publishers.

Fried, Oskar (1871–1941), German conductor who knew Mahler and became an enthusiastic interpreter of his symphonies in the years between the wars. Mahler admired his conducting of the Second Symphony. His letters to Fried are published in *Mahler's Unknown Letters*, Made first recording of a Mahler symphony (No. 2).

Gropius, Walter (1883–1969), distinguished and influential architect, director of the Bauhaus Academy (1918–28). He was the cause of Mahler's 1910 matrimonial crisis. Alma Mahler married him in 1915 but the union was short-lived. In 1934 he settled in England and went to the U.S. in 1937.

Groves, Sir Charles (1915–92), the first English conductor to perform all Mahler's symphonies, including the Cooke version of the Tenth, with his orchestra, the Royal Liverpool Philharmonic. This he did in the 1960s.

Gutheil-Schoder, Marie (1874–1935), soprano who was one of the outstanding singer-actresses of Mahler's Vienna régime. She became a notable Elektra.

Gutmann, Emil (1877–1922(?)), German impresario with an agency in Munich and later in Berlin. Organized first performances in 1910 of Mahler's Eighth Symphony, for which he coined, to the composer's displeasure, the nickname 'Symphony of a Thousand'.

Haitink, Bernard (b. 1929), Dutch conductor of the Amsterdam Concertgebouw Orchestra, 1964–88, who has recorded Mahler's nine symphonies and the *Adagio* of the Tenth.

Hammerschlag, Paul (1860–1933), Austrian banker, later president of the Austrian Bankers' Society. Born on same day as Mahler and studied law at Vienna University. On board of Vienna's Konzertverein. Gave Mahler recording cylinders of original Chinese music.

Hellmesberger, Joseph (1828–93), Austrian conductor and violinist (leader of a string quartet) who was director of the Vienna Conservatory from 1851 until his death. His son Joseph (1855–1907) was also a violinist and a conductor of ballet and was for a short time conductor of the Vienna Philharmonic after they had rid themselves of Mahler.

Jahn, Wilhelm (1834–1900), director of the Vienna Hofoper from 1881 to 1897, when he was succeeded by Mahler.

Karpath, Ludwig (1866–1936), Austrian music critic, a profession he adopted after Mahler had engaged him as a bass in Budapest and dismissed him a few days later. Worked for *Neues Wiener Tagblatt* 1894–1923. Supported Mahler as director of the Vienna Opera, but thereafter was ambivalent.

Klemperer, Otto (1885–1973), German conductor who worked with Mahler and attended all rehearsals for the first performances of Symphonies Nos. 7 and 8. His interpretations of Mahler were notable for clarity and absence of excessive expression. His opinion of Mahler the conductor was unequivocal: 'Toscanini was the greatest conductor of his generation, but Mahler was a hundred times greater.'

Křenek, Ernst (1900–91), Austrian composer who was at one time married to Mahler's daughter Anna and prepared the first performing version (1924) of *Adagio* and *Purgatorio* of Symphony No. 10.

Krisper, Anton (1858–1914), Austrian composer. For two years was a fellow-student of Mahler's at Vienna Conservatory. Abandoned music after failure of his opera at Prague. Became insane.

Krzyzanowski, Heinrich (1855–192?), Ausrian writer and teacher, elder brother of Rudolf Krzyzanowski and fellow-student of Mahler in Vienna. Wrote a novel in 1885 and lived in Munich and Berlin befor returning to Vienna. Mahler remained very fond of him and helped him in many ways. From New York in 1909 he arranged to send money to Heinrich because he had heard he was in 'grave financial difficulties'.

Krzyzanowski, Rudolf (1859–1911), younger brother of above and also a fellow-student of Mahler's at Vienna Conservatory, where he studied violin and piano, changing to organ and composition and graduating in 1878. He and Mahler spent walking holidays together. Became opera conductor at Laibach in 1883. Succeeded Karl Muck as first conductor in Prague, 1892–5. Appointed second conductor to Mahler at Hamburg 1896–8 by Pollini without consulting Mahler (who had not heard from Krzyzanowski for years). Pollini played one off against the other.

Langford, Samuel (1863–1927), music critic of the *Manchester Guardian* from 1906 until his death. It can justifiably be claimed that he was the first English critic to appreciate Mahler at his real worth, as is shown by these extracts from his obituary of Mahler published on 19th May (p. 9): 'The greatest of present-day symphonists . . . While in a sense [his music] is thoroughly popular, it has so far missed popularity because it was not designed for it . . . Mahler is as lightfooted as the most alert worldling could be. He is never in a hurry. Almost more than that of any other composer, his music may be said to dance . . . In his Third Symphony Mahler first shows himself a composer who can break bounds with an air of transcendent genius.' Langford attended the great 1920 Mahler Festival in Amsterdam and his notices of it are still worth reading.

Lipiner, Siegfried (1856–1911), Austrian writer, poet and philosopher who met Mahler during Vienna student days. Their friendship was close until the advent of Alma who disliked him (a feeling that was mutual). Published books of philosophy and poetry and earned his living as librarian of Austrian Reichsrat.Friendship with Mahler was repaired in 1910, when Mahler re-read his books and had a long talk with him about attitudes to death.

Löhr, Friedrich (Fritz) (1859–1924), Austrian archaeologist who became secretary of Austrian Archaeological Society in Vienna until his death. Very close friend of Mahler from 1876 until the end of Mahler's life and recipient of many revealing letters.

Marschalk, Max (1863–1940). German critic and composer, brother-in-law of the playwright Gerhart Hauptmann. Mahler wrote of him in 1896: 'He knows and understands my work better than anybody.'

Mengelberg, Willem (1871–1951), Dutch conductor of the Concertgebouw Orchestra of Amsterdam, 1895–1945, and at one time of the New York Philharmonic. A passionate advocate of Mahler, who said of him in 1906: 'There's no one else I could entrust a work of mine to with entire confidence.' Performed all Mahler's major works at the festival in Amsterdam, 1920. Between 1903 and 1920, Mahler's name occurred in his programmes over 230 times.

Mildenburg, Anna von (1872–1947), Austrian soprano noted for her Isolde, Brünnhilde and Fidelio. In Mahler's Hamburg and Vienna companies. Was engaged to Mahler in Hamburg. Married the poet Hermann Bahr in 1909.

Mitchell, Donald (b. 1925), English publisher and critic, authority on Britten. His *Mahler: The Early Years, The Wunderhorn Years* and *Songs and Symphonies of Life and Death* are detailed studies. He also edited the second English edition of Alma Mahler's *Gustav Mahler: Memories and Letters* and co-edited *The Mahler Companion.*

Moll, Carl (1861–1945), Austrian painter, pupil of Emil Jacob Schindler

(1842–92) whose widow Anna (18??–1938) he married in 1897, thus becoming stepfather to Alma Schindler, later Mahler's wife. He much admired and liked Mahler, who in his turn was deeply attached to his parents-in-law. In later years Moll became a Nazi and committed suicide when the Red Army entered Vienna.

Pfitzner, Hans (1869–1949), German composer and conductor of Romantic music whose opera *Die Rose vom Liebesgarten* Mahler conducted in Vienna.

Pollini, Bernhard (1838–97), German tenor who became a noted theatre-manager, combinig adventurous policy with profit. Manager of Hamburg Opera from 1873.

Richter, Hans (1843–1916), Hungarian-born conductor who became a noted Wagnerian and conducted the first *Ring cycle*, 1876. Conductor of Vienna Opera, 1880–98, and of Hallé Orchestra, Manchester, 1899–1911.

Roller, Alfred (1864–1935), Austrian stage-designer who worked with Mahler in Vienna from 1903 and created famous productions of Mozart, Beethoven, Wagner and Gluck.

Rosé, Arnold (1863–1946), leading violinist, Vienna Philharmonic and Opera Orchestras, for fifty-seven years. He founded and led the Rosé Quartet. He married Mahler's sister Justine in 1902. She died in 1938, the year Rosé fled to London, where he lived until his death. Their daughter Alma died in Auschwitz where she had conducted an orchestra; their son Alfred (1902–75) became an American citizen. Arnold's brother Edward (1855–1942), a cellist, married in 1898 Mahler's youngest sister Emma, who died in 1933.

Rückert, Friedrich (1788–1866), German Romantic poet who had a keen interest in Turkish and Oriental verse-forms. Several composers set his work to music.

Schalk, Franz (1863–1931), Austrian conductor who became assistant to Mahler at the Vienna Hofoper in 1900 and was director, 1918–1929. Mahler regarded him as pedestrian and incompetent and suspected him of intrigue. Responsible for spurious editions of Bruckners Symphonies. In 1924 conducted first performance of *Adagio* and *Purgatorio* from Mahler's Tenth Symphony in Vienna.

Schoenberg, Arnold (1874–1951), Austrian composer whose 'system of composing with twelve notes' revolutionized music in 1923. Beginning as a violent opponent of Mahler's music, he rapidly became an ardent champion.

Seidl, Arthur (1863–1928), German music critic and teacher who was an influential propagandist for Mahler, Strauss and others.

Solti, Sir Georg (1912–97), Hungarian conductor, who became a naturalized Briton. Recorded nine of Mahler's symphonies, including notably a magnificent performance of the Eighth.

Specht, Richard (1870–1932), Austrian music critic and essayist who wrote biographies of Mahler, Strauss, Brahms and Puccini. Published analyses of Mahler's late works. It was to Specht at Munich in 1910 that Mahler described his Eighth as 'a gift to the nation'. Founded Vienna periodical *Der Merker* in 1909, editing it until 1919.

Stein, Erwin (1886–1958), Austrian music-critic who settled in London. His book *Orpheus in New Guises* contains valuable essays on Mahler; and he has left vivid detailed descriptions of Mahler's Viennese opera productions.

Steiner, Josef (1857–1913), Austrian lawyer, who was one of Mahler's boyhood friends. They spent holidays together on country estate of Steiner's aunt. Wrote opera libretto on *Herzog Ernst von Schwaben* for Mahler, 1875. They lost contact after 1879, when Mahler gave Steiner an autograph manuscript of *Das klangende Lied*.

Walter, Bruno (1876–1962), Austrian conductor who was assistant to Mahler in Hamburg and Vienna, a close friend and for the rest of his life a fervent advocate. His interpretations were perhaps softer-centred than is now fashionable, but they are an irreplacabe link with the composer. Conducted first performances of Symphony No. 9 (1912) and *Das Lied von der Erde* (1911). Wrote monograph on Mahler (1936).

Weingartner, Felix von (1863–1942), succeeded Mahler as director of the Vienna Hofoper in 1907 and became one of the world's leading conductors of his day.

Wood, Sir Henry J. (1869–1944), English conductor of extraordinarily catholic and adventurous taste who was the first to conduct a Mahler symphony (No. 1) in England and later conducted the first English performances of Symphonies 4, 7 and 8 and *Das Lied von der Erde*.

Zemlinsky, Alexander von (1871–1942), Austrian conductor and composer who taught Schoenberg and became his brother-in-law. A close friend of Alma Mahler. His opera *Es war einmal* was conducted by Mahler (who composed part of its first-act finale) in Vienna in 1900. He went to America in 1938.

Zichy, Count Géza (1849–1924), Hungarian composer and one-armed pianist who had been a Liszt pupil. Intendant of Budapest Opera, 1891–4.

Zuckerkandl, Emil (1849–1910), Viennese anatomist who was a close friend of Alma Mahler's stepfather, the painter Carl Moll. His wife Bertha was related by marriage to Paul and Georges Clemenceau, both of whom were drawn into the Mahler circle.

Appendix D

Select Bibliography

Adler, Guido, *Gustav Mahler* (Vienna-Leipzig, 1916).

Adorno, Theodor W., *Mahler: eine musikalische Physiognomik* (Frankfurt, 1960).

Banks, Paul, 'Mahler 2 – some answers?' in *The Musical Times*, Vol. 128, No. 1730, April 1987.

——, 'Hans Rott and the New Symphony' in *The Musical Times*, Vol. 130, No. 1753, March 1989.

——, 'Aspects of Mahler's Fifth Symphony: performance practice and interpretation' in *The Musical Times* Vol. 130, No. 1755, May 1989.

——, (with Mitchell, Donald) 'Gustav Mahler' in *The New Grove Dictionary of Music and Musicians*, Vol. 11 (London, 1980). Reprinted in *Turn of the Century Masters* (London, 1985).

Barford, Philip, 'Mahler: A thematic archetype' (*Music Review*, Vol. 21, No. 4, November 1960).

——, *Mahler Symphonies and Songs* (B.B.C. Music Guides, London, 1970).

Bauer-Lechner, Natalie, *Erinnerungen an Gustav Mahler* (Leipzig-Vienna-Zürich, 1923). English ed. trans. Dika Newlin, ed. and annotated by Peter Franklin, *Recollections of Gustav Mahler* (London, 1980).

Bekker, Paul, *Die Symphonie von Beethoven bis Mahler* (Berlin, 1918).

——, *Mahlers Sinfonien* (Berlin, 1921).

Berg, Alban, *Letters to his Wife*, trans. and annotated by Bernard Grun (London, 1971, German ed., 1965).

Blaukopf, Herta (ed.), *Gustav Mahler Richard Strauss Briefwechsel 1888–1911* (Munich, 1980). Eng. trans. Edmund Jephcott, *Gustav Mahler Richard Strauss Correspondence 1888–1911* (London, 1984).

—— (ed.), *Gustav Mahler: Unbekannte Brief*, (Vienna, Hamburg, 1983). Eng. ed. *Mahler's Unknown Letters*, trans. Richard Stokes (London, 1986).

Blaukopf, Kurt, *Gustav Mahler oder der Zeitgenosse der Zukunft* (Vienna, 1969). Eng. ed. *Mahler*, trans. Inge Goodwin (London, 1973).

——, *Mahler: a Documentary Study* (London, 1976).

—— and Herta (ed.), *Mahler, His Life, Work and World* (London, 1991); rev. and enlarged edn. of *Mahler: a Documentary Study*.

Bloomfield, Theodore, 'Two undetected misprints in Mahler's *Das Lied von der Erde*' in *The Musical Times*, vol. 130, No. 1755, May 1989.

Busoni, Ferruccio, *Letters to his Wife*, trans. Rosamond Ley (London, 1938).

Cardus, Sir Neville, *Gustav Mahler: his Mind and his Music*, Vol. I: *The First Five Symphonies* (London, 1965).

——, 'Mahler' in *Ten Composers* (London, 1945), reprinted in *A Composers' Eleven* (London, 1958).

Carner, Mosco, *Of Men and Music: collected essays and articles* (London, 1944). Republished in revised edition (still containing the Mahler articles) as *Major and Minor* (London, 1980).

Carr, Jonathan, *The Real Mahler* (London, 1997).

Clements, Andrew, 'Das Lied von der Erde' in *Song on Record*, Vol. I (ed. A. Blyth) (London, 1986).

Cooke, Deryck, *Gustav Mahler* (B.B.C. publication, London, 1960).

——, 'Mahler's Unfinished Symphony' (*The Listener*, 15 Dec. 1960).

——, 'Mahler's Tenth Symphony: sonority, texture and substance' (*Composer*, No. 16, July 1965).

——, *Mahler's Eighth Symphony* (Royal Liverpool Philharmonic Society, Liverpool, 1964).

——, 'The History of Mahler's Tenth Symphony' in *Gustav Mahler: a Performing Version of the Draft for the Tenth Symphony* (full score) (London, 1976).

——, *Gustav Mahler, an Introduction to his Music* (London, 1980).

de La Grange, Henry-Louis, 'Mistakes about Mahler' (*Music and Musicians*, Vol. 21, No. 2, October 1972).

——, *Mahler*, Vol. I (New York, 1973; London, 1974).

——, Vol. II *L'age d'or de Vienne (1900–7)* (Paris, 1983).

——, Vol. III *Le Génie foudroyé (1907–11)* (Paris, 1984).

Revised and published in English as *Gustav Mahler. Vienna: The Years of Challenge (1897–1904)* and *Gustav Mahler. Vienna: Triumph and Disillusion (1904–1907)* (Oxford, 1995 and 2000).

Del Mar, Norman, *Richard Strauss: a critical commentary on his life and works*, Vol. I (of three) (London, 1962).

——, *Mahler's Sixth Symphony, a Study* (London, 1980).

Engel, Gabriel, *Gustav Mahler: Song-Symphonist* (New York, 1932).

Franklin, Peter, *The Life of Mahler* (Cambridge, 1997).

Gartenberg, Egon, *Mahler, the Man and his Music* (New York and London, 1978).

Hefling, Stephen E., 'Mahler Autograph Re-discovered: Das Lied von der Erde' in *News About Mahler Research* (International Gustav Mahler Society) No. 13, March 1984 (Vienna, 1984).

Heyworth, Peter (ed.), *Conversations with Klemperer* (London, 1973; rev edn 1985).

Holbrook, David, *Gustav Mahler and the Courage To Be* (London, 1975).

James, Burnett, *The Music of Gustav Mahler* (London, 1985).

Jones, Ernest, *Sigmund Freud, Life and Work*, Vol. II (London, 1955).

Kaplan, Gilbert E., 'How Mahler Performed his Second Symphony', *The Musical Times*, Vol. 127, No. 1718, May 1986.

Kaplan, Gilbert E., 'The Birth of a Symphony' in *Gustav Mahler, Symphony No. 2 in C minor*, facsimile (New York, 1986).

——, 'The Birth of a Symphony' and 'How Mahler Conducted the Second Symphony', in booklet issued with MCA Classics recording of Symphony No. 2 in C minor (MCAD-2 11011), 1988.

——, (ed.), *The Mahler Album* (New York and London, 1995).

——, *Gustav Mahler: Adagietto; facsimile, documentation, recording* (New York, 1992).

Karpath, Ludwig, *Begegnung mit dem Genius* (Vienna-Leipzig, 1934).

Keller, Hans, 'The Unpopularity of Mahler's Popularity' (*The Listener*, 15 April 1971).

Keener, Andrew D., 'Gustav Mahler as Conductor' (Music and Letters, Vol. 56, Nos. 3–4, 1975).

Kennedy, Michael, 'Mahler Song-Cycles' in *Song on Record*, Vol. I (ed. A. Blyth) (London, 1986).

Klemperer, Otto, *Meine Erinnerungen an Gustav Mahler* (Zürich, 1960). English ed., *Memories of Mahler* (London, 1964).

Kolodin, Irving, *The Story of the Metropolitan Opera, 1883–1950* (New York, 1953).

Kralik, Heinrich von, *Das grosse Orchester. Die Wiener Philharmoniker und ihre Dirigenten* (Vienna, 1952).

Kucerova, Dagmar, 'Gustav Mahler v Olomouci' in *Hubedni Veda*, No. 4, (Prague, 1968).

Langford, Samuel (ed. Cardus), *Music Criticisms* (London, 1929).

Lebrecht, Norman (ed.), *Mahler Remembered* (London, 1987).

Mahler, Alma Maria, *Gustav Mahler: Erinnerungen und Briefe* (Amsterdam, 1940).

——, English ed., *Gustav Mahler: Memories and Letters* (trans. Basil Creighton) (London, 1946); 2nd (enlarged) ed., edited with introduction by Donald Mitchell (London, 1968); 3rd ed. enlarged with new appendix and chronology by D. Mitchell and Knut Martner (London, 1973).

——, (ed.), *Gustav Mahler Briefe, 1879–1911* (Berlin-Vienna-Leipzig, 1924). For English edition see under Martner, Knud.

——, *Introduction* to facsimile of Symphony No. 10 (Vienna, 1924).

Mahler-Werfel, Alma, *Diaries 1898–1902* (selected and trans. by Antony Beaumont) (London, 1998).

Martner, Knud (ed.) *Selected Letters of Gustav Mahler*, trans. Eithne Wilkins, Ernst Kaiser and Bill Hopkins; orig. ed. selected by Alma Mahler, enlarged and with new intro., illus. and notes (London, 1979).

Matthews, Colin, *Mahler at Work: Aspects of the Compositional Process* (Univ. of Sussex, diss., 1978).

Mildenburg, Anna von, *Erinnerungen* (Vienna, 1920).

Mitchell, Donald, *Gustav Mahler: the Early Years* (London, 1958, rev. 1980).

——, 'About Mahler's Early Symphonies' (*The Listener*, 26 Feb. 1959).

——, 'Early and Mature Mahler' (*The Listener*, 25 October 1962).

——, *The Wunderhorn Years* (London, 1975).

——, *Songs and Symphonies of Life and Death* (London, 1985).

—— (with Banks, Paul), 'Gustav Mahler' in *The New Grove Dictionary of Music and Musicians*, Vol. II (London, 1980). Reprinted in *Turn of the Century Masters* (London, 1985).

—— (ed.), English 2nd ed. of A. M. Mahler's *Gustav Mahler: Memories and Letters* (London, 1968); 3rd ed. enlarged with new appendix and chronology by D. Mitchell and Knud Martner (London, 1973).

——, *Gustav Mahler: the World Listens* (Amsterdam, 1995).

—— (ed.), *New Sounds, New Century: Mahler's Fifth Symphony and the Royal Concertgebouw Orchestra* (Bussum, 1997).

—— and Reilly, Edward R., *Gustav Mahler: facsimile edition of the Seventh Symphony* (Amsterdam, 1995).

—— and Andrew Nicholson (eds), *The Mahler Companion* (Oxford, 1999).

Newlin, Dika, *Bruckner-Mahler-Schoenberg* (New York, 1947).

Prawy, Marcel, *The Vienna Opera* (London, 1969).

Redlich, Hans Ferdinand, *Bruckner and Mahler* (London, 1955, revised 1963).

——, 'Gustav Mahler' (entry in Vol. VIII, *Die Musik in Geschichte und Gegenwart*, Cassel-Basle-London-New York, 1960).

Reich, Willi, *Schoenberg: a critical biography*, trans. Leo Black (London, 1971).

Reilly, Edward R., *Gustav Mahler und Guido Adler: Zur Geschichte einer Freundschaft* (Vienna, 1978), in Eng. as *Gustav Mahler and Guido Adler: Records of a Friendship* (Cambridge, 1982).

Roller, Alfred, *Die Bildnisse von Gustav Mahler* (Vienna-Leipzig, 1922).

Roman, Zoltan, *Gustav Mahler's American Years 1907–1911: a Documentary History* (Stuyvesant, NY, 1989).

Specht, Richard, *Gustav Mahler* (Berlin, 1905).

——, *Gustav Mahler* (Berlin-Leipzig, 1913).

Stefan, Paul, *Gustav Mahler: eine Studie über Persönlichkeit und Werk* (Munich, 1910, revised 1912 and 1920). English ed. trans. Edward Clark (New York, 1913).

Stein, Erwin, *Orpheus in New Guises* (London, 1953).

——, 'Mahler and the Vienna Opera' in *The Opera Bedside Book*, ed. H. Rosenthal (London, 1965).

Truscott, Harold, 'Some Aspects of Mahler's Tonality' (*Monthly Musical Record*, Nov.–Dec. 1957).

——, 'Gustav Mahler' in *The Symphony*, Vol. 2 (ed. R. Simpson) (London, 1967).

Vignal, Marc, *Mahler* (Paris, 1966).

Walker, Frank, *Hugo Wolf, a Biography* (London, 1951, revised 1968).

Walter, Bruno, *Gustav Mahler* (Vienna-Leipzig-Zürich, 1936). 1st English ed. trans. James Galston (London, 1937); 2nd English ed. trans. supervised by Lotte Walter Lindt (London, 1958).

——, *Theme and Variations, an Autobiography*, trans. James Galston (London, 1947).

Wellesz, Egon, 'The Symphonies of Gustav Mahler' (*Music Review*, Vol. I, Nos. 1 and 2, 1940).

Mahler

Whaples, Miriam K., 'Mahler and Schubert's A minor Sonata, D.784' (*Music & Letters*, Vol. 65, No. 3, 1984).

Weismann, Sigrid (ed.), *Gustav Mahler und Wien* (Stuttgart and Zürich, 1976). Eng. ed. *Gustav Mahler in Vienna* (London, 1977).

Williamson, John, 'Mahler and Veni Creator Spiritus' in *Music Review*, Vol. 44, No. 1, February, 1983.

Willnauer, Franz, *Gustav Mahler und die Weiner Oper* (Vienna, 1993).

Appendix E

Mahler's 're-touchings' of Beethoven

In February 1900 Mahler caused a printed explanation of his 'retouchings' of Beethoven's symphonies – and specifically the Ninth – to be distributed among the Vienna Philharmonic audience after he had been severely criticized for attempting to 'improve' Beethoven. In it he said:

> ... Because of his total deafness, Beethoven had lost the essential intimate contact with the reality of physical sound in the world just at the time in his creative development when a very powerful increase in understanding urged him to find new ways of expression and towards hitherto unthought-of drastic treatment of orchestration.
>
> Just as well known as this fact is the other, namely, that the nature of the brass instruments of his time excluded the proper formation of succeeding notes which are needed for the formation of a melody. Just this very lack of perfection led to the improvement in the manufacture of these instruments and it would be a crime not to use them to give a more perfect rendering of Beethoven's works. Richard Wagner, who all his life by word and deed was passionately trying to rescue Beethoven's works from abysmal performances which had become almost unbearable, in his article 'On the Correct Performance of Beethoven's Ninth' indicates how to conduct this work in the way Beethoven had intended it to be heard, and most conductors have followed Wagner's advice.
>
> The conductor of today's concert [i.e. Mahler] ... does not differ in essentials from the limits drawn by Wagner. Nobody could possibly call this a re-orchestration or, still worse, an 'improvement' of Beethoven's composition. The customary increase in the number of stringed instruments has made it equally necessary to increase the number of wind instruments, and this was done solely to balance the volume of sound and not to give instruments a new significance. This point, as with any other concerning the interpretation of this work, in parts as well as in whole, can be proved to be correct by study of the score. This will lead to the conviction that the conductor ... did not allow either 'tradition' or instinct to creep into it: he was determined not to sacrifice one iota of what the Master demands and did not allow any particle to become lost in the welter of sound.

Index